OLDHAM COLLEGE

Pebblegogy

Ideas and activities to inspire and engage learners

Shane Sutherland

Jane Brotchie

Sarah Chesney

Published by Pebble Learning Ltd

e-Innovation Centre
University of Wolverhampton
Shifnal Road
Telford
TF2 9FT
UK

First published 2011
© Pebble Learning 2011

ISBN: 978-0-9565641-1-5

The right of Shane Sutherland, Jane Brotchie and Sarah Chesney to be identified as the authors of this work has been asserted by them in accordance with Section 77 and 78 of the Copyright, Designs and Patents Act 1988.

Design and cover: Pebble Learning
Printed and bound in Great Britain by Bell & Bain Ltd., Glasgow

Contents

List of figures

Acknowledgements

As a founding architect of PebblePad I ought to have found it relatively easy to explain what the system is and what it stands for. However, as with so many intimate projects, it is sometimes difficult to articulate the ideas and concepts that exercise the mind almost daily, into sensible and understandable prose. I could not have accomplished this without the patience, perseverance and prodding of my fellow authors, Jane Brotchie and Sarah Chesney.

Jane and Sarah have also worked incredibly hard at editing the diverse range of submitted activities into a body of learning designs that are coherent, clear and consistent across the 12 themes into which they have been organised. I cannot thank them enough for their brilliance.

That they have had so much to do is testament to the generosity and commitment of the PebblePad community who responded so positively to our call for example activities. We are aware of the many challenges and pressures our colleagues face in colleges and universities and so are always astounded by the time and effort they are prepared to invest for the benefit of the wider community.

These exceptional people contributed activities to *Pebblegogy* or were instrumental in helping form the overall shape of the book:

Ben Andrews, Lilian Austin, Karl Behrendt, Zelma Bone, Kath Botham, Liz Bregazzi, Rachel Challen, Megan Chiswell, Kerry Cochrane, John Couperthwaite, Richard Culas, Charlie Davis, Lyn Doolan, Jo Doughty, Angela Eddy, David Eddy, Miriam Edwards, Alison Felce, Kevin Garner, Suzanne Gough, Yann Guisard, Claire Hamshire, David Heesom, Julie Hughes, Carole Hunter, Lester Jones, Krishna Lambert, Caroline Marcangelo, Nicole McNab, Peter Mills, David Morley, Brendon Munge, Deborah O'Connor, Graham Oakes, Harry Owen, Alyssa Phillips, Trisha Poole, Heidi Probst, Emma Purnell, Geoff Rebbeck, Moira Savage, Wyverne Smith, Cyle Sprick, Bronwyn Sprick, Judie Taylor, Shevahn Telfser, Victoria Thoms, Andrew Turner, Santanu Vasant, Warwick Wheatley, Matthew Willett, Dennie Wilson.

They represent the following institutions:

Brunel University, Coventry University, Charles Sturt University, Flinders University, La Trobe University, Manchester Metropolitan University, RMIT University, Sheffield Hallam University, Thanet College, University of Birmingham, University of Cumbria, University of Derby, University of Manchester, University of Winchester, University of Wolverhampton, University of Worcester.

I would like to close by thanking my colleagues Colin Dalziel, Matthew Wheeler and especially Alison Poot who spent many hours proof-reading chapters of the book and testing activities to make sure we had included the right instructions. And finally, a Mexican wave for Tom Teichmann who has grown from placement student into PebblePad's very own specialist developer, iconographer, web designer, newsletter compiler, photographer, event co-ordinator and now *Pebblegogy* book designer.

I apologise most profoundly if I have missed anyone who has contributed to this wonderful book, and close with a final thanks to all those whose efforts have made this endeavour possible.

Shane

June 2011

Pebblegogy: an introduction to the book

What is Pebblegogy? In some respects nothing more than a fabrication; a word conjured up to suggest that there are certain pedagogies promoted, reinforced or even awakened in PebblePad – and which are unique to it. And yet, as you read this book you will notice that, whilst the word is a fanciful construct, PebblePad does spring from a clearly discernable pedagogical foundation – and when its underpinning principles align with the right actors and the right conditions it has the potential for truly transformative learning and teaching.

The actors we have in mind for this book are tutors and other designers of learning. We start with the assumption that you already agree that good teaching always has the needs, experience, knowledge, capability and motivations of the learners in mind: that you cannot design inspiring, engaging and rewarding learning activities without being cognisant of what learners bring to the party. And so this is not a book designed to be used by learners but rather a book that sets out to explain what this thing called PebblePad really is, why it is shaped as it is, and what learning purposes it can serve.

PebblePad is unique. There are no other systems like it. There are lots of tools that do some things in a similar way or provide some of the functionality of PebblePad, but there are none that are so clearly and obviously designed to promote learning for and from experience – wherever that experience occurs. At first you may not realise how different PebblePad is from other tools you might typically experience in an educational environment. It shares more in common with Web 2.0 tools and yet at the same time it offers much more depth and purpose than they are able to. You really have to understand PebblePad to be able to get the best from it and Part A of this book is designed to bring you as close to our ideas and ideology as we are currently able. Experience gained using PebblePad will do the rest.

In the first chapter of Part A, *PebblePad: the Personal Learning Space,* you will learn more about the ideas behind the system, whilst *Chapter 2: Designed for Learning* focuses on the various tools and functions that make up the whole. *Chapter 3: The Principles of PebblePad* is essential reading because it is these principles that determine what the system is and what it stands for, and they provide a reference point for how the system will develop in the future. A thorough understanding of the principles will stand every practitioner in far better stead than any in-depth knowledge of the functions could ever do. *Chapter 4: Planning Purposeful Activities* provides a useful model of activity design which will be helpful for practitioners who want to expand their repertoire beyond the offerings presented in Part B

– or for those who want to unpick, understand and reconstruct any of the activities available herein. *Chapter 5: Doing Things Differently* is a wonderful offering from PebblePad's very first (2004), and foremost, practitioner, Julie Hughes. Julie has drawn upon her vast wealth of experience to contribute a guest chapter oozing with astute hints, tips, insights – and health warnings. Part A concludes with *Chapter 6: Pebblegogy in Practice*, a synopsis of the questions and suggestions addressed so far and many readers will find this an invaluable guide to planning their own first forays into PebblePad.

Part B presents 38 activities inspired by contributions from members of our generous PebblePad community – which means that the designs are tried, tested and authentic. The activities are organised into themed sections and provide a rich selection of 'recipes' you can use straight from the book or use as inspiration for your own learning designs.

Why a book on Pebblegogy now?

The reason that it has taken six years to write a book about Pebblegogy is that it has taken until now for a clear view of practice to emerge. The principles upon which PebblePad is founded have remained consistent throughout its development but many of those principles were alien to academic institutions when PebblePad first appeared on the scene. Of course, there have always been teachers in those academic institutions who saw in PebblePad a tool that aligned with their approach to learning and teaching, and who championed its use. Examples of excellent practice have developed over time and we have all been beneficiaries of those who generously shared their knowledge and experience with the wider community.

We are now at a point when there is not only a vibrant and varied body of practice but also at a point where the needs and understanding of academic institutions has evolved to be much more in tune with a personal learning space like PebblePad. At the same time that awareness is growing in universities and other seats of learning, an increasing number of progressive professional organisations have adopted PebblePad to serve the needs of their organisation and their members.

Whilst the global economic climate has naturally impacted on how universities do business there are many policy and strategy shifts that took root before the financial crisis and which have simply been accelerated more recently. It is unclear how a greater concern for clearly evidenced graduate attributes or employability skills can be addressed without tools like PebblePad. The same is true for almost all models of recognising prior learning and achievement, or for supporting and valuing work-based learning. The drive for more responsive curricula and for niche programmes designed to service directly the needs of employers; an increase in the number of organisations offering professional accreditation; and increasingly formal requirements for evidencing continuing professional development are some of the many changes and challenges to learning organisations that can be readily – and effectively – addressed through the use of tools like PebblePad.

So, why a book called Pebblegogy now? Because there are more and more reasons why the effective use of PebblePad is of increasing importance to learners, to tutors, to colleges and universities, to employers and to the professions. Time and experience are on our side though. We have been able to draw upon over six years of practice by enthusiastic and creative tutors in more than a hundred organisations to share their knowledge and experience of inspiring and engaging learners through PebblePad and to present those ideas to you here. We hope the book inspires and engages you to continue finding creative ways to use PebblePad.

Shane, Jane and Sarah

Part A

Understanding PebblePad

chapter 1 | PebblePad: the Personal Learning Space

This chapter provides an introduction to PebblePad for people who are using, or plan to use, PebblePad to support the learning of others – whether you are a tutor, lecturer, learning technologist or professional developer.

PebblePad has long carried the strap line 'not *just* an eportfolio', though for some years the *just* has felt rather superfluous. So, if PebblePad is *not* an eportfolio, what *is* an eportfolio and how does PebblePad differ? The briefest trawl of the literature will reveal that there is still no widely held definition of what an eportfolio is – though our preference tends toward those definitions that simply describe an eportfolio as a digital presentation:

> *A purposeful aggregation of digital items – ideas, evidence, reflections, feedback etc, which presents a selected audience with evidence of a person's learning and/or ability. (Sutherland and Powell, 2007)*

If you accept this definition you will notice that PebblePad allows learners to create different kinds of eportfolios:

- webfolios are (typically) narrative-based presentations of *evidence*;
- profiles are competency-based presentations of *evidence*;
- blogs are chronologically ordered presentations of *evidence*;
- activity logs are ordered collections of *evidence* characterised by tags, points or hours.

A personal learning space

PebblePad is not, then, an eportfolio; it is a system containing multiple tools to support the creation of different kinds of eportfolio depending upon the needs of the author and their intended audience. And so it might be argued that PebblePad is an eportfolio *system* – a collection of tools and functions used for creating eportfolios. However, many PebblePad users routinely use the input wizards (action plan, meeting, thought etc.) to create assets never destined to be included within any kind of presentational eportfolio. The value for these learners is in using the scaffolding and supporting prompts to make meaningful entries to support their learning – wherever that learning is situated. Many learners will go on to share their records seeking reassurance, recognition or reviews from trusted others. It is these uses that suggest it is much more than an eportfolio *system*. PebblePad provides a space where learning can take place that is personal, eclectic and idiosyncratic and so we have chosen to refer to it as a *personal learning space*.

At first it appears problematic to reconcile the notion of a personal space in an institutional context. After all, the majority of readers of this book will belong to organisations that make PebblePad available to their members – most often, universities to their staff and students. However, two principles make PebblePad different from other institutional systems: ownership and control. Whilst the institution maintains ownership of the system and controls who has access to the system as a whole, it is the individual user who has ownership of all of their own *assets* and absolute control over who has access to view (comment, or collaborate on) their work.

Some would argue that spaces such as these should be wholly independent of the institution and that individual learners should be free to choose from the plethora of social networking systems currently available. This idealistic argument misses three important points. The first is that the user's choice to use a personal learning environment (PLE) that includes Facebook, Blogger, Twitter etc. is compromised immediately they are required to fulfil any institutional act – typically assessment, and many studies are now showing that students resent this imposition. The second point is that many of these *free* social tools carry an implicit contract whereby they are provided in exchange for data about the user and their behaviours, rendering them particularly unsuitable for some students working and learning in professional contexts. Thirdly, whilst these tools are often brilliant in their designed function they are not specifically designed to support or scaffold learning – PebblePad is.

The personal learning space is not substituting for either the personal learning environment or the institutional learning environment; its significance lies in the fact that PebblePad can connect and interact with both in ways that are under the control of the learner.

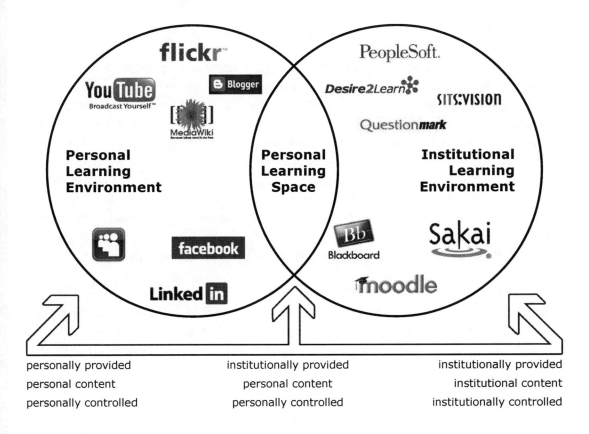

Figure 1.1: *The Personal Learning Space situated between the Personal Learning Environment and the Institutional Learning Environment*

Whilst PebblePad is typically adopted by organisations to support a particular strategy such as the development of graduate attributes, the move towards authentic assessment, or an emphasis on professional education and development, the inherent design of PebblePad promotes the sense that it is 'my space', a personal space but a space from which I can choose to connect with others. It is a space where my thoughts, ideas and aspirations can be more easily articulated through the supporting structures it contains. It is conversational, though not always in an easy way. This space challenges me, encourages me to deconstruct, analyse, reflect and reconstruct and it provides opportunities for social enrichment of my learning experiences. Of course, my personal learning space also allows me to create multiple eportfolios for myriad purposes and aimed at diverse audiences.

How PebblePad supports learning

PebblePad supports good teaching and learning. It has a reflective structure, supports individual and social constructivism, and is essentially dialogic in nature. Although it is possible to enjoy a certain level of self-mediated dialogue, supported by the scaffolding in the system, dialogue is always enhanced by audience: validated by valued others. It is a tool wholly founded on improving learning and we believe it to be unique in its design and conception. However, it is just a tool and, whilst it is based on sound educational principles and borne out of extensive pedagogical practice, it relies, like any tool, on the people who utilise it to use it knowingly, insightfully and deliberatively. Just as there is an art and a science to teaching so there is both capacity and understanding associated with the best uses of PebblePad. The function of this book, then, is to provide many examples of how PebblePad can be used by tutors and others to support learning effectively.

What does effective use of PebblePad look like? Given that PebblePad is used by well over a hundred organisations to support processes as diverse as assessment, appraisal, work-based learning and professional development there can be no single view of effective practice. However, where use of PebblePad does add value to learning it is likely to:

- □ guide users through acts like planning and reflecting;
- □ surface the process of learning in tangible form;
- □ promote improvement through timely feedback;
- □ encourage sharing, reviewing and peer support;
- □ engage others outside of the normal teaching context;
- □ value diverse forms of evidence such as audio and video;
- □ recognise learning from experience and learning over time.

Because tools like PebblePad are so novel, and so distinct from the institutional tools that preceded them, we are developing new models of learning, new ways of thinking, acting and being. These ways of working are closely associated with the design and functionality of this space and it is clear to see that the learning designs evidenced by this book have enough in common with each other to warrant distinction from mainstream pedagogies. Whilst there is still much to learn if we are to fully realise the truly transformative nature of personal learning spaces, there has been sufficient progress and success to render it not unreasonable to think of what we do as somewhat unique, an emergent pedagogy – the practice of Pebblegogy!

Designed for Learning

This book is about how PebblePad can serve different learning purposes rather than being a technical manual about using the tools. An understanding of what PebblePad can offer is an important starting point, however, so this chapter introduces the main components of the system for those who are not familiar with it. If you know PebblePad well, you may prefer to skip this chapter or turn to it for reference if you need to remind yourself of any of the components and functions.

The design philosophy

PebblePad is designed with flexibility and usability in mind. It is a generic system, designed to accommodate the recording of experience independent of place, time or context. It is as relevant to the new student as to the professional with years of work experience. The interface is purposely simple and friendly, making the system accessible even to those with minimal IT skills. There are, however, many options for customisation and personalisation for the more advanced and confident user. While PebblePad has its origins in the university environment it is now widely used in the professions, and is increasingly used by independent learners. Its design philosophy is one of learner ownership and control:

- It is a space for personal learning that belongs to the learner not the organisation who provides it;
- it is populated by the learner to reflect their rich and diverse learning experiences;
- it is primarily concerned with supporting learning, including learning leading to or resulting from authentic assessment
- it is for lifelong and life-wide learning – not a single event, assessment or course;
- it allows learners to present multiple stories of learning, experience and achievement, rather than being a simple aggregation of competences;
- and, importantly, access to it is controlled by the learner who is able to invite feedback from myriad others to support personal growth and understanding.

We will expand on some of these ideas in the next chapter, *The Principles of PebblePad*.

To facilitate the use of PebblePad in an organisational context, additional 'organisational' tools have been designed to enable the submission of selected items for feedback and/or assessment by tutors, moderators and examiners without compromising the privacy of the learner's personal space.

A core component of the PebblePad design, and what sets it apart from other 'eportfolio systems', is the inbuilt wizards that support the process of personal learning. These wizards prompt the learner to consider diverse aspects of their experience and provide a step–by–step process for the creation of learning records (called assets) within the system. This scaffolded creation of assets, as distinct from simply uploading existing files, encourages the learner to make sense of, and reflect on, their experiences to a much deeper level.

PebblePad is based on the idea that we each learn many different things in different places and at different times. A typical user may record a meeting with their mentor in the morning; create a project action plan in the afternoon; and reflect on their part time volunteering later in the evening. It is a very open system that does not limit the user to a single purpose. Indeed, users should be encouraged to record all of their learning and experiences partly because the act of recording can be a learning experience in itself, but also because the greater the range of records, the richer the connections and patterns that emerge over time.

PebblePad can be used to great effect by students planning experiments and trials, those working on problem-based learning, students working on group projects, trainee nurses on their placements, work-based learners recording their skills or teachers maintaining their record of professional development activities. But it can also be used in many more contexts and to support many different learning purposes – as you will find out when you read the range of activities featured in Part B.

How PebblePad works

All items a user has stored in PebblePad are known as 'assets'. The term *asset* was chosen as it is more inclusive than *file* which tends to describe an externally generated object. It is also more personal than *record* which often refers to an item recorded about the user by someone else. The term *artefact* is sometimes used by other systems but, because it suggests that something is from the past, rather than something capable of further development over time, it too was felt inappropriate. So, whilst *asset* is not immediately embraced by all, it does imply that the items created or uploaded are valued by, and of value to, the user.

Users can create an unlimited number of assets in their account, which can be used and repurposed to suit different ends. For example, a user creating webfolios to support job applications can create tailored versions of their 'employment' webfolio for each application they make.

It might help to think of assets as being one of three broad types: uploaded files, single assets and aggregating or presentational assets.

Uploaded files

Uploaded files are any externally generated files that are uploaded into PebblePad and include normal office documents, video, audio and images. When files are uploaded to PebblePad they are automatically linked to an 'asset holder' which acts like a container for the file and allows the file to be shared with other users and for comments, feedback and grades to be added to it without changing the file itself. Because uploaded files are slower to open and require more steps to edit, many users prefer to use PebblePad's own assets. So, for example, instead of asking users to complete an action plan in Word, use PebblePad's inbuilt action plan 'wizard' even if it may mean explaining to users what to enter into each field or recognising that not all of the fields are needed.

Users can upload files directly into their asset store. PebblePad supports any kind of *safe* file including video, audio and images. The maximum size of file that can be uploaded is 10mb though this is dependent on internet connection speed. On slower connections, a safety mechanism on the server may time out before such a large file can be uploaded.
As well as allowing single files to be uploaded, PebblePad also supports the upload of multiple files from a zip archive. When uploaded, PebblePad unzips the archive making the individual files available. There are three broad types of uploads available:

- ☐ **Multiple files**: a standard zip archive with a collection of files which are each stored individually when 'unpacked'.
- ☐ **Gallery**: a collection of files containing only images. After upload, all the files in the gallery will be tagged with the name given to the zip folder. This allows a gallery page to be quickly added to a webfolio by adding a tag as a page.
- ☐ **Website**: this option allows users to upload a website or linked HTML documents. There must be an index.htm or default.htm "home page" for the site which will be the starting point when anyone views the website. PebblePad will display a single file in the asset store and will allow the website to be linked, shared and opened like other assets.

Single assets

Single assets are created by working through one of the wizards that help scaffold the recording process for the user. Whilst the wizards contain many steps and prompts they are only there to loosely support the recording process and so, other than the title, none of the steps are *required* fields. Users sometimes get anxious that they are not using the correct wizard but it really does not matter which wizard is used as long as the scaffolding has been useful to the learner. For example, it is equally valid to record a tutorial using the meeting wizard, the activity wizard or the thought wizard as each prompts the user to describe what took place and to record what was learnt from it. Use of the *correct* wizard is normally only a requirement if it is to serve a formal process such as assessment – in which case the user will be told which type to use.

 Ability

> *Ability*: allows users to record skills, competences and other attributes which they feel are significant or which are required for the purposes of assessment, accreditation or validation. Users can describe their ability, skill or competence in their own words or copy an official description of the attributes being recorded. When users claim a skill in association with a profile, an ability asset is created. (For a description of profiles, see *Tools that support assessment, grading and feedback* later in this chapter).

 Achievement

> *Achievement*: allows users to record any successful endeavour which is significant to them. Any achievement which might be useful in the future as part of a webfolio or CV can be recorded. Users can describe achievements in their own words or include copies of official documentation as evidence of achievement: for example, transcripts, certificates, photos of trophies or medals.

 Action plan

> *Action plan*: allows users to create plans designed to help them achieve a particular outcome or goal. Action plans can be created by users to guide personal or professional development or as part of an activity or project planning process. The action plan tool includes a 'steps to success' function where larger goals can be broken down into smaller steps, and a SWOT analysis section.

Activity

Activity: allows users to record any significant event or experience, normally directly related to their personal or professional development. This might include attendance at a workshop or training course, presentation of a paper at a conference, or involvement in a project. Activity assets can provide useful evidence towards an overall development record, project work, appraisal or review, as well as providing a record against which progress can be monitored.

Experience

Experience: allows users to record any event or experience which is of significance to them. Typically, the experience record is used to record lengthy experiences such as work-related roles. Any experience which might be useful in the future as part of a webfolio or CV should be recorded.

Meeting

Meeting: allows users to record details of significant meetings with others, such as tutors, careers advisers, or fellow students working on a project. Just like action plans, the meeting asset includes a facility for recording outcomes and for planning how and when the outcomes will be addressed.

Thoughts

Thoughts: allow users to record journal entries, structured reflections, significant incidents, ideas or notes. PebblePad provides a range of options for recording thoughts from a simple single stage process to more detailed structures to guide users through the recording process. Posts to a blog are also saved as thought assets, allowing them to be reused or linked with other assets.

Aggregating or presentational assets

Aggregating or presentational assets bring together other items to provide a richer picture of the user's experience or learning. Users can create multiple examples of each kind of presentation and it would be normal for a user to have multiple blogs, webfolios and CVs as the requirements of each viewing audience would be different. Although the presentational assets are described separately here, they also behave like single assets in that they can be shared, copied, commented upon, and can be linked to and from other presentational assets. For example, a graduation webfolio could contain links to a user's first and second year webfolio, their placement blog and their competency profile.

These tools are available to every user and follow a step-by-step process that enables quick and easy production of high quality presentations to support a wide range of purposes such as assessment, appraisal and job applications etc.

The presentation tools enable users to aggregate, link and, as with all assets in PebblePad, display them to different audiences both internal and external to the system.

 *Activity log*

This asset has to be turned on in the settings by anybody wanting to use it. It allows users to bring together items they would like to use to demonstrate activity during a given period. Activity logs display as a single page that lists entries in date order. Multiple activity logs can be created for different purposes such as appraisal, recording continuing professional development (CPD) and managing time on projects.

The activity log enables users to indicate how many hours (or Professional Development points) must be completed and, as items are added to the activity log, displays the number of required hours remaining so that progress can be monitored.

 Blogs

Blogs consist of a single webpage made up of chronological journal-type entries. Blogs are valuable to gather and share ideas or to quickly record events or activities without using the fuller structure of other PebblePad wizards. Blogs are created, published and shared in the same way as all other assets and they can be added as a page in a webfolio. Users can post entries straight to blogs or post existing or new assets to them. Entries posted straight to a blog are also saved as individual 'thoughts' in the asset store.

There are three types of blog in PebblePad:

- An **individual blog**, which is personal to the user. Unlike other blog tools on the Internet, a PebblePad blog remains private to the user until they decide to share it (like other PebblePad assets).

- A tutor can set up a blog for a group of users on a gateway. This is a collaborative blog and is known as a **gateway blog** and is accessed through the **gateway resources**.

- A **tutor blog** is used by members of staff on a gateway to communicate on such issues as the assessment processes, validation, and plagiarism, and is useful as a tracking mechanism for external assessors, moderators and examiners.

CV Builder

The 'CV Builder' allows users to create an electronic CV by drawing upon information entered into the 'About Me' tool in PebblePad, as well as other assets from the asset store. The CV content is customisable with users able to select which information from 'About Me' to include: personal details, qualifications, employment, references, referees, and so on. Users can create multiple CVs that can be shared in the same way as any other PebblePad asset. CVs can also be copied to a word processing package, which enables layout and design changes to be made.

Webfolio

The webfolio is PebblePad's primary presentational tool and, if it was not used for so many other purposes, might easily be renamed 'eportfolio'. It is best thought of as an evidence-based website that allows users to present stories about themselves, their work, or about their learning and development. They can contain any number of pages which can be added to, edited, or deleted at any time. Pages can also contain links to other assets within the asset store to give a rich picture of activity. A wide choice of templates, colour schemes and image options allow the user to customise each webfolio they create.

Organising and tracking assets with tags

Tags allow users to identify assets as being similar in some way. For example, assets may be the result of a particular unit of study and demonstrate a graduate attribute. Using tags makes it easier to locate, organise or display related items so a user could choose to view all items which demonstrate an attribute and choose the best examples for their assessment. A number of default tags are preset in PebblePad but users can easily create their own: for example, project, hobbies, module code, graduate attribute. Assets can have multiple tags applied to allow them to be categorised in a number of ways.

Within a webfolio, a tag page can be added and all items with the selected tag will be listed on the page.

Tools that support assessment, grading and feedback

PebblePad contains a number of institutional tools to support assessment, grading and feedback. The system also has tools to build forms to support individual or group development and self-evaluation questionnaires that allow users to audit their current knowledge, skills and abilities.

Gateways

Gateways are effectively the institutional space that sits alongside the personal space. Gateways are the area where users can publish their work for viewing by other users such as tutors, examiners or peers, for assessment or feedback. Access to gateways is based on group permissions with differing permissions being assigned to users depending on their role. In a typical gateway the following groups are available: administrator, owner, tutor, user, and reviewer. Different permissions can be given to each user group within each gateway: so, for example, on one gateway users may be able to publish assets but not view other people's work, while on another gateway users may be able to view each other's work in order to peer review it.

Gateways support a variety of uses including assessment, mentoring, group projects, and sharing resources with large groups of people. They provide permissions which allow blind marking/double marking, (anonymous) peer review, archiving and structured feedback.

 ### *Profiles*

Profiles are self–evaluation questionnaires that allow users to audit their current knowledge, skills and abilities. Profiles are often used to record and evidence progress towards graduate attributes, professional standards or subject competences. Users complete a profile by rating their skill level against a defined scale and/or by attaching evidence to support their claims to have a particular skill. Once completed, profiles are saved as assets within the asset store and can be shared or linked to like other assets.

Profiles are created within the 'Profile Builder' tool. Institutions assign 'Profile Builder' permissions to staff that require this capacity. Profiles can be published to individual users or published to groups. Reports of profile responses can also be generated.

 Forms

Forms can be created to support any type of activity: for example, a form to reflect on a complex experience or a form which helps users plan for an activity such as a placement or a lab experiment. Forms scaffold user responses through short and long text fields, multiple–choice, rating scales, and multi–column tables. Users can also be asked to attach evidence to support their responses. Once completed, forms are saved as assets within the asset store.

Forms are created using the 'Form Builder' tool. Institutions assign 'Form Builder' permissions to staff that require this capacity. Forms can be published to individual users or published to groups. If a form and its responses are published through a gateway, a report of responses can be generated.

Making assets available to others

There are three ways of making assets available: sharing, publishing and sending to the web. In all three ways of sharing, the link is 'live' so any updates can be seen immediately.

 Sharing

Sharing is the normal way a user allows another person to view one or more assets. It is not possible for anyone, including administrators, to view the entire asset store of another user without knowing their username and password – which should obviously always be kept secret.

When sharing the user chooses the level of access the recipient will have – as well as the length of time an item is shared for.

As well as sharing with other PebblePad users in the organisation it is also possible to share with 'external' people such as potential employers or external mentors.

 Publishing

Publishing describes the process of sending assets to a gateway where they can be viewed by others, typically for assessment. Although users have control over what they send to a gateway they do not have control over who sees their asset or how it is handled on the gateway. The gateway 'owner' determines the membership and permissions on a gateway – and needs to do so in order to facilitate organisational processes such as assessment.

Publishing is actually a linking process which allows those with the correct permissions to follow links from the gateway to assets submitted to it. This process allows work-in-progress to be published to a gateway and for those with the required permissions to be able to view an up-to-date version of the work and provide on-going feedback as it develops.

 Send to web

This feature allows users to publish their work allowing others to access it without the need of a password. There is still some protection in that PebblePad assets cannot be found by Internet search tools such as Google unless they are permanently linked to from another static web page.

In summary

This chapter provides a very simple overview of the various tools and functions available in PebblePad. It does not explain the detail of how each tool works, though throughout the activities in the second part of this book you will see how many of the tools and functions have been used in practice.

If you find that you do need to know more about how different parts of PebblePad work then help is always close at hand. Throughout PebblePad you will find **?** icons next to most fields. Clicking on one of these will display a hint about the field and clicking on the hint box will launch PebblePad's online help directly at the relevant section. Most sections contain written support, example images and help videos. You can also launch the main help from the large **?** icon in the bottom right corner of the right-hand pad.

The Principles of PebblePad

chapter **3**

This chapter outlines the pedagogical principles that have informed the design and development of PebblePad. We have provided a summary at the end of the chapter for quick reference.

Whether you are a practitioner, curriculum designer or professional course developer, understanding the underpinning principles of PebblePad will help you to harness its potential when you design learning activities. Learners too will benefit from understanding these principles when they start to use the personal learning space.

1 PebblePad supports personal learning

A group of people can share a common experience but may learn different things from it. A group of students may follow the same course of study, but each will make sense of their learning in a different way – as we know, what is taught is not always what is learned. Personal learning, then, is the sense that each learner makes of their own experiences.

PebblePad is a personal learning space whose prime purpose is to provide a place and a process to record learning experiences and achievements, encouraging learners to become accountable for themselves and their learning. It is about recording things learners do, things they are planning to do or things that they are proud of. The reason for recording is to make better sense of experiences, so that a learner can make links between one experience and another and so form new learning.

By recording learning events and experiences at, or close to, the time they happened it is easier to build an authentic record which allows learners to look back and see what they have learned, how they have changed and how they have developed. The narratives that a learner constructs later can then explain how the events relate to each other *over time* rather than just their moment by moment significance. Without this evolving record, it is hard to avoid interpreting past events through today's lens – where we are now and how we think today. Using PebblePad over time, learners can revisit and review past experiences for many different purposes and, like a kaleidoscope, new patterns will emerge.

Personal learning is not to be confused with 'personalised learning' when that term is used to describe an educational strategy to modify and adapt teaching according to the needs of individuals: for example, making podcasts available to learners who prefer auditory learning. It is possible to use PebblePad to personalise learning experiences for different learning preferences, but when we talk about personal learning we are referring to the idea that users of PebblePad are managing their own learning in a personal space where learning is 'done by me' not 'done to me' (de Freitas and Yapp, 2005). To support this kind of learning, tutors and course designers tailor the curriculum to meet the individual needs of students but, perhaps more importantly, they shift the focus from curriculum and planned learning outcomes to a focus on the learner and the experience and interpretation of their learning. Personalised learning, in this sense of the term, is an internalising process where learning is connected to personal lived experience and each learner constructs their own meaning through reflection in their PebblePad and through dialogue with their tutor or mentor. There can still be meaningful and valuable learning activities that take place elsewhere online (in a Learning Management System, for example) or face-to-face, but PebblePad can help learners prepare for, record and capture, and reflect on, the learning.

2 PebblePad offers a safe and private place which is owned and controlled by the user

PebblePad is owned by the learner. It is a fundamental principle of PebblePad that nobody else can enter another's PebblePad. There is no interface for an administrator to log into learners' accounts because that would contradict the core principle of personal ownership. Users may choose, at any time, to allow others to view and interact with one or more of their assets but no–one ever has access to their entire PebblePad.

Each user of PebblePad can experiment, record, plan, reflect and play with ideas, secure in the knowledge that their work is private. In an institutional context, whether this is a university or a professional association, what this means is that the institution maintains ownership of the system and controls who has access to the system as a whole, but the individual user owns all the assets within their PebblePad and has absolute control over who has access to their work.

This is more than a privacy issue, it is about where the locus of control is situated within the learning relationship. The PebblePad personal learning approach can, and does, work well alongside institutional learning systems but they differ in two key dimensions: control and ownership.

▢ *Control*: In a Virtual Learning Environment (VLE) or Learning Management System (LMS), whether it is Moodle, Blackboard or other system, the course is managed and owned by the tutor and administrator. A typical activity might be that the tutor requires students to post and respond to a forum a minimum number of times. The forum belongs to the course and everything that the student does on the LMS course can be seen by the tutor, who may also control what permissions students have to view other people's work. In a LMS, the student is the 'guest' in the learning space and the tutor is the 'owner'. In PebblePad, the roles are reversed: the student is the owner and the tutor is the guest (see Figure 3.1).

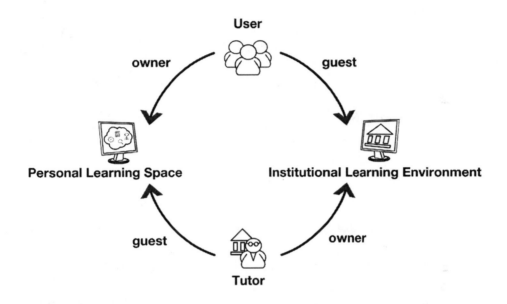

Figure 3.1: *The locus of control in the Personal Learning Space and the Institutional Learning Environment*

▢ *Authorship and ownership*: During the time that students are enrolled in a LMS course they might, for example, engage with the forums and add to the resources – but once the course is over, their evidence of engagement is no longer available to them. They are normally taken off the enrolment to allow new students to access the course. Unless they have made some external record of what they achieved, the students' evidence of learning has gone too. By contrast, there is no end point of 'un-enrolment' within the personal learning space. Everything that the students creates in PebblePad continues to be owned by them (see Figure 3.2).

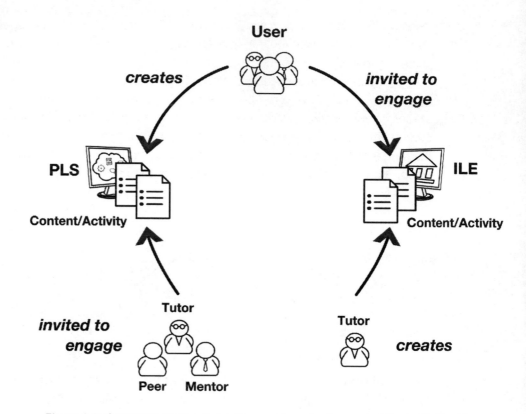

Figure 3.2: *Ownership of work in the Personal Learning Space and the Institutional Learning Environment*

Understanding the differences between the LMS and PebblePad, rather than viewing them as competing technologies, allows us to make the most of both and to offer users a unified learning experience. Both can be used as complementary systems and PebblePad has plugins available for popular LMS's. These bring the two systems together by making a range of PebblePad facilities available within the LMS: for example, one option is for learners to create PebblePad assets directly from the LMS without having to log onto PebblePad. So, if learners are working through some content in the LMS, they can create a reflective thought about the subject area they are working on. Unlike posting to a discussion forum in the LMS, this thought is personal and private unless the user chooses to share it.

3 PebblePad is multi-purpose – but purposeful

You will get the best value from PebblePad when you use it, and encourage others to use it, for multiple purposes. The purposes will change over time in a learner's lifecycle, perhaps first as a student and then as a developing professional; they can be seen as a series of 'touch points' which continue throughout formal education and professional development.

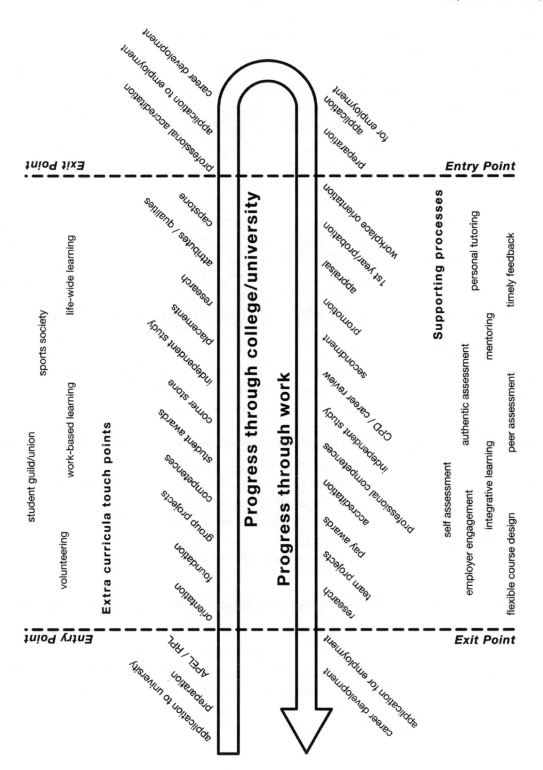

Figure 3.3: *Educational and professional touch points*

PebblePad can be used for personal and professional development planning, continuing professional development, recognition of prior learning, tracking of graduate skills, plus any number of other educational and professional processes. Tutors might use it to help students learn, to demonstrate their own professional development or record experiences and ongoing research. PebblePad can be used to write a CV and to make a job application. It can be used for appraisal, accreditation or for managing projects. It can do all this and more. As the use of PebblePad grows, people add new ways of using it every day, as the learning designs later in the book illustrate.

Regardless of who you are or what you are using PebblePad for, the structure and scaffolding within the system makes its use purposeful. Far from being a 'file dump', PebblePad helps you make sense of experience and create a record of that experience that you can draw upon for all sorts of reasons, for all kinds of audiences.

4 PebblePad supports learning wherever it happens, whenever it happens

Any experience offers opportunities for learning. Most institutional tools are typically designed to capture learning that takes place in formal places in structured ways. PebblePad supports the idea that learning is 'context-free': it takes place all the time, not only in the subject groupings that we divide learning into in educational settings. A chance conversation with a child might help an apprentice understand a work problem. A television programme might help a student make sense of something they've read or heard in the classroom. A walk in the mountains might spark a discovery that helps a scientist with a research problem. By making these links across contexts, we continue to learn and develop. One problem with ideas and insights is that they are often fleeting, nebulous or half-formed. PebblePad helps learners capture these thoughts, develop them over time, and make sense of them, perhaps through sharing them with relevant others.

Although organisations try to separate out formal curricula-based learning, individual learners are engaged in sense-making and new learning all the time and PebblePad provides the thread that binds together all these contexts. This idea of transferable learning holds true for tutors and for students as they use PebblePad for professional development or a course of study. For students, the concepts and ideas they learn in one module may have a huge impact on things they learn in another module. Similarly, students who are working to support their studies may find their workplace learning helps them to develop skills of relevance to their studies.

The fact that it is context-free doesn't preclude a manager, mentor or tutor saying: 'For this particular module, project or placement, I want you to do these particular things in PebblePad…'. In other words, context will *inform* how you use PebblePad but it does not *constrain* what you do in PebblePad.

5 PebblePad helps to surface and scaffold the process of learning

Traditionally, in formal education, assessment has tended to concentrate on the *product* of learning and has put too little value on the *process* of learning. Whether the outcome is a piece of academic writing, a piece of design, a drawing or a dance performance – if all the tutor sees is the 'thing' at the end, it is very difficult to judge the individual effort and development that has taken place to get to this point.

PebblePad offers powerful presentational tools such as its webfolio which can showcase both the *products* of learning and the plans, comments, reflections and other assets that chart the *process* of learning. Whilst the presentation tools are powerful, and for many users highly motivating, the input wizards (action planning, meeting, thought, activity etc.) are designed to support the process of learning. In combination, then, PebblePad supports learning through surfacing and exposing learning processes and by providing frameworks and scaffolding that actively generate learning and understanding.

Surfacing learning

Educational institutions that focus on 'products' sometimes find they become evermore concerned with the originality of student work, which means investment in mechanisms to 'police' this. That becomes less of a problem if you can see the process the student went through – where the challenges were, how the student overcame them, what sparked moments of insight, how well the work was planned and executed. With PebblePad, this can all be documented for external evaluators to view. Additionally, tutors can monitor, support and, if necessary, intervene in the process when they can see how the student is developing.

Just as a student can get credit for including their workings-out in a maths exam, when PebblePad is used within an appropriate learning design, it can expose the processes of learning. For example, an individual's contribution to a group outcome may be hard to establish through traditional teaching processes but PebblePad offers the tools that can capture individual and group effort. This is valuable for the learners themselves because they can review how they have approached the task and what they have learned. It is also valuable for those who are evaluating the task because they can gain insight into how the group process evolved. This might reveal, for example, that there is a common breakdown in one part of the process and the tutor can plan more support for later cohorts of students to develop the skills needed.

Scaffolding learning

An essay, a presentation, a performance or a project report can be a daunting prospect for many students. Tools in PebblePad – such as the action planning, activity and meeting wizards – are designed to lead the students through a process that builds up to the final product in managed stages. The student then goes through a scaffolded set of activities that lead to a particular purpose. The hope is that the experience of using these prompts and frameworks will encourage learners to return to them to help with any further study, research or work projects in the future, helping to develop lifelong habits of learning.

6 PebblePad is underpinned, and informed, by a reflective structure

At every step of the way PebblePad users are prompted to consider 'Why?', 'So what?', 'What if?' and 'What now?' This inbuilt reflective structure is what transforms PebblePad into a space where learning is generated rather than simply collected and evidenced.

PebblePad regularly challenges the user with questions: 'What did this mean to me?', 'What will I do with this learning?'. The underpinning design of the personal learning space calls into question what the learner knew before and makes explicit their tacit knowledge, whilst guiding the learner to new understandings of their experience. How the learner chooses to engage with this process is in their hands – the wizard tools allow the user to skip questions if they are not meaningful or relevant to a particular situation.

Encouraging learners to move beyond descriptive reflection can be difficult and most reflective frameworks propose a series of prompts that guide the learner through different levels of reflection (Moon, 2004). The reflective prompts within PebblePad are particularly helpful for those who are still learning how to record, reflect and to make sense of their experience. For these learners, who may not yet have developed the necessary mental frameworks to support the reflective process, the tools provide a structure that nudges the user to move beyond simple description of events and activities to a deeper level of analysis or forward projection. But it is not only novices in reflective practice that find this structure useful; skilled reflective thinkers tell us they find the scaffolding helpful because it allows them to concentrate on making sense of the experience rather than having to think about ways to frame the experience.

PebblePad tools are technically easy to learn and use, but what they ask of the learner can be intellectually demanding. Learning to think and practise reflectively is not an easy option, it demands some rigour which some learners might resist. In time, though, with repeated use of PebblePad tools, learners come to recognise the personal and professional benefits.

7 PebblePad gets people talking and helps users construct their narratives

The reflective structure is conversational, prompting further thought and exploration. Since anything created in PebblePad can be shared with one or more others in both private and group spaces, the capacity for comments, feedback and collaboration facilitates dialogue between users in these spaces. This sharing and dialogue contributes to the creation of much richer, more meaningful records of learning.

Many reflective models suggest that reflection is best done with a mentor or 'critical friend' (Titchen, 2003) through 'reflective conversation' (Ghaye, 2010). A dialogue and continuing feedback between a tutor and student, or a mentor and mentee, can be stored in PebblePad and can then provide another record of learning. In addition, users can collaborate within their personal learning space as well as peer review each other's work.

This conversational approach supports a narrative style of presentation, a style that has been described as story-telling or patchwork writing (Winter and colleagues, 1999). The webfolios, for example, encourage more than a listing of achievements or actions. The way that they are created encourages learners to move beyond a 'tick box, done that' approach and move towards talking about what they have done, why they did it, how one experience led to another and how they made discoveries along the way. The learner can give links to assets created in their learning journey – blogs, action plans, meetings, achievements – as well as link to examples of work and final outcomes, using images, video or other means that suit their story.

A webfolio can be read for its 'top-level' narrative, the story of the learning that has taken place. But if you want to dig deeper into how the learner has reached these conclusions or formed this story, you can follow the links to assets and further evidence to different levels of depth. The viewer or reader can engage with the webfolio in different ways, which makes it immediately more useful to a wider audience. For assessment or accreditation purposes you may need to dig deep into the webfolio for evidence of attainment, whereas an employer may be more interested in the personal learning journey, secure in the knowledge that the evidence is there to be checked.

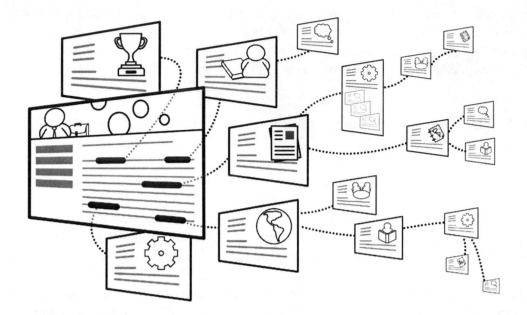

Figure 3.4: *The different layers of narrative in a webfolio*

Someone using PebblePad over the years may create multiple webfolios, which can themselves be linked together. In this sense it is possible to create a 'meta-narrative' which encapsulates one person's education, work, personal and professional development.

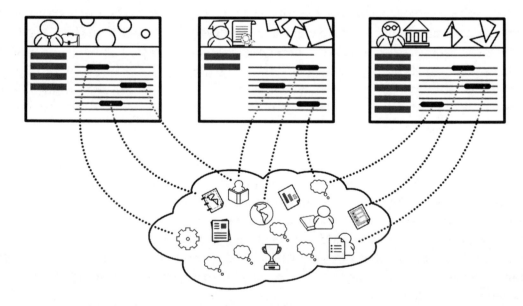

Figure 3.5: *A meta-narrative: multiple representations of a learner*

8 PebblePad can accompany learners throughout their lives and across all their activities

Over time, learners' needs change but the assets are always there in PebblePad to revisit and to use in different ways. PebblePad users take their records with them as they develop and learn, change direction, and take on new challenges throughout their study and working lives.

They are life-wide learners who continue to evidence learning in many different ways. One learner might, for example, be on a photography course using Flickr to showcase images, another might be creating 'how to' movies on YouTube or contributing to forums in an online community of practice. All around us outside PebblePad is evidence of our learning that can be linked to, or captured and stored in PebblePad. Some items of 'external' evidence may be more secure than others: those that are public can be easily linked; those that are more secure can be linked by allowing PebblePad to authenticate to another system; and those that are more sensitive, high-stake, or generated in a less stable Web 2.0 tool, can be imported to PebblePad using open standards.

Endnote: walking the talk

Although *Pebblegogy* will give you plenty of insight into how these principles are being put into practice, the best way is to use PebblePad yourself. Once you engage with the personal learning space you start to experience how it can support and develop your own personal and professional goals, as well as those you may teach, manage or mentor. Indeed, modelling good practice and using PebblePad yourself is probably the best way to build enthusiasm for those you teach, manage or support.

Summary of principles

PebblePad supports personal learning

A group of people can share a common experience but may learn different things from it, make sense of their learning in different ways, and want to document or evidence their learning differently. The flexibility of the PebblePad interface supports all of these individual differences and enables you to engage in personal learning in your own way.

PebblePad offers a safe and private place which is owned and controlled by you, the user

PebblePad is totally private. It is a fundamental principle of PebblePad that nobody else can enter your PebblePad. There is no interface for an administrator to log into your account because that would contradict the core principle of personal ownership. You can choose, at any time, to allow others to view and interact with one or more of your assets but no–one ever has access to your entire PebblePad.

PebblePad is multi-purpose – but purposeful

PebblePad can be used for any number of educational, professional and personal processes. It can be used by anyone who wants to record, reflect on and learn from experience. Regardless of who you are or what you are using PebblePad for, the structure and scaffolding within the system makes its use purposeful. Far from being a 'file dump', PebblePad helps you make sense of experience and create a record of that experience that you can draw upon for all sorts of reasons, for all kinds of audiences.

PebblePad supports learning wherever it happens, whenever it happens

Any experience offers opportunities for learning. Most institutional tools are typically designed to capture learning that takes place in formal places in structured ways. PebblePad supports the idea that learning is 'context-free': it takes place all the time, not only in the courses you study in educational settings. PebblePad helps you to identify, record, and create links between learning experiences wherever and whenever they occur.

PebblePad helps to scaffold and surface the process of learning

The wizards and forms in PebblePad support users through the process of creating meaningful records of experience and linking these records to develop rich understandings of learning. This scaffolding not only benefits users but also makes the process of learning evident for anyone with whom these records are shared. Supervisors, tutors and/or peers can assess not only the product of the learning activity but more importantly the process of skill and knowledge acquisition. Together with the capacity for on-going formative feedback, PebblePad becomes a powerful tool for teaching and learning.

PebblePad is underpinned, and informed, by a reflective structure
At every step of the way PebblePad users are prompted to consider 'Why?', 'So what?', 'What if?' and 'What now?' This inbuilt reflective structure is what transforms PebblePad into a space where learning is generated rather than simply collected and evidenced.

PebblePad gets people talking and helps users construct their narratives
The reflective structure of PebblePad is conversational – it prompts further thought and exploration. Anything created in PebblePad can be shared with one or more others in both private and group spaces. The capacity for comments, feedback and collaboration facilitates dialogue between users in these spaces. This sharing and dialogue contributes to the creation of much richer, more meaningful records of learning.

PebblePad can accompany you throughout your life and across all your activities
Over time, your needs and interests will change but the assets you have stored in PebblePad are always there for you to revisit and to use in different ways. Because PebblePad is 'context-free' you can continue to evidence learning and experiences wherever you go and whatever you do. PebblePad has the flexibility to be of value to you in any environment and at any stage of your life. Ideally it is the place where you record, reflect on, and learn from your journey and share it with others.

Planning Purposeful Activities

In this chapter we provide some suggestions and a model for how you might think about designing learning activities. In many ways, the suggestions are generic and you might find them useful for designing activities unrelated to the use of PebblePad. Of course, that's to be expected as good learning always results from considering the interplay of certain ingredients such as purpose, content, methods and assessment. PebblePad happens to be one of many ingredients you might choose to include – particularly in the light of reading this book.

Too often people choose to use PebblePad to 'add some variety' to their teaching, or because they are somehow 'required to'. On occasion, people choose to use the blog, the webfolio or an activity simply because 'they haven't tried them before'. Designing teaching around the tools available or because they are in vogue is unlikely to yield great results and will probably result in a group of frustrated learners resentful that PebblePad has been inflicted upon them. In these cases, it would be better if PebblePad was not used.

However, do not read this as a rebuttal against experimentation – because piloting, trialling and testing ideas in the curriculum is what keeps it fresh, creative and innovative. The starting point for said innovation, though, should always be: 'What do I want my learners to achieve as a result of this?' not: 'What tool shall I use this week?'

Learners and learning

It is hard to imagine how a learning design process could begin without some understanding of who the learners are; what their current level of skill, knowledge and experience is; and what they hope to gain from *this* lesson, unit or course. Consider the role that learners have to play in the ultimate success of the design at every stage of the process that follows.

Aims, outcomes and purpose

Curriculum development, learning design, session planning, call it what you will, starts with understanding what your purpose is. What do you want to achieve and what do you want the learners to achieve? At the broader levels of design, purpose is often written in terms of what the tutor's or institution's aims are: *To develop entrepreneurial graduates able to contribute to a fair and just society*. Of course, aims don't have to be so embroidered, they can refer to your intentions for a single session: *To experience collaborative problem-solving techniques*. Aims, then, are statements of *teaching* intent.

Aims are typically less amenable to assessment than those statements of purpose written to describe learning from the perspective of the learner. These statements are often referred to as learning outcomes, though they may also be referred to as objectives, competences or planned learning behaviours. Outcomes are a statement of what the learner *will be able to do* at the end of the session. These are *specific* action statements and are achievable stepping stones that lead towards those more generally expressed teaching aims described above. Outcomes say what the student will be able to *do* or *think* or *feel* or *say* as a result of the planned learning.

Aims and outcomes are different, then, in that one describes tutor intentions and one describes student learning; though in terms of planning, one is no less important than the other. Aims can be thought of as providing a very useful sense of direction with outcomes providing the steps along the way. Because PebblePad can be used to support everything from single episodes of learning through to course-wide requirements, we need a model of learning design that treats the smaller steps and the wider intentions as being broadly the same and so we will use the term *purpose* to describe what it is that we are trying to achieve through our planning.

So, not forgetting that a knowledge of the learners underpins all of our planning, purpose sits at the centre of our learning design model. It is the starting point because once we know what we want our learners to achieve, we are better able to consider what content is relevant, decide how it will be 'taught' or otherwise learnt, and consider how it will be assessed.

Content and method

Content describes what is being taught. It is the thing that is to be learnt; the subject matter. However, for this model we will treat content not in terms of specific subject knowledge like *describing the parts of a flower* but in its general characteristics. For example, content could be characterised as:

- a body of knowledge
- a way of thinking
- a way of acting
- a way of feeling
- a skill or capability.

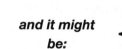
and it might be:

- concrete or abstract
- new or familiar
- predetermined or serendipitous
- prescribed or negotiated

An understanding of the nature of the content is important in considering the method that is used to convey it; the kinds of exercises and activities you might incorporate. Again, method can be described in very specific terms – such as *an idea storm* or a *lecture* – but it is useful to consider the characteristics of the method:

- □ tutor- or learner-centred
- □ expository or experiential
- □ prescribed or negotiated
- □ structured or spontaneous.

If you were considering using a PebblePad wizard or function as your *method* promoting engagement you might need to consider whether the activity ought to be:

- □ individual or collaborative
- □ private or shared
- □ simple or complex
- □ immediate or developed over time
- □ a single asset or a collection (such as in a blog or webfolio).

Why is it important to understand the characteristics of the content and the method? Simply because tension exists between some kinds of content and some methods of delivery. Conversely, choosing a method that is in sympathy with the content enhances the learning experience. Let's explore this with the following example.

Content and method in tension

The purpose of this three hour session is to develop academic writing skills, focussing in particular on the correct use of quotations, paraphrasing and referencing.

The content could be characterised as knowledge-based and concrete. The learners are familiar with the content but not yet confident.

The tutor organises the students into groups of three and tells them to spend the first part of the session in the learning centre making a list of resources (websites, online supports, books etc) that provide help and information about the subject. In the second half of the session the groups are to order their lists to show which resources appear to be most useful. They record their findings on a webfolio, which allows them to make links to electronic resources. This is then displayed in the classroom when the students briefly explain their ordering rationale to the other groups.

Imagine the session is being observed, perhaps as part of a peer review process. What would the observer note? The content is a staple of many first year modules and the method is active, participatory and concludes with the groups sharing their learning with others. It includes elements of information retrieval, of evaluation and presumably, of negotiation and presentation. So both the content and the method are valid *independently* but they are not aligned (Biggs, 1999). In other words, they do not support each other because the method, though apparently appropriate, does not provide the students with an opportunity to practice *how* to quote, paraphrase or reference.

Assessment

Imagine now that the tutor has planned to assess the students. If the tutor chooses to assess a short piece of academic writing created by the students it would be reasonable to argue that this is unfair. Although the students have gathered together a number of resources about academic writing they have not yet had the opportunity to assimilate the information and to practise its application. What if the tutor chooses to assess the presentation skills of the students? Presentation was included within the method but there is no evidence of preparation or of rehearsal. Would the assessment be of individual presenters or the group as a whole – or indeed of the design of the webfolio? What if all of the students presented in one group whilst, in another, a single student acted as the group's spokesperson? The most appropriate assessment would be of the quality or usefulness of the data sources found by each group and the reasoning behind their ordering.

This assessment would be out of line with the content but in sympathy with what the students actually did.

Activity design

It is a feature of good design that the content and method are in sympathy with each other. However, other elements of the learning design can still conspire to mis-align the overall plan. Perhaps the most obvious of these other elements is the assessment – be it formative or summative. We would argue, then, that the form of assessment selected should accurately assess what has been taught and draw upon methods familiar to the learners.

Writing about purpose, then content, method and assessment should not be taken to suggest that the model we are working towards is linear or *rational* (see Print, 1993), it should actually be viewed and used as a dynamic model. That is, any subsequent changes to any of the elements demands a reconsideration of the others because the overall value of the learning experience is always contingent upon how all of the elements relate to each other. A simple representation would look like this:

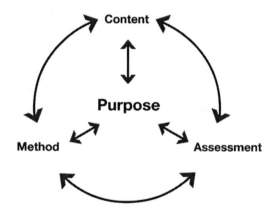

Figure 4.1: *Simple activity design model*

So this is how the session described above might be redesigned to ensure all of the elements of the model worked in alignment:

Content, method and assessment in sympathy

The purpose of this three hour session is to develop academic writing skills, focussing in particular on the correct use of quotations, paraphrasing and referencing.

The content could be characterised as knowledge-based and concrete. The learners are familiar with the content but not yet confident.

The tutor engages the students in a short discussion on the importance of academic writing conventions. She then provides some example texts which contain both incorrect and correct uses of quotations, citations and paraphrasing. As a whole group the students are encouraged to identify the errors. Once the students demonstrate sufficient group understanding, she organises them into groups of three, provides them with a page of text containing 20 known errors. The tutor explains that some of the errors are simple or obvious, whilst others are more difficult or subtle. There is one point available for each simple error spotted and three points for the more complex errors – without emphasising the point, an element of competition has been introduced to the activity.

After the allotted time, the groups take it in turn to describe an error, points are awarded and the overall points gained by each team gives the tutor some sense of the groups' general understanding.

Now that she has some confidence in the students' ability to identify mistakes, the students are presented with three short passages, by different authors but about the same subject. Their next task, which is completed as a self-directed activity, is to draw equally upon the three texts and to write a 200 word compilation which includes at least two examples each of referencing in the text (paraphrasing), direct quotation, and longer quotes. The students are told to write their compilation as a thought record and to post it to a gateway. In the gateway they have been organised into tutor groups which mirror the groups they have been working in face-to-face.

The gateway allows the tutor to set up a peer review activity and each group member is asked to provide feedback on other group member's work – an opportunity to put into practice the skills they developed in class. The act of feeding back on the work of others also helps reinforce knowledge and understanding of the referencing rules that formed the core of this activity. Because the tutor is able to view the compilations and the peer comments she can evaluate the success of the session and, if necessary, intercede in any disagreements that arise.

In the redesigned version of the session there is much clearer alignment between content, method and assessment. The method itself allows students to progressively work through activities designed to develop their understanding of the content. As well as developing their content knowledge, they have an opportunity to practise their evaluative skills which they use again during the peer assessment activity. The method supports the content and the use of a peer assessment activity provides further learning opportunities for all of the students, whilst also supporting the tutor's evaluation of the design.

Using PebblePad for this single activity also aligns with the tutor's plans for the broader module design:

'Fit' with the broader module design

The focus for the tutor in this activity has been on the 'rules' of referencing being better understood and practised in a writing activity – the interpretation of the original texts and the quality of the writing is of less importance. However, the tutor has insisted that the students keep a blog throughout the module because she knows how much easier it will be for the students to complete the end of unit essay if they can refer back to the ideas, thoughts and reflections that they have recorded during the module. With this in mind, and conscious that one of her broader aims is to develop independent learners, she tells the students to upload the compilation and comments to their blogs, along with a reflection on what they learnt during this activity.

To help encourage the students she offers to provide tutor feedback on the writing. Students are invited to share their blog posts with the tutor and to request feedback on specific aspects of their work.

It is clear in this design that the tutor is also thinking about how this session fits with other sessions and of the broader module purpose. The students are encouraged to take ownership of what they have learned through the entries they make on their blogs. This is not mandated, but is strongly encouraged by the way the final essay is structured. Furthermore, the tutor offers to provide additional feedback if a blog post is shared with her and if the student is able to articulate the nature and scope of the feedback required – rather than simply requesting *general feedback*.

Tutor and student concepts of self

The way the session is planned and delivered shows that the tutor is conscious of the short and longer term purposes of her interventions. The conception that she has of herself as a tutor is implicit in the way she has designed the session. The methods that she chooses are consistent with a view she holds about how her students learn best. Of course, if the students' view of themselves, their conception, is at odds with the design, then what might have been a successful learning encounter with another group of students may be much less successful with this particular group.

So, let us extend the activity design model to reintroduce the learners and to take account of the tutor.

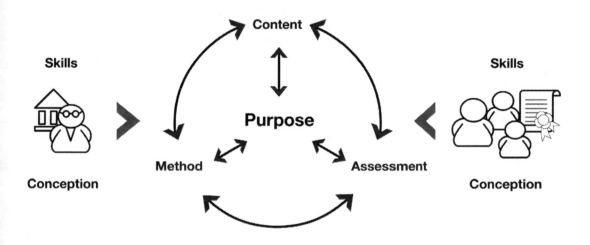

Figure 4.2: *Pebble activity design model: tutor and student conceptions*

An understanding of how different actors view their roles is important to the successful use of PebblePad – especially where an activity relies upon any form of iteration: for example, the student does some work, the tutor feeds back, the student replies to the comments or amends the work. As we have discussed in earlier chapters, PebblePad works best where conversation or dialogue takes place between those who use it. From the perspective of the learners they can choose to share and converse with friends, colleagues, peers, employers and others. Indeed, good learning designs have the potential to suggest ways in which learners can go on to use PebblePad independently, to make sense of learning beyond the curriculum, supported by people they choose to engage with. This type of use of the tool is most likely to be prompted or modelled by someone initially involved in their formal, planned or structured learning. It is also likely that the kind of tutor to be found providing ongoing, iterative feedback or supporting comments is likely to be the kind of tutor who has a conception of themselves as an active agent in the learning process. This is not someone whose only contact with their students is once a week in the lecture theatre.

Similarly, learners will have a conception of their role in the learning transaction. However, unlike the tutor, whose conception is more likely to remain constant throughout all of her teaching, the learners' conception can be modified through well designed learning activities and appropriate support from the tutor. Nevertheless, the tutor needs to have some sense of how learners understand their role. For example, do students see themselves as:

- active or passive?
- self-directed or dependent?
- individual or social?
- competent or novice?

If the learners view themselves as broadly passive and dependent then the tutor, having a view of herself as being responsible for developing independent learners, would try to modify that view. She would do this by embedding approaches and techniques within the content, method and assessment that, for example, enable the learner to take more responsibility for their own learning through peer assessment or by introducing activities that encourage reflective learning.

Skill development

At some point there is an overlap between changing a *conception* and developing *skills*. For example, a learner might think of themselves as always *acting in the moment* – of being unreflective. On many professional programmes the construct of a reflective practitioner is core to the makeup of the curriculum and so the development of both a reflective approach and reflective skills is essential. One could also point to the increased attention paid to notions such as graduate attributes, employability skills and other skills framed around sustainability, entrepreneurship and leadership. To take just one of those examples, it is easy to see how the development of entrepreneurial skills would increase the likelihood of a learner forming a conception that they were *entrepreneurial*.

Consideration of the skills of the learners has so far been discussed in terms of how it contributes to their conception of self-as-learner. We also need to consider the skills that learners will need in order to successfully engage with the methods used to deliver the content: and subsequently to be able to complete the assessment.

Contextualising this squarely in the realm of an assessed PebblePad activity, imagine you have asked the students to:

Reflect on your personal and professional contribution to a community project drawing upon the principles and practices explored during your studies.

You are required to make an entry to your project blog every day; the final entry for each week must be a summary of what you have learnt that week and what your short term goals are for the following week. The blog as a whole does not need to be shared with your tutor but can be shared with other project members and your project mentor. However, the summary post must be added to your project webfolio each week. You will receive feedback on your webfolio every second week.

You will be assessed by webfolio which must be published to the Community Project Gateway. The webfolio must contain two pages entitled 'Project Preparation and Project Reflections'. The preparation page should contain a 500 word overview of how you prepared for the placement, including links to any action plans, meeting records or other supporting assets. The reflection page must provide a 1000 word summary of what you contributed to the project, what you learnt from this experience and what you plan to do as a direct consequence of it. You must make links on this page to all six of your weekly summaries, indicating through the webfolio narrative the key learning points from each linked summary. You may also link to any supplementary blog posts that support your overall summary.

Let us consider the skills needed for the students to successfully complete this assignment:

Learning skills

- relate theory to practice;
- reflect on experience;
- plan to improve performance;
- plan to achieve a goal;
- review, consolidate, extend and apply knowledge and understanding.

PebblePad skills

- □ create a blog;
- □ post to a blog;
- □ share an asset;
- □ create a webfolio;
- □ publish to a gateway;
- □ make links to assets.

So, the tutor needs to ensure that students either have these skills or have opportunities to develop them throughout the unit or project, otherwise they are discriminated by the assessment itself.

If the students do not have some of these skills, then the tutor needs to incorporate plans for them to be developed; that is, ensure that the original content and methods are extended to allow for the development of the skills needed to actively and successfully participate.

But what if the tutor does not have the necessary skills to develop those of the learners? In some ways, this is not immediately important, especially if the tutor is able to call upon the skills of others such as, for example, learning technologists, student mentors or learning centre colleagues. What is essential is that the tutor has sufficient skill (and resources, such as time) to ensure that the learning activity itself is not compromised. In the activity above, the tutor would need to know how to create a gateway, perhaps how to set a deadline, how to view webfolios through the gateway and how to add feedback to them or to assets linked to them. A failure to add timely feedback might result in learners repeating errors throughout the project and ultimately losing grades or points for the assignment.

Design summary

We have tried to show how successful learning design is the result of a careful consideration of the interaction of the factors and actors in a planned learning experience. It has been necessary to exclude many other features and components of the learning ecology known to have an influence on learning. For example, we have not discussed resources such as handouts, tipsheets, people and time. We have not discussed group sizes, levels or subject areas and we have consciously avoided any discussion of prescribed syllabus, the wider curriculum and the vagaries of validation processes.

By way of summary, turn to the following pages where you will find a simple list of questions that might help scaffold your design conversations. Bear in mind, however, that although a list might appear to suggest a step-by step process, the reality is that every part of the model has some bearing on every other part.

PebblePad's approach to activity design

1. **Purpose**: Decide your purpose. What should learners be able to do as a result of this activity and where does this activity fit in the wider learning context?

2. **Content**: What content needs to be covered? What form does it take?

3. **Methods**: What methods are best suited to this content? Are the methods consistent with the assessment I have in mind?

4. **Assessment**: Does the assessment measure the learning I planned? Do the students have the skills for this kind of assessment? Does the assessment contribute to further learning? Are there opportunities for practice, for increments, for formative feedback?

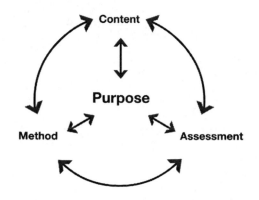

5. **Tutor skills**: Do I have the skills to make this activity a success? How can I develop my skills or get support for my ideal design?

6. **Teaching approach**: Is my approach to teaching consistent with what I am planning to do? Have I the resilience, aptitude and commitment for the activity I have planned?

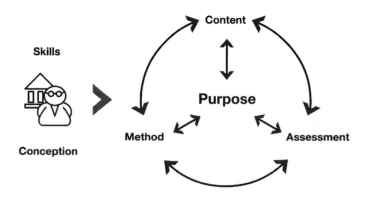

7. **Learners' skills**: Do the learners have the skills they need to be successful? What opportunities exist for skill development, rehearsal, practice, challenge and extension?

8. **Learners' approach**: How open to this kind of learning are the learners? What

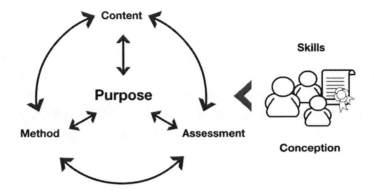

preliminary work may be necessary to prepare them for a different approach to their learning?

9. **Realign**: Remember that this is a dynamic model. A change to the assessment should provoke a reconsideration of whether the method and content are still appropriate and whether all three still support the purpose.

10. **Consider multiple players**: Rather simplistically, this model has only considered the conception and skill of a single tutor, the tutor-as-designer. In the very common context of multiple tutors, work-based mentors, supervisors and casual support much more concern should be given to how these other actors perceive their role in the learning and teaching transaction and the skills they bring to bear upon it.

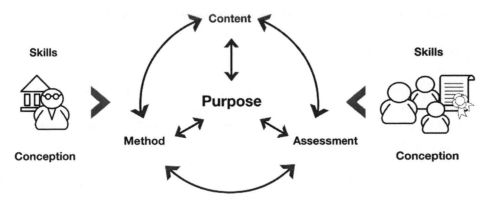

Doing Things Differently: Bungee Jumping with PebblePad

Julie Hughes
Principal Lecturer (Post Compulsory Education) and National Teaching Fellow

The inspiration for compiling this book has been the work of PebblePad users themselves, who have adopted the principles of PebblePad and taken them to places we would never have imagined. To give you a real flavour of PebblePad in action, we invited one of the most experienced PebblePad users, Julie Hughes, to tell us about her journey supporting teachers and learners with PebblePad.

So, you've been thinking about using PebblePad for a while? Or you've been using it and you want to develop what you and your students do with it? Or you are being 'urged' to use it and you'd like a pedagogic justification and roadmap to help?

This chapter will explore how the principles identified earlier, in *Chapter 3: Principles of PebblePad*, might translate into practice and how educators might prepare themselves, in part, for the rollercoaster ride ahead. The chapter starts from the basic tenet that PebblePad-based learning and teaching has the wonderful potential to challenge both students and their educators to do things differently. PebblePad is a disruptive technology which challenges the educator to re-think and re-do their pedagogy (Beetham and Sharpe, 2007, p.3). This is part of the rollercoaster and necessary pedagogic bungee jumping, to adopt Ron Barnett's (2007) metaphor for learning. So be prepared, whether a novice or more experienced user of the system, for some highs and lows in implementing and embedding new approaches and take heart from the fact that this is to be expected.

Getting started

You may have been to a staff development session or you may have seen how colleagues use PebblePad in their programmes but be aware that you are already making assumptions about its use. You need to immerse yourself in PebblePad to be able to begin to imagine its potential in your context. It's time consuming but you do need to explore and experience PebblePad for yourself to use it well to support individual learners and learning communities. Start with your curriculum, its design, its principles and values and consider how and where simple PebblePad-based activities might extend and enhance the learning experience. It's much better in the long term to start small and simple and feel in control of the intervention than roll out an ill-thought through, mass activity that leaves students and educators with a negative experience. In this instance, it's not unusual for others to project negativity onto PebblePad itself rather than examine the lack of planning and pedagogic reflection prior to its use. If this occurs in the first semester of a programme it is very hard to reassure colleagues and convince students to engage at a later stage of their learning. Some colleagues simplistically assume that PebblePad will do the pedagogic work for them; whereas others plan overly ambitious complex activities that leave students confused and sometimes frustrated. Wherever possible give yourself time to plan, reflect, practise and share your intended use of PebblePad. And whenever possible, undertake this as part of a team or community.

This is where an established PebblePad community can provide invaluable support, guidance and a safe opportunity for sharing experiences. An institutional, regional, or national PebblePad user group (meeting face-to-face or virtually) can offer compelling stories from practice as well as hints and tips that can save you from reinventing the wheel. Remember that you are not alone. The PebblePad community is a friendly, collaborative one and whilst not yet available to us, the next generation of PebblePad is designed to make it much easier for tutors and other users to work together to improve opportunities for learning across the international PebblePad community.

Actions:

- ☐ *Learn how to use PebblePad. You need to model and value the practices that you expect from your students.*

- ☐ *Access PebblePad from different computers/locations/devices. This will flag up any security issues and limitations that you need to be aware of.*

- ☐ *Find out how your IT systems talk to PebblePad – for example, passwords, information integration.*

- ☐ *Find out what institutional support there is for you and your students and publicise this. Can students call IT services about a PebblePad issue?*

- ☐ *Consider IT suite access. How much will you need? How often?*

- ☐ *Explore the videos and handouts available from PebblePad and from institutions. Could you use or repurpose them?*

- ☐ *Evaluate continually. It's ok to tell students that this is your first time using this fantastic new system and that their views and experiences are important to you and to your future use of PebblePad.*

Introducing PebblePad

If you start from your curriculum and your values it is straightforward to introduce, justify and contextualise the use of PebblePad as an expansive learning and teaching space: for example, the need for critical incident sharing in a group of new professionals or for dialogue-based learning journals. Ask yourself the questions:

- Why use PebblePad?
- What is it adding to the teaching and learning experience?
- Where is this pedagogic intervention adding value?
- Where could these practices be built upon further in a student's programme of study?

If you cannot answer the questions you need to revisit your initial intentions and reconsider your use of PebblePad. PebblePad may not be the appropriate technology to use in certain contexts and its success or failure in your programmes will depend upon the fit between what PebblePad can do and how you use it. This is why you need to have thought carefully through the pedagogic implications of engaging with students in this learning space.

If this is your first time using PebblePad, be prepared – it will take longer than your earlier face-to-face interactions as you and your students are learning to use the system and explore its potential. It is useful to consider Garrison and Vaughan's (2008) definition of blended learning as a thoughtful fusion of face-to-face and online activities. So, to return to your curriculum design you need to ask: "Am I using this PebblePad activity *as well as*?" (bolt on) or: "Am I using it *instead* of" (integrated)? Some colleagues have fallen into the trap of bolting on PebblePad activities in addition to standard face-to-face learning and teaching activity. As you can imagine, this adds considerably to the workloads of both tutors and students. PebblePad offers you the opportunity to thoughtfully fuse and expand face-to-face learning with individual and group online learning.

If this is your first time teaching online you will need to consider your online identity and the shift in digital literacies. Some colleagues struggle to find their online identities and voices in spaces such as PebblePad. This is because learning and teaching identities are more democratised in PebblePad as the 'power' rests with the owner of the asset and the permissions granted to others. This may also be viewed as powerfully transgressive and disruptive – in a positive way. One of my colleagues, Cathie, said that teaching in PebblePad was about *learning to let go* and this can be a painful struggle for some educators.

As many of our students arrive with experience in online talk spaces it is important to consider how (our) formal language use might inhibit or even shut down an emerging conversation. Standard feedback practices are usually highly formal, structured and monologic (one-way with no requirement for feedback). PebblePad is insistent in its demand for dialogue and this function is one of its most powerful learning tools. Therefore colleagues may need to expand their feedback repertoire and practices to include a more dialogic and conversational stance through the use of prompts and questions. It is important to reflect upon our feedback style and consider the shift to 'thinking through our fingertips' in these spaces: in other words, writing as a stream of consciousness, uninhibited by conventions of proper academic grammar. Overly formal writing by an educator in a talk space such as a shared blog, can intimidate and inhibit further group conversations. Often this is the result of a lack of experience of teaching in these spaces and a need to shift one's self-perception as a teacher from 'teller' to 'talker'.

Actions:

- ☐ *Be clear about where PebblePad-based learning fits in the curriculum and aligns with assessment.*

- ☐ *Negotiate and establish the netiquette of the space and its practices – for example, interactions with others – this is a learning space just like our classrooms and it is important to clarify expectations.*

- ☐ *Experiment with online feedback techniques – written, audio and video.*

Creating expectations and the conditions for talk and reflection

As a more experienced PebblePad user, it is possible to use the webfolio and blogging tool to support transitions into and out of the institution. Based on our experiences of using blogging at the University of Wolverhampton, the discussion that follows illustrates how PebblePad may be used as a socialisation and orientation tool to support the development of digital literacies, to create an expectation for dialogue-based peer learning and to facilitate critical reflective practice.

First, let's consider the learners and the challenges we faced.

Using blogs and blogging to support transitions into and out of university

The learners are both graduates undertaking a full time one year Post Graduate Certificate in Education (PGCE) teaching qualification for the post-compulsory sector and mature students beginning a part time foundation degree in an education subject related to their work role.

Both cohorts face a challenging professional course where they will be required to demonstrate their development as critically reflective practitioners. Both programmes require the sharing of critical incidents from practice within sub-divided learning groups.

The programme teams wanted to model blogging behaviours as professional reciprocal dialogue beginning pre-course or at induction to support the transition into study.

There are a number of challenges that face the learners and the tutors. Foundation degree students are often very nervous about the transition into higher education and lack academic confidence. New students cannot access PebblePad until they are fully enrolled in the university and the team felt that this was a missed opportunity to engage with new students. In both programmes, students are required to be reflective practitioners. Established earlier practices positioned reflection as a solitary activity 'assessed' at the end of the programme of study. There was no potential for dialogue and responding to feedback and, additionally, paper portfolios and paper journals were conceived as static repositories.

Using PebblePad, we were able to address a number of these issues:

- Blogging in PebblePad introduced an expectation for dialogue and exchange with peers and tutors whilst on the programme. Individual and collaborative blogging is now an integrative assessed part of both programmes.
- The ability to create a webfolio with an embedded blog, and to then share via the web, allowed pre-course activity and early socialisation that was reported to be vital to students' sense of belonging in and to the university. Prior to this, students in college-based provision did not have access to the wider university learning community.

    ☐   Using PebblePad has allowed PGCE students to export and develop their blogging practices in their Professional Formation applications to the IfL (Institute for Learning).

From our experience of using blogs for socialisation and orientation, here are some of the key considerations.

Allow access to the blog before the course

Being able to access a group blog before the course has proved to be highly successful with foundation degree students over several iterations. Through the blog, students share their hopes, fears and expectations, which is both a powerful learning activity and a springboard into a higher education community. Students report feeling relieved: 'I'm glad I'm not the only one feeling this way' has been a common comment. It is important to get the tone of the blog prompts right for the target audience and to provide timely supportive feedback to encourage more contributions.

Aim to move from tutor ownership to collaboration

Initially it is important to retain 'control' of blog permissions, as multiple posts with no or few comments can be chaotic and operate simply as a message space. Students who are experienced with posting to the web (using Facebook, for example) may be a little frustrated by their lack of ownership and it is important to talk through your choice of permissions and the implications of giving 'collaborate' permission to a group. After induction, a publicly shared blog may be withdrawn from the web to support confidential critical incident sharing. It is vital that ground rules and expectations for the learning environment are negotiated and agreed, particularly in professional contexts where settings and references to individuals must be anonymised.

Develop individual reflective practice

All students on the PGCE have an individual blog, shared only with their personal tutor on a gateway. Evaluation repeatedly tells us that students highly value this activity which contributes considerably to their development as students and as teachers. Fostering and modelling a critically reflective stance supports the movement into a wider community of practice for peer learning through critical incident sharing. The role of feedback in both individual and collaborative blogs is crucial to developing a questioning and analytical stance. Feedback from the tutor should be challenging and forward looking, using questions to encourage students to talk back to the feedback, thereby encouraging a deeper analysis.

Use 'Blog Buddies' and 'Pebble Pals'

In every cohort there will be individuals that shine because of PebblePad, either because they respond particularly well to the emphasis upon engaged reflective practice and the peer learning opportunities, or because they are agile PebblePad users. Use them! Students with well-developed practical skills make great Pebble Pals (peer mentors for their own and future cohorts) and Blog Buddies who act as critical friends on the group blog. Blog Buddies can be invited onto a shared blog either by sharing the whole blog with them or, if there is a need to retain confidentiality, through the sharing of the individual thought asset. Students who have been immersed in this supportive, dialogic learning culture are often prepared 'to give something back' to the next wave of *Pebblers*.

Share critical incidents

Asking all students to share a 'critical' incident from placement on the blog provides a powerful opportunity for problem-based peer learning and professional reflective learning. The tutor models challenging, but constructive, feedback and students learn from this to give feedback to their peers that challenges assumptions, practices and outcomes. Some incidents require ideas or solutions and the peer approach supports the group to look to each other, and not just the tutor, for guidance. It is important that the incidents are theorised beyond surface practicalities and critical readings of theory applied to practice are incorporated into the group blogging over time. This applied and theorised reflection builds into the summative assignment in a patchwork manner (see *Theme 7: Collaborative Learning* for more about 'patchwork text'). Students are encouraged to view their blogs and webfolios as cumulative stories which they will take with them into their employment and wider learning.

For those readers who might want to replicate our work in PebblePad, here are some very specific points to think about.

Create a structured blog with learning activities/prompts to share with a group

Stop! Think about the size of the cohort and what this blog activity is trying to achieve. If working with large groups, you will need more than one blog or you will need to structure your posts to support smaller group interaction. Too large a group will result with a message board type stream of comments that can overwhelm some contributors/readers and can inhibit deep learning.

If you are working with a large group and you want to split them into learning sets create a structured blog, copy and rename each separate blog (e.g. Group 1/2/3/4). You can then embed each blog as a page within a webfolio template. This will allow you to manage and monitor the divided groups and provide opportunities for peer learning within groups and across the cohort.

Remember that blog posts will appear backwards so plan for about four blog posts initially.

- Post number 4 should be the welcome post (as it will appear at the top of the blog page) which should provide information on how to navigate the blog, add content and change the viewing appearance/layout. If this blog is going to be shared with the web/external participants, this information must be shared with the bloggers as well as a reminder about appropriate netiquette and an invitation to introduce themselves. It is vital to be clear about where the blog is posted and who has access to it. Confusion about this may have an impact on contributions and concerns about confidentiality. The tutor(s) should then add an introduction to themselves within the blog post.

- Posts number 3 and 2 should be related to the course of study and/or to expectations of higher education study, for example: 'What does it mean to be a reflective practitioner in an early years setting?', 'What are your expectations for the foundation degree?' If this blog is shared within PebblePad and all contributors are aware that this is confidential you might ask: 'How are you feeling about higher education study?' 'What sort of teacher do you want/ hope to be?'

- Post number 1 should be a more informal chat space where students can ask questions etc.

Use the web and gateways to share the blog

For pre-induction activities, send to the web. You can either send the URL directly in an email or shorten first (with bit.ly/tinyurl). On programme activities, send to a gateway and give students instructions on how to subscribe.

Use structured blogs to help students move beyond description

If the blog posts remain quite descriptive, advise students to use the structured thought prompts and then post them to their blog. Alternatively, you can provide additional writing frames: for example, learning autobiography, action plan prompts.

Sometimes reflection and blogging can seem daunting and it is important to model and prompt reflective writing. Blogs can host any PebblePad asset type and a structured blog that contains a simple or complex form can provide a useful scaffold. Over time, students can post action plans, experience records etc. to their blogs as well as their open thoughts.

And, finally, here are ten tried and tested tips for planning your blogging activity.

Ten tips for planning your PebblePad activity

1. If using this with large groups plan your gateway structure and permissions carefully and ensure that all staff are aware of the gateways function.

2. Create handouts in good time so that a less experienced PebblePad user can test it for you – it is very easy to miss out a stage. Nervous students will be very put off if they can't follow the handout.

3. Whenever possible demonstrate using PebblePad in an IT suite.

4. Whenever possible work in pairs – if there are two of you, you can work with 30 students at a time and they can copy, auto-publish and begin to populate in 30 minutes.

5. Think about the support your colleagues will need – you may want to plan an 'Away Day' where you have hands-on activities and horizon gazing.

6. Plan some workshops for less experienced students. Use more experienced students as Pebble Pals (peer mentors) and Blog Buddies.

7. Think about your feedback practices and allow additional time early in the semester to provide lots of formative feedback to get the blogging going.

8. Evaluate mid-semester to get a sense of what is working and what you need to develop. If you are confident enough, use the blog to gather this evaluation.

9. Keep the institutional drivers of retention, achievement and progression in mind. Make a note of times when you are aware that blogging is supporting these drivers and extract any comments that directly address this. After the assessment period consider and correlate if this approach has had any impact on grades – and if it has, publicise it!

10. Be patient, sometimes it takes two or three iterations before it works in the way you'd anticipated. Don't get disheartened, this is a culture shift.

Growing PebblePad cultures – and not in a petri dish

It is vital to grow your PebblePad community for these practices to flourish. As identified above, our students are a rich resource who have much to teach us about successful learning in spaces such as PebblePad. Students exposed to PebblePad-based learning and teaching have told us that the benefits include: feeling supported in the transitions into higher education study; it personalises what could be a mass impersonal experience;

it provides a valuable tutorial and welfare role; and it provides valuable opportunities for peer learning, anytime anywhere learning. The space offered by PebblePad gives students time to think and compose themselves in a blog setting rather than a physical classroom; it also provides the opportunity for warm-up/rehearsal of academic literacies and on-going reflective writing, iterative formative assessment and feedback. Importantly for teacher education students (PGCE/FD), many recreate their own learning experiences with their own students, with the result that there is an increased use of technology in general and an expectation that tools and online spaces used should encourage talking not telling.

Tutors converted to these ways of working stress that it allows greater insight into individuals. It is a great retention tool as it allows a tutor to monitor and intervene in a non-public manner. For more experienced users of PebblePad, the workload may reduce as the PebblePad community of practice support and help each other. There is also the advantage that assessment is staggered as there is no end-loaded assessment period. Tutors who embrace PebblePad-based learning also enjoy the shift in their teacher identity and practices which can create democratic and vibrant learning and teaching.

Institutionally, PebblePad-based learning may support achievement, retention and progression if used in a holistic manner. It is possible to create the expectation for alumni networks and continued communication with the institution. For employers and roles in the wider society these ways of being can facilitate and create important transferable skills such as reflection, problem solving, working with others online, developing an awareness of audience, the need for different registers and the development of some digital literacies.

What next?

All of the above require what Barnett (2007) terms 'a will to learn in uncertain times'. Now, more than ever, educators must be prepared to enter into unknown territories. This pedagogic bungee jumping is vital if we are to adapt to support 21st century learners. This book, and the examples from practitioners in Part B, offer educators a scaffold and safety net to experiment within. PebblePad-based learning and teaching has well and truly arrived.

6 Pebblegogy in Practice

By way of concluding this first part of Pebblegogy, we have gathered together a set of questions that will help you when you are thinking about designing activities in PebblePad. These are all discussed in previous chapters, so this checklist is intended as a series of reflective prompts that you can return to over time. In some organisations, the design and delivery may be shared between different people but, for simplicity, we are assuming that the activity is designed and delivered by the same person.

Consider the learning culture and establish support

Before you begin, consider:

How will you make time to plan, practise and reflect so that you are a confident user of PebblePad?

Who in your department/organisation do you need to get on board to ensure that the activity will be a success and that you have the support you need? Can you link to a PebblePad community?

What is the learning culture in your department/organisation? For example, is there a willingness to share, peer review and collaborate? If not, what discussions or work might need to take place to gather support for doing these things in PebblePad?

Think about your context

Think about your curriculum, the way your subject is taught, its design, principles and values

At which points in the curriculum design will PebblePad activities help to extend, continue or link learning?

Think about the learners

Who are your learners and what do they bring? What aptitudes or challenges will be relevant to designing your PebblePad activity?

Think about yourself

How do you see yourself as a teacher/tutor/facilitator/mentor? Do you think your role is to tell, to guide, to support, to facilitate…? How will this translate to the personal learning space that your learners will inhabit in PebblePad?

Be clear about your purpose

Think about the learning and the learners

What are the pedagogic implications of using PebblePad? (What value does it add, how is it integrated into the course design?)

Think about how PebblePad will help

Is PebblePad the right choice for the activity and why? Some purposes, such as delivering a body of theory may be better addressed on the Learning Management System or in the classroom. In this case, PebblePad can be used alongside to enable reflection and personal record-keeping.

How would you explain your reasons to someone who was not familiar with PebblePad? Be prepared to justify your use of PebblePad to others and try to do this in terms of the learning value that can be achieved.

Scope the activity

Now you can think in more detail about the parameters of your activity:

How many students will you be working with and what implications will this have on your workload (giving feedback etc.)? Be realistic about how much time this new way of working may take initially. Factor in a potential reduction in time later down the line. If you are teaching in a team, discuss these timeframes with all concerned.

Have you planned regular team meetings to discuss progress?

How will you support less experienced colleagues?

Where are your learners in their 'lifecycle' and how might this affect their willingness to engage? Identifying the 'touch point' (see *Chapter 3: Principles of PebblePad*) may help you to understand what will motivate learners to use PebblePad. For example, your students may be much more willing to engage in an activity when they see it is going to be useful in getting a job or securing accreditation later on.

What is the timeframe?

What do you know about the skills of your learners? What will you need to do to ensure they have the necessary skills to engage with the activity?

Can you involve others to help you? Remember that there may be willing students who pick up the necessary skills straight away who can be valuable in supporting others.

How much time do you have to plan and prepare the activity? A complex activity may take a long lead-in time to set up, but can pay dividends in the long-term if it can be repeated and saves on tutor time in other ways. A simple activity can help to build your confidence and the confidence of your learners.

What implications do your answers to the above have for the kind of activity you can realistically plan and manage? In Part B each activity displays a set of icons to indicate teacher complexity, student ability, preparation time, duration and number of students. These will help to guide you to activities that may suit your purpose.

Design the activity

Outcomes and 'fit' (revisit Chapter 4: Planning Purposeful Activities for more detail)

What are the learning outcomes for the activity (i.e. curriculum-specific) and how do they fit with the overall course/programme aims?

Are there other outcomes that may be useful for your learners? (For example, the activity may ask for a webfolio to be developed and this may be useful after the activity ends for presenting to employers or for postgraduate research beyond the curriculum).

How is the PebblePad activity integrated with other activities in the curriculum? Does it sit outside the flow of other activities or does it fit with them? Are you aware of any other use of PebblePad in other modules/programmes/projects? If so, are you replicating/expanding?

Ownership and control

What level of control do you plan to retain or release, for example with sharing permissions? Are your learners ready for a high level of self-directed learning in the personal learning space or will they need more help using the scaffolding tools in PebblePad?

Aligning the learning purpose to the tool

Is the chosen PebblePad tool or asset the right one for this activity? For example, do you want to demonstrate competency using a profile? Do you want to engage in dialogue using a blog? Do you want to plan a project using the action planning tool and a webfolio? Do you want to present a programme of work and experience using a webfolio? Or maybe you want to use a combination – in which case, are you linking the assets in some way? Remember, the learning should drive your choice of tool (and not the other way around).

Feedback and assessment

How will you deliver online feedback: for example, will your use of language be formal/informal? What limits or boundaries will you make to your availability?

Will feedback be formative or summative or a mixture or both?

Will you incorporate peer review or other people in the formative feedback?

Will the activity be assessed? If so, how? Consider whether a final assessment is the best approach for your learners. A series of small tasks along the way offer opportunities for formative feedback and can be more manageable than a large task at the end of a course or module.

Is the assessment aligned to the learning outcomes?

Who will be involved in assessment: peers, yourself, external examiners, employers?

Sharing and viewing permissions

Who else is likely to view the assets during and after the activity? Are there some parts of the activity that will remain private in the learner's personal learning space or will you expect all assets that are completed during the activity to be shared? Consider how you will ensure learners fully understand the implications of the range of permissions they can set.

Skills and knowledge requirements

What skills or knowledge will the learners need in order to complete the activity – either in using PebblePad or in subject-specific areas? Will you use PebblePad, the LMS or face-to-face workshops to deliver this? Or a blend?

Will you share the tutoring/mentoring/facilitating with others? Do they have the skills and understanding they need to use PebblePad and, if not, how will they acquire these?

Have you looked at this from a user's perspective?

What preparation will be needed, such as user instructions or handouts? Are you aware of resources that already exist within the community that may prevent repetition of effort in creating new ones?

Preparing the online space

What ground rules and expectations do you have for the learning space? For example, the netiquette for interacting with others or commenting on others' work, the importance of confidentiality in professional contexts. How will you negotiate and agree these with your learners?

Do you need to take any actions or further development yourself to become confident about your own online identity?

Tracking progress

How will you build in evaluative processes: continuous checks to see that learners are on track?

Reflect and learn

What went well?

What were the pedagogical benefits of using PebblePad?

What were the administrative benefits of using PebblePad for this activity? For example: reduction in paper, administrative processes easier to monitor, easier to retrieve archived assignments, first and second markers are looking at scripts simultaneously.
If you repeat the activity, what will you change or improve?

What did the learners think of it? How do you know?

How will learners take this activity forward into other parts of the curriculum (or other 'touch points' in their study/career)?

Share your success

Have you shared the process with other tutors (or managers/stakeholders) in your department/organisation so that the activity can be repeated without you or in other parts of the organisation?

Have you shared the process with others (colleagues, institution, PebblePad community) so that they can learn from it and adapt it for their context?

Have you considered how to achieve on-going involvement of external examiners who may be new to PebblePad?

Remember there is a supportive community of PebblePad users who can help you if you feel daunted by the questions here. Take heart from the experiences of others and the fact that those who have taken the leap to working in a different way are reporting huge benefits for learners, tutors and learning organisations. As you will see in Part B of *Pebblegogy*, there are many examples of inspiring and engaging activities to draw upon but only you can decide what will work in your particular teaching and learning context. If you are starting off, bear in mind Julie Hughes' advice: keep it simple and build from there. As you grow in confidence designing activities in PebblePad, you and your learners will start to enjoy the transformative potential of the personal learning space.

Part B

Activities for Learning with PebblePad

B Activities for Learning with PebblePad

Introduction to the learning themes

As we discussed in *Chapter 3: The Principles of PebblePad*, there are many 'touch points' in a life of study, work and learning when PebblePad can be used for a variety of purposes. At each one of these touch points, whether that is entering university or collaborating with peers on advanced professional development, a particular learning purpose might arise. So, in Part B, we have clustered a selection of activities under twelve learning themes which illustrate how PebblePad can be used to, for example: develop evidence of employability (*Theme 10: Preparing for Employment*); assess group work skills (*Theme 5: Promoting Group Work*); or integrate individual learning across a programme of study (*Theme 9: Preparing for Accreditation*). Each theme offers ideas that will help tutors and learning designers to design activities that will support their curricula. We hope, too, that as you grow more familiar with the range of possibilities offered by PebblePad, that you will be tempted to extend your use of PebblePad to support your own learning goals.

How the activities were developed

The activities have been developed from the contributions of tutors, learning and curriculum designers and other practitioners in Australia and the UK who generously gave their time to share their ideas with the wider PebblePad community. The activities are not intended to be 'case studies'; we have used a liberal amount of editorial licence to make them readily applicable to different contexts. Whilst some of the contributions have been retained in their entirety, most have been edited to make them usable for a wide audience in a range of different contexts and some contributions have been conflated with others where they each shared a similarity of purpose. These activities are tried and tested and, where possible, we have given more detail about them in the 'activity in context' section. Others have been developed as composites of common learning designs that are used widely by PebblePad practitioners.

As we edited, categorised and compiled the activities, we started to think of them rather like recipes where the PebblePad tools provide the ingredients and the cook/learning designer combines them with flair and creativity to achieve specific results. Like a cookbook, we have clustered the activities so that you can dip into Part B for ideas and inspiration.

We have tried to make the activities as generic as possible but it is up to you to adapt them to the needs of your learners and the purpose of your learning design. Remember that if you change one element of a learning design you may need to check that other elements are still in alignment, as we discussed in *Chapter 4: Planning Purposeful Activities*. Make sure that learners have opportunities to develop any PebblePad skills that are required for successful engagement with the activity: for example, creating a blog, sharing an asset or publishing to a gateway. This may be integrated into the activity or you may decide to develop a separate set of introductory activities. You will find some ideas for these in *Theme1: First Steps with PebblePad*.

The activities that feature in the following themes are an eclectic mix of distance and blended learning models. Since PebblePad, by its nature, can support all aspects of distance learning most of these activities could be adapted to an entirely distance online learning approach with minimal changes.

Finding activities to suit your learners

To help you find activities that meet your needs and those of your learners, each activity has a series of icons which will help you to assess the time, effort and type of activity that is being described. These are only a rough guide, and bear in mind that all the activities can be adapted to your own purposes.

Achieving consistency in terminology is quite a challenge when educational institutions and professional organisations in Australia and the UK use a wide range of terms for their packages of learning. Rather than adding to the complexity by creating a new lexicon, we have opted for consistency within activities where we have adopted local terms.

The icons

Tutor complexity

Student PebblePad ability

Preparation time

Duration of activity

Number of students

The main PebblePad assets

	Ability		Blog		Meeting
	Achievement		CV		Profile
	Action plan		Experience		Thought
	Activity		Form		Webfolio

Using the instructions

For each activity we have included instructions for tutors in how to set up, and deliver, the activity in PebblePad, followed by instructions for the learners. If you are using the instructions with your own students, you may want to break the steps down further than we have here – or you may find that you can abridge them if your learners are quite familiar with the PebblePad functions. It is up to you to adapt them to your context.

The icons shown alongside the tutors and students actions/instructions indicate tools or functions used during the setup or completion of the activity.

Cross referencing

Many of the activities serve more than a single purpose and could appear under different themes. For example, a collaborative activity may also have an element of peer review built into it, or a professional development activity may also improve academic skills. So, for each theme we have suggested ideas for cross referencing to others where you will find further ideas that can inspire your own learning designs.

Remember also that these 'recipes' are just the starting point. As your confidence with PebblePad grows you will be able to take parts of one recipe, combine them with another, add a couple of flourishes and arrive at an activity that is uniquely suited to the needs of your students and your curriculum intent.

Companion website

A Pebblegogy website is being developed to augment the activities here and to offer further ideas to inspire and engage your learners. Further details are available from the PebblePad site: www.pebblepad.co.uk/pebblegogy

theme
01

First Steps with PebblePad

Although PebblePad is designed to be intuitive and easy to use for new users, on many courses of study tutors choose to run introductory workshops so that learners can try out the PebblePad tools in a risk-free environment before they embark on critical assessed activities.

Even those who are nervous of computers usually find that they can produce pleasing results with only a short induction into how to use the tools and it is possible to design fun and engaging activities that can work in either a face-to-face environment or entirely online.

As with all the activities in this book, careful planning is the key. To begin, consider the learners. What challenges do they face? These may include, for example:

- different levels of information technology skills
- preconceptions about the technology (which may range from a reluctance to engage to over-confidence)
- lack of familiarity with the language and purpose of 'reflection' in learning
- other external distractions such as timing of the introduction (it may be freshers' week, or part time students may have work or family commitments).

While external distractions are something the workshop facilitator probably has little control over, the timing of the PebblePad introduction needs to be early in a course of study so that learners can get into the habit of using PebblePad. Whether the induction activities are online or face-to-face it will be important to create a safe and supportive environment where learners can explore PebblePad at their own pace. There should be opportunities to voice concerns and anxieties, which will go some way to addressing the first two challenges. The tutor or facilitator will need a clear understanding of the principles of PebblePad so that the reflective, supported personal learning approach can be modelled from the outset.

This may be the time to introduce the purpose and practice of reflective learning in a gentle reflective exercise, which can then be reinforced in future activities. To understand how PebblePad can support this learning, the user needs to experience how to use the prompt questions within the wizards and to understand how tutors and peers can exchange comments within the system. It is very important to emphasise that PebblePad is a secure, private space where the learner controls who sees what. Learners will be reassured to hear that the only way someone can look at the contents of the account is if they have the username and password for the account. Even the system administrator cannot log into an account and take a look.

The purpose of an introductory workshop is usually to build confidence and help learners to engage with the PebblePad tools, so be prepared to answer questions.

PebblePad FAQs

Here are some of the questions that may be asked in an introductory session. If they are not, make sure that learners are aware of these key messages.

Can I use PebblePad to include experiences outside this course?

Yes, definitely. The ethos underpinning the PebblePad approach to learning is that learning occurs both within a course and away from formal learning environments, so PebblePad can be used for anything that supports your development, whether that is working at a fast food restaurant or planning a holiday.

Is there a file limit to how much I can upload?

The file limit is 10mb. Large files can cause problems for people viewing them, so file sizes should always be kept as small as possible.

I already use Web 2.0 tools: why should I use PebblePad?

Web 2.0 tools are great and you may already be blogging in WordPress, be uploading video files to a YouTube account and sharing documents on GoogleDocs. You can continue to use these tools, and some can be imported to your PebblePad account. You can, for example, embed Flickr photos or YouTube videos. But the important considerations that PebblePad offer are durability, security and privacy. Some Web 2.0 tools are here today, gone tomorrow. PebblePad is here to stay. If you are discussing topics that are sensitive or private, you know that working within PebblePad, they will only be shared with those people you choose to share with.

What is an asset?

The **Create New** menu initially has assets to record or plan single 'things' or 'events' and the 'more' option takes you to assets that allow for building presentations or collections of evidence. (Showing the learners a webfolio of a former student at this point can really help learners envisage what they are working towards.)

What is a gateway?

When you send an asset to a gateway, it is a secure and risk free method of handing something in to the institution. Your asset doesn't actually leave your PebblePad account but a link to the item you have 'sent' is added to the gateway. Assets sent to the gateway area are open to scrutiny from other tutors and external examiners. Using a gateway tutors can, within reason, allow other appropriate people – such as moderators and external examiners – to view submitted assets.

How do I share assets?

Assets can be shared with trusted peers and can be presented to an audience outside of the institution (assets can be shared with anyone with an email address) and unshared just as easily, emphasising the concept that the learner is at the heart of PebblePad.

(It can be useful to demonstrate a sample asset such as an action plan, an activity record or a webfolio that includes feedback and comments from peers.)

Can I export my work when I leave?

You can export your work using standards-based export facilities. Once you have left the institution you get a free personal account for a minimum of a year and then longer term you can keep your account for a small fee.

Where can I get further help?

The PebblePad help button, a question mark icon, is located on the right hand side of the PebblePad screen and throughout PebblePad you will see a question mark icon next to most fields. Clicking on this reveals a short hint and clicking on the hint box will open the online help at the correct section.

Looking for more ideas ?

If you are interested in more starter activities, look for the 'beginner' . You may also find further ideas in *Theme 2: Orientation and Induction*.

---

activity

01.1

Getting to know each other in PebblePad

This is a socialising activity which borrows from the idea of 'speed dating'. It helps students to get to know each other, have fun and start to use the 'CV' and 'About Me' tools in PebblePad.

Activity Overview

Low		Assets
Beginner		
Low		
Session		
Class		

What challenges might this address?

When the requirements of a course require trust and cooperation with peers, it is important to allow some time early on to get to know each other and to learn the basics of PebblePad. Using PebblePad tools/categories to trigger face-to-face interactions as part of an early socialisation process allows the student the dual benefit of having prepared information for the interpersonal interaction, and also establishing some familiarity with the personal learning tool that they will be using.

Learning new technology does not have to be boring and the element of gaming and fun that this activity introduces helps learners to engage with the tools in preparation for later study.

Learning design

Prior to the workshop, the tutor creates a handout that has blank fields taken from the 'About Me' tool in PebblePad. The tutor chooses which fields are most appropriate for the group. It is probably best to stay with the more factual fields that might appear on a CV (personal details, languages, education and employment) than to ask belief and value questions at this stage. This activity suits a group of between 15 and 20 students and takes place in a workshop that has space to move around, and access to PCs. In the workshop each student is given the handout and asked to complete the questions on it. Two rows of 10 chairs are then set up and students sit on a chair and use the fields on the handout to introduce themselves to one another (as in speed dating!). Students systematically move on after a two minute exchange, until each student has met all the other students in the group. Students ask each other how they have filled in the different categories and share their information. With the completed paper copies now filled in and possibly some enhanced information derived from the conversations, students log onto PebblePad and enter the information into the appropriate categories. Then, using this information, students complete a brief CV and submit it to the appropriate gateway for the tutor to view and comment on.

Tutor actions

What you need to do in PebblePad to set up the activity

Prior to the activity:

☐ Select which categories you would prefer your students to fill in from the **About Me** section in PebblePad.

☐ Copy these onto the handout you will distribute in class.

☐ Create a **gateway**. Add students to the **user group**. The default permissions do not need to be changed for this activity.

During the activity:

☐ Once the students have sent their **CV** to the **gateway**, comment on each one, acknowledging their **CV** and achievements. If you find yourself adding similar comments to a number of CVs think about using the **comment bank**.

Instructions to the learner

You can adapt these instructions to your learners and to your context

☐ After you have completed the face-to-face activity, log onto PebblePad.

☐ Go to **tools** and select **about me**. Fill in each category that corresponds with the handout you have just completed. Select **add to my CV** once you have completed a category. Alongside each new piece of information you add there is an icon which indicates whether it will be added by 'default' to your new CV. In future you can create multiple CVs and the information you include can be different each time.

☐ When you have finished with a category click save and close.

☐ Now go to **create new** and **more**. Select **CV**. Put your name as the title.

☐ In step 2 choose a banner to suit your character.

☐ In step 3 select the categories your tutor has included on the handout. These will be added to your **CV** with the details you filled in, in **About Me**.

☐ To view the **CV** click on the **magnifying glass** in the right hand corner. A new window opens. Read your **CV**. Close the window.

☐ Send your **CV** to the **gateway**.

☐ Your tutor will read and comment on your **CV**. When he has done this, you will be alerted by an update on the **current activity** pane in PebblePad.

The activity in context

This activity has been used with second year students, studying to become physiotherapists at LaTrobe University, Australia. Students were relatively unknown to each other because of a multidisciplinary first year.

Practitioner tips

This activity can be used as part of an induction process, introducing new members of staff to one another.

activity
01.2

Introducing blogging for reflective practice

This activity provides a first introduction to PebblePad using the blog tool. This simple use of PebblePad can help to build confidence amongst learners who may go on to develop webfolios to meet course requirements. It develops digital literacy skills and introduces students to the concept of reflective practice.

Activity Overview

👥	Low	Assets
📖	Beginner	⚙️
📋	Low	
🕐	Semester	
👪	4+	

What challenges might this address?

Introducing PebblePad early on in a course does not mean you have to introduce all its tools in one go. This simple approach, using the blog tool, allows the learners to access PebblePad and to start their explorations in a straightforward and easy activity. It also shows how assessment and dialogue with a tutor/mentor can take place through PebblePad.

Learning design

Students in this activity post regularly to a blog for the duration of the semester. The students are introduced to the activity in a two hour workshop in a computer lab. In the first part of the workshop the tutor explains the value of reflection and describes the process in a simple manner. A more sophisticated model for reflection is developed later in the course. For the purposes of this workshop, reflection is introduced as the process of going back over something recalling thoughts and memories; examining what happened, identifying what worked well and why; and thinking about ways to develop and improve in the future. It is emphasised that reflection is a purposeful activity that leads to better outcomes.

The activity, which is a pass/fail assignment, is to write at least eight posts with a word limit of 250 words each week during the semester. The blog posts have to include the following professional topics:

- discipline specific issues;

- thoughts on placements;

- transition to university life;

- time management;

- challenges to studying.

In the second part of the workshop, students create a blog, add an introductory post and send the blog to the assessment gateway. This has two purposes:

1. The tutor can check, during the workshop, that all the students in the cohort have successfully completed the submission part of the assignment even before the assignment has been completed.

2. The students have completed one of the eight posts before leaving the workshop.

Students are advised that only eight posts will be assessed by the tutor, but they can write more if they wish. This manages the tutor's workload, should the activity become very successful and students write more than eight posts.

At the end of the semester students are awarded a pass or a fail. Awarding a fail is rare because the tutor can use the gateway to monitor student engagement with the blogs and remedy any problems before the assignment due date.

Tutor actions

What you need to do in PebblePad to set up the activity

Prior to the activity:

- Create a **gateway**. Add students to the **user group**. The default permissions do not need to be changed for this activity.

- Set the **gateway** to lock at the end of the semester.

During the activity:

- At regular intervals read the **posts** and acknowledge the contributions the students have made to their **blog**. Explain to the students that you may not reply to every **blog** every week but that you will try to look at all contributions at some point in the semester.

☐ Once the assignment deadline has passed, read eight of the **posts** made in each **blog** and give **feedback**. If you are giving similar comments on each of the blogs, use the **comment bank** to reduce your work load. Award a pass or fail grade.

☐ When you have awarded either a pass or a fail grade, **confirm/release the grades** and **release** the **feedback** in **manage assets** on the **gateway**.

Instructions to the learner

You can adapt these instructions to your learners and to your context

☐ Log onto PebblePad.

☐ In **create new** and **more** select **blog**. Give the **blog** your name as the title and put a brief description of the **blog**, reminding yourself that the purpose of this activity is to reflect on your professional practice.

☐ For step 2 choose a **banner** to suit your character.

☐ For step 3 select **view** and **post to blog**. A new window opens and, in the top right hand corner, select **post new**. Add your reflection in the text box that appears and select **submit** to add this thought to your **blog**.

☐ In the **view** of the **blog**, you will see your **thought** added to the **blog**. Close this window. Now select **send to**. **Send** this **blog** to the **gateway** your tutor has set up. Once you have sent the **blog** to the **gateway** you do not need to do this again as it will be automatically updated every time you add a new **post**. When you want to add a **post** to your **blog**, go to **view**, **my assets** and then select the **blog**. Choose **view** and **post to blog**.

☐ Your tutor will be able to view the **blog** as you add to it. Your tutor will occasionally read your **posts**, but not necessarily every week.

☐ After the assignment due date has passed, you will not be able to add to this **blog**, but if you are enjoying the process of reflecting on your learning in this way, why not start a fresh **blog**?

☐ When your tutor has given your **blog** a pass/fail, you will receive an email notifying you that your **blog** has been graded.

The activity in context

This activity is based on one developed with first year nursing students at Charles Sturt University, Australia. Reflection is a graduate attribute required by the professional regulatory body. Students use PebblePad to develop their eportfolio further on in their degree so using the blog tool is a good starting point for using PebblePad. The students have a lecture and tutorial on reflection and critical thinking along with a two hour computer lab session where the group designs their blog page and submits their first introductory 'thought' via the gateway. The marking criteria require the students to show progression of thought, not simply a narration of their experiences. Only the subject coordinator and the on campus lecturer have access to the reflective blogs. The security and the confidentiality provided by PebblePad allow the students a safe place to reflect. This item of assessment (which is a pass/fail) has been introduced and has run successfully for three sessions. The subject is run internally over four campuses: with a distant education cohort, this equates to over 400 students.

Practitioner tips

Explain the difference between a 'thought' and a 'blog'. You can do this by describing the blog as a book and the thoughts are like the pages within the book.

activity
01.3

Seven steps to success with PebblePad

This activity provides a comprehensive introduction to PebblePad in the context of a two hour computer lab workshop. The seven steps introduce new users to PebblePad to some of the key tools (action plan, activity, webfolio) and concepts (sharing, commenting, tagging) ready to start learning in PebblePad. The workshop introduces digital literacy skills and learning activities to support the transition to university and can also be

Activity Overview

🏫	Low	Assets
📖	Beginner	📄 🎫 ⚙️
📑	Low	Optional Assets
🕐	2 hour workshop	👥
👥	unlimited	

useful in new groups where peers are still getting to know each other. It may be useful for troubleshooting early in the semester for students who have difficulty logging on and using their account.

What challenges might this address?

When you are introducing PebblePad to new students who may not yet have acquired the skills and discipline of self-directed learning, it can be more effective to organise workshop sessions for students to learn and work together. Such sessions can also build enthusiasm and interest in using the tools as learners can see, and share, instant results in PebblePad.

When a new technology is embraced, sometimes the technology is blamed for frustrations and/or failure of submission. This class at the beginning of semester introduces all students to PebblePad, which ensures at minimum that they are able to log onto the system, and can submit to a gateway. Beyond this, the workshop provides everyone with the information they need to use the system well and it is particularly helpful for those who are less confident in their IT skills.

Learning design

This is a two hour workshop in a computer lab. Some institutions have developed their own resources to support students who are using PebblePad. If your institution hasn't created its own resources, you can use the PebblePad's inbuilt help by clicking on the help icon.

Prior to the workshop, students are asked to find and bring with them a suitable digital photograph of themselves, or an image they would like to include in their portfolio. They are also asked to prepare some thoughts about why they chose to study the programme they are enrolled in.

At the end of the session students should be able to:

- Describe what a PebblePad account is and have an awareness of how PebblePad may be used for learning and assessment at university.
- Locate and access their PebblePad account and begin to construct an eportfolio using a webfolio.
- Create PebblePad assets such as a webfolio, a blog, an action plan and activity and identify different types of assets using tags.
- Share a webfolio with their tutor.
- Locate class mates (neighbours) through PebblePad, add them to their contacts and share assets with them.
- Have an awareness of digital literacy concepts (e.g. tagging, blogs, webfolios) and confidence in share permissions and electronic submission of assignments.

The workshop is divided into seven sections, or steps. The discussion at the end is an opportunity to ask questions and to check understanding. Some of the frequently asked questions (FAQs) in the introduction to *First Steps with PebblePad* might be useful here.

Step 1. Learning about PebblePad

Show the students in the workshop where to access PebblePad resources and PebblePad tipsheets, including the help embedded in PebblePad.

Using the resources available, students are asked to access the resources and find answers to the following questions:

- What is a PebblePad account?
- How do I access my PebblePad account?
- How do I start using PebblePad?
- How is a webfolio used in my course?

   ☐   What kinds of things can I include in my webfolio?

   ☐   Will I ever use my work created in my PebblePad account in my career?

Step 2. Accessing PebblePad

Show the students how to log onto PebblePad.

Students then explore the PebblePad asset creation wizards. Students are encouraged to create the following sample assets with suggestions about how the assets may be used:

   ☐   Action Plan

   ☐   Activity

   ☐   Blog

Step 3. Create a new webfolio to introduce students to peers and tutor

Explain to the students that a webfolio can be created for a particular assessment task, audience or activity. It is possible to have lots of different webfolios or mini eportfolios for different purposes in a learner's PebblePad asset store. Show the students examples of former students' webfolios.

Show the students how to create a simple two page webfolio. Ask them to create a webfolio themselves.

Page 1 is titled 'About Me'. Use the help tools in PebblePad to learn how to upload a photograph of yourself.

Page 2 is titled 'The reason I chose this course'.

Step 4. Introduction to peers on the course.

Explain to the students that PebblePad allows sharing of assets with specific permissions including comment and collaborate. The learner controls the permissions when they send their assets to another person.

Students introduce themselves to their neighbours, and try to locate them in PebblePad by searching for their names, and adding them as contacts. The webfolio is then shared with the neighbour with comment permissions so that the peer can comment.

When students get to this step, they may ask if they *have* to share their webfolio containing the 'about me' section, as some of their thoughts are private. This is a great place to discuss share permissions, the portfolio being owned by the student, with privacy assured and permissions set by the student. It is also an opportunity to discuss portfolios for different audiences and for different purposes.

Step 5. Tag an asset so that you can find it at a later date

Demonstrate how to use the tag tool.

Students select one of the assets they have just created and assign a tag to it. They then try to locate this asset using **search**, **tags**.

Step 6. Send your webfolio to a gateway

Explain to the students how the gateways work and the differences between sharing with another person, and sending the asset to a gateway. Sending an asset to a gateway creates a link between the asset and the gateway, and when doing so, the learner accepts the permissions set by the tutor on the gateway.

Students send the webfolio they have just created to the gateway created by the workshop facilitator.

The tutor can show their view of the gateway, demonstrating how the tutor can see all submissions on the gateway, but pointing out that the students cannot see other people's webfolios in the gateway.

Step 7. Any Questions?

This is the students' opportunity to ask questions and share initial reactions to using PebblePad.

Tutor actions

What you need to do in PebblePad to set up the activity

Prior to the activity:

☐ Create a **gateway**.

☐ Add students to the **user group**. The default permissions do not need to be changed for this activity.

During the activity:

☐ Be aware that PebblePad tipsheets and resources are embedded throughout PebblePad. Click on the **question mark icon** to reveal short hints. Clicking on the hint box will open the online help at the correct section.

☐ Have a sample **webfolio** ready to show the students during the workshop.

Instructions to the learner

You can adapt these instructions to your learners and to your context

☐ Prior to the workshop, locate a digital image that you are happy to share with your peers and tutor. Please bring this to the workshop.

☐ Your tutor has designed a number of tasks for you to complete during this workshop. Browse the resources that your tutor has recommended.

☐ Log onto PebblePad.

☐ Go to **create new** and select **action plan** (or any other **asset** such as **blog** or **activity**) and complete this **asset**. If you need help first look in the **help** section in PebblePad which is a **question mark icon** in the right hand corner of the pane. You will be able to search for help about filling in an **action plan**.

☐ Save this **asset** by clicking on the **green tick**.

☐ In **create new**, click **more** and then select **webfolio.** Using the **question mark help icon** again to guide you, create a **webfolio** with two pages.

▫ Page 1 is called 'About Me'.

▫ Page 2 is called 'The reason I chose this course.'

☐ When you are satisfied with the descriptions your have written about yourself, save the **webfolio.**

☐ To access the **webfolio** again, go to **view**, **my assets**. Click on the **webfolio** and then select **view**. A new window opens and this is what others will see when you share it with them. Now close the view window and select **send to**. Send this **webfolio** to the **gateway** your workshop facilitator has identified.

☐ A new window opens. You will be able to see your **webfolio**, and you will see a notice if others have also sent their **webfolios** to the **gateway**. However, notice that you cannot see anyone else's work. The **gateway** is where you will send your assignments when they are due. You will receive an email via your normal email client confirming that you have sent your **webfolio** to the **gateway**.

Searching for your assets

☐ Go to **view**, **my assets** and click on the **webfolio.** Click on **more options** and **tag** this **asset**. **Tags** are an effective way of organising your PebblePad **assets**. Choose an appropriate **tag**, or create a new **tag** for this asset. Again, use the **question mark icon** if you need further assistance.

☐ Now repeat this last step for the **asset** you created in the first part of this workshop (e.g. **action plan**).

☐ Select **view** and then **search**. You can **search** for your **assets** using the **tag** tool. This is an effective way of searching for **assets** as your PebblePad account grows.

Sharing with your peers

☐ In **tools**, select **my community**. Select **add a contact** and add your neighbour's name. Search for them on the PebblePad system. Repeat with another neighbour's details.

☐ Now go back to **view**, **my assets** and select your **webfolio.** Using **send to person**, send the **webfolio** to your neighbours whose names now appear as a list in **your contacts**. Give them **comment permissions**.

☐ You will receive an email when one of your peers has shared with you. To **view** their **webfolio**, go to **view** and **received**. Click on your peer's **webfolio** and read it carefully. Using the **comment** icon, respond to their introduction in a positive way.

The activity in context

This workshop activity is based on one that is run with first year Medical Radiation students at RMIT University in Australia.

Practitioner tips

Suggest that if a learner gets stuck with any of the processes, they ask their neighbour for help before asking for your assistance.

Orientation and Induction

In *Chapter 3: Principles of PebblePad*, we introduced the idea of 'touch points': those points of transition when we are moving, for example, from school or college to university; from university to work placement or postgraduate study; entering employment; work-based learning; or being promoted. At any of these touch points we may face the challenges of being in a completely new environment with new procedures. Handled well, with effective orientation and induction procedures, these transitions can be transformative experiences. Conversely, the consequences of poor induction processes can be very costly – resulting, in extreme cases, in students dropping out of a course or losing a newly appointed member of staff. For the individual who fails to make the transition there is, of course, a high emotional cost which is less easy to quantify.

Orientation and induction processes allow a period of settling in and becoming familiar with a new culture of work and learning. If an institution or organisation is to retain all of its diverse intake of new students and newly appointed staff on a wide scale, there needs to be system-wide support that recognises and addresses the challenges facing new entrants. Traditionally, for undergraduate students, this period is called freshers' week (UK) or orientation week (Australia) and it is an institutionally recognised length of time that is devoted to students familiarising themselves with university life. Similarly, there may be a period of induction events for postgraduate students and customised programmes for international students. Staff, too, are usually given a period of induction to their new role.

Although induction is commonly thought of as a finite period, it is becoming clear that many new students (and employees) may need continuing transitional support over a much longer period than a week or two from a range of significant people including peers and tutors.

To avoid high drop-out or leaver rates, institutions can adopt specific good practice measures. The UK Student Transition and Retention (STAR) project, led by the University of Ulster (2005, see http://www.ulster.ac.uk/star/) applied Chickering and Gamson's (1987) principles to develop effective induction processes and this is a framework that can be adapted to other contexts besides higher education:

1. Encourage contact between students and faculty

2. Develop reciprocity and co-operation among students

3. Encourage active learning

4. Give prompt feedback

5. Emphasise time on task

6. Communicate high expectations

7. Respect diverse talents and ways of learning.

Many of the activities featured in this book focus on one or more of these principles. In the activities presented here, the focus is on very early intervention and support.

PebblePad is designed to support active learning, reciprocity and co-operation. New students and newly appointed staff benefit from prompt and timely feedback on their achievements, no matter how small or insignificant these may appear to the tutor or long term employee. This feedback is easily built into PebblePad activities through the commenting permissions. Learners who may be isolated or lacking in confidence can be integrated into a team or group by setting tasks that ask students to share their work and to invite comments from their peers, tutors or mentors. The security and privacy of PebblePad can reassure new entrants, who may be already nervous about sharing details, that it is a safe environment in which to introduce themselves. PebblePad can support all of these approaches, even when the tutor is dealing with large cohorts of students, or the newly appointed member of staff cannot meet up face-to-face with their mentor. Feelings of isolation can be reduced with careful planning and a welcoming atmosphere, whether this is online or face-to-face.

The following activities are low risk and aim to support all learners through this exciting, confusing and potentially stressful time. Although they take a minimal amount of time to prepare and complete, their impact can be far-reaching, allowing students or employees to find their feet without the fear of failure or looking incompetent. Investing in such activities helps professional relationships to develop and mature, especially when they are part of a system-wide approach to supporting new learners and employees.

Looking for more ideas ?

If you are interested in *Orientation and Induction*, you might find further useful activities in *Themes 3: Planning Personal and Professional Development*, *5: Promoting Group Work* and *1: First Steps with PebblePad*.

activity 02.1 | Using case studies to reflect on the transition to university life

This activity is part of a wider induction process to support students in the transition from secondary to university education and to ensure that they are developing the necessary skills to manage their studies on a clinical course.

Activity Overview

Low	Assets
Beginner	
Low	
Semester	
Cohort	

What challenges might this address?

The first few months at university can be daunting for new undergraduate students. At the same time, academic staff often report that students are ill prepared for managing their learning in lectures, small group teaching sessions and in self-directed studies. New students may be unfamiliar with self-directed and reflective learning and it is important for their future studies that they are introduced to these approaches early in the programme. Designing this activity in PebblePad helps students to work in a self-directed manner, whilst having access to support and feedback from their peers and their mentor. This provides a simple example of the potential benefits of reflection and of using PebblePad. The case study approach helps students to understand that the challenges they face as learners on this course are shared by others – and that there is help available if they need it.

Learning design

This activity sits within a sequence of induction activities that focus on the student learning journey, support structures and welfare, and the professional perspective of the course.

The activity is based on two case studies that portray two fictional students. These fictional students are at a similar stage to the students examining the case studies, and they are challenged by the transition to university life. The students analyse the case studies and have to reflect on the similarities between themselves and the fictional students.

The activity takes place in week 6 of the first semester and lasts a whole week. In the preceding week 5, the students attend short lectures that explain the reflective learning approach on the course and the importance of reflection to professional practice. At this stage, they are introduced to PebblePad.

During the activity week there are two scheduled sessions, one at the beginning of the week and one at the end, both led by a facilitator. In the first session, the facilitator asks the students to discuss the case studies within the whole group. The students discuss these two case studies and begin to identify common themes. The case studies are written to prompt discussion in the group about, for example:

- the different ways in which people learn (learning styles);
- managing time when there is no one there to tell you;
- handling stress that may arise in tackling new situations and meeting new people;
- understanding how to make the most out of lectures;
- knowing where to find help for academic or pastoral issues.

Later in the session, students work in small groups and choose one theme (arising from the earlier discussion) to discuss in depth. They are asked to explore how the students in the case studies can effectively manage this issue – for example, effectively managing their time. The students then plan a presentation for the session at the end of the week that is centred on this theme.

The group works together throughout the week to prepare for the group presentation at the second facilitated session.

During the week, all students complete a personal PebblePad diary in a blog, to record, for example: how their group are working together; how they find working with the others; and how they feel their approach to learning in the early weeks of the course compares with the two case studies under discussion.

Each group makes their presentation at the second session, and the facilitator allows sufficient time for questions and discussion with the larger group.

Following the presentation session, students complete a form based on a reflective learning model that they have studied earlier. This form is completed and shared, along with the blog, with their personal mentor.

The personal mentor is expected to review all student submissions and provide some feedback to the assets.

Finally, a meeting with the student is arranged by the personal mentor to discuss how the student managed the group activity, and any issues that might need to be addressed in their own transition to university life and studies.

Tutor actions

What you need to do in PebblePad to set up the activity

Prior to the activity:

- [ ] Create a **gateway**. Add students to the **user group**. The default permissions do not need to be changed for this activity.
- [ ] Add personal mentors to the **tutor** group. Use **manage tutor group** to divide the students up into groups of approximately six.
- [ ] Add the resources for this activity to the **gateway resources** area. This will include the two case studies. There is no need for all the resources to have **copy permissions** as this will duplicate the files in each user's account and take up space.
- [ ] In **form builder**, create a **form** called Week 6 for the students' individual reflections. Include the following fields:
  - What you have learned about:
    - a) working in groups
    - b) planning presentations
    - c) finding information
    - d) the extent to which you identify with the fictional students
    - e) how you will apply this knowledge over the coming year.
- [ ] **Publish** this **form** to the **gateway**.

During the activity:

- [ ] Log onto PebblePad.
- [ ] Go to **view** and then **gateway**. You can **view** the **blogs** and attached **forms**

that your students have completed during the week. Add a **comment** to each **blog** acknowledging the work the student has done.

Instructions to the learner

You can adapt these instructions to your learners and to your context

- ☐ Log onto PebblePad.
- ☐ Select **view** and **gateway**. Go to the **gateway** your tutor has identified and look at the **gateway** resources. This area contains details about the task and copies of the case studies you have been given in the first face-to-face session of the week. You can return to this area to re-use the resources if necessary.

You are going to keep a **blog** throughout this week, making a note of your own and your group's progress in completing the task. In the **blog** include

a) Your thoughts about the group session at the beginning of the week.

b) What you have found out.

c) How you searched for information and assessed its reliability.

d) References for the books, journal papers and websites used.

e) Sources you would recommend and those you would avoid.

f) A diary of how you spent your time.

g) Thoughts about the process you are going through, particularly about working in a group, and also about preparing to present your findings to your group.

- ☐ Go to **create new**, **more** and select **blog**.
- ☐ Give the **blog** your name as title. In the description briefly outline the theme your group is addressing.
- ☐ For step 2 choose a **banner** to suit your character.
- ☐ For step 3 select **view and post to blog**. A new window opens and in the top right hand corner, select **post new**. Add your reflection in the text box that appears and select **submit** to add this thought to your **blog**.
- ☐ In the **view** of the **blog**, you will see your **thought** added to the **blog**. Close this window.
- ☐ When you want to add a **post** to your **blog**, go to **view**, **my assets** and then

select the **blog**. Choose **view and post to blog**. Add a new **post** regularly throughout the week.

□ After the group presentation at the end of the week, in PebblePad go to **create new**, **more** and select **form**.

□ Select the reflection on the Week 6 **form** and complete it.

□ Now go to **view** and select your **blog**. Select **more options** and **add/edit link**. Link your **form** to the **blog**.

□ **Send** this **blog** to the **gateway**.

□ Your personal tutor will be able to view the **blog** in the **gateway**. Your personal tutor will read and **comment** on your **blog** and completed **form**.

The activity in context

This is based on a compulsory course activity for all Year 1 medical students at the University of Birmingham, UK. It is a large cohort (400 students) led by the module lead for a semester 1 module, 'Learning Medicine', and facilitated by a group of 22 academic staff, with over 130 personal mentors. All reflective reports are submitted for review and feedback to the relevant Personal Mentor for each student. The tutors find the structured approach works very well for Year 1 undergraduate students who are unsure about reflection and welcome the prompting available in the PebblePad forms. Students like that they can store assets and other media formats in a single location as similar facilities are not available through the learning management system or other portals.

Managing information overload during orientation

By recording orientation events, this activity helps learners to cope with the mass of information that they need to absorb during orientation – whether at university, placement or in a new job. In this activity the learners are encouraged to use the activity wizard to record significant events and to publish them to a gateway where their 'mentor' can monitor their progress and identify any issues as early as possible – and so provide support and encouragement. This activity is suitable for any new members of an organisation, though it is written with new students in mind. The mentor may be a personal tutor or may be a more experienced learner who has volunteered to support new entrants.

Activity Overview

Low	Assets
Beginner	
Low	
2-3 weeks	
Cohort	

What challenges might this address?

A typical orientation process gives learners a schedule of events that they should attend. In sequence they are told about the students' union, the library, other learning supports, online tools, academic procedures... the list goes on. What sense they make of this torrent of information, or how they are responding to it intellectually and emotionally, is difficult to surface and so difficult to support.

Using a simple tool in PebblePad (the activity wizard) this process can be supported whilst prompting the learner to both record and reflect on the events they attend.

For the tutor/mentor it provides a useful method for finding out how new learners are coping with their orientation. It also provides a feedback mechanism directly to individual learners and highlights common issues which can be shared through the blog. An added benefit is that the activity also demonstrates the value of recording events so that more meaning can be extracted from them. The records also serve as valuable reference points later on.

Learning design

This activity is likely to begin in a computer lab, though, if preferred, a tipsheet could be created to guide learners through the process.

Learners are introduced to PebblePad and the concept of it being a tool that they can use to support their learning and to collect evidence over the duration of their learning journey as they develop their skills.

They are told that there are lots of tools within PebblePad that they are welcome to explore, and which they are likely to use at different times during their studies, but for this activity they only need to know about the activity wizard and how to publish to a gateway.

The mentor decides which orientation events the learners should engage with and record in the activity wizard. The events could be about the students' union, the library, other learning supports, online tools, or academic procedures. Each of these events (or a selection that the mentor has confirmed) must be recorded using the activity record and each must be published to a gateway.

The mentor will keep a check on the activities being posted, will add feedback both as encouragement and as support for the learners, and will answer any common issues to a frequently asked questions (FAQ) blog on the same gateway.

The mentor could also choose to use the messaging function on the gateway to send reminders, hints or tips to some, or all, of the cohort.

Tutor actions

What you need to do in PebblePad to set up the activity

Prior to the activity:

- ☐ Create a **gateway**. Add students to the **user group**. The default settings do not need to be changed for this activity.
- ☐ Add mentors to the **tutor group**, using **manage tutor group** if the cohort is large.
- ☐ In **gateway resources** add a **gateway blog**, and call it 'Orientation FAQs'. Use the description field to describe the purpose of the **blog**. Set the options to **view** only if you want learners to be able to **post** new questions to the **blog**.

During the activity:

☐ In the face-to-face workshop, show the learners how to access and complete an **activity** record, explaining what the expectations are for content, style and length and which activities they need to record.

☐ Show the learners how to send the **activity** to a **gateway**.

☐ Monitor assets published to the **gateway**. Use the **column headings** to organise the assets by published date or by learner. Give **feedback** to students.

☐ Common issues or questions can be added to the **gateway blog** and hints or tips arising can be sent as **group messages**.

Instructions to the learner

You can adapt these instructions to your learners and to your context

☐ Log onto PebblePad.

☐ Select **create new.**

☐ Select **activity** and complete the activity specified by your mentor. You will need to create a new **activity** for each event your mentor wants you to engage with. You can choose to record all of the events you go to but only send the required ones to the **gateway**.

☐ To **edit** an **activity**, go to **view** and **my assets**. Select the **activity** and **edit**.

☐ Once completed, **send** the **activity** to the **gateway**. You will not be able to see your peers' activities, only your own.

☐ Keep an eye on your **assets** in your **asset store** – if they turn bold it is because some feedback has been added by your mentor.

☐ Your mentor will give you feedback on your **activity** record.

☐ Your course team has created a **group blog** that you can use if you have a question about the process. This can be viewed by going to **view, gateway** and then selecting **gateway resources**. The **blog** is called 'Orientation FAQs' (frequently asked questions). You may have permission to add a question; if not, email your question to your mentor and the answer will appear on the **blog** as soon as possible.

☐ Once orientation is over you might like to return to your **activity** records to remind yourself how you felt and what you learned during your first days at university.

The activity in context

This activity is a composite of common learning designs that are used widely by PebblePad practitioners.

Practitioner tips

During the induction period, respond to queries on the 'Orientation FAQ' blog as soon as possible. Later in the course, you can manage student expectations about when and how often staff respond to queries, but during the induction period a swift reply will be appreciated.

If, as a mentor, you are repeating the same comment, use the comment bank to reduce your workload.

activity 02.3

Mentoring through online dialogue

The purpose of this activity is to encourage newly appointed professional staff to habitually record their continual professional development (CPD) and to share these records, in a PebblePad blog, with an appointed mentor. The intention is that, after a period of time, staff will feel supported during a challenging period in their career and be able to recognise that they are continually developing whilst carrying out everyday duties.

Activity Overview

👥 Low		Assets
📖 Beginner		⚙
📑 Low		
🕐 3 months		
👥 4+		

What challenges might this address?

In a number of professions there is a need to record and reflect on non-formal development, with staff learning on the job. Non-formal development includes conversations with colleagues, reflecting on incidents in practice, or being part of a team. Capturing the learning that happens during these events is not always easy. Using a PebblePad blog to quickly record and reflect upon the event can improve practice and confidence and, in certain situations, can provide evidence of development for organisational processes. If a member of staff is new in post, just recording and reflecting in isolation can be a challenge. This activity draws in a mentor, appointed to support the member of staff. The mentor is required to read the staff member's posts and comment on them. This strengthens organisational processes already in place for induction, and provides support that does not require face-to-face meetings.

Learning design

In an induction pack, newly appointed members of staff receive a guide to accessing and using their PebblePad account to support this transitional period in their career. They receive, by email, the name and email of their appointed mentor (not their line manager). The mentor is aware that a newly appointed member of staff will be sharing a blog with them via PebblePad, and that, as a mentor, they are expected to respond to the blog with positive, supportive comments.

Both the newly appointed member of staff and the mentor are made aware of the privacy and security of a PebblePad account. In addition, the newly appointed member of staff is given instructions about sharing and unsharing an asset to emphasise that they are in control of their blog and all that is shared with the mentor. Although privacy and security are critical to both members of staff feeling confident in using this system as part of the induction process, there are also reminders that this is a professional dialogue and that there is still the need for confidential information (such as customer or patient names) to be omitted from any posts.

In the medium term, the newly appointed member of staff can use the blog posts to identify areas of non-formal development and if appropriate, use these incidences as evidence for organisational processes such as a review or an appraisal. Longer term, the newly appointed member of staff is a potential mentor themselves, and they have a record of their reflections when they were first in post.

Tutor actions

What you need to do in PebblePad to set up the activity

Prior to the activity:

Create separate guides to using PebblePad for newly appointed staff and mentors. Both guides should include:

a. Instructions on how to log on, how to create a **blog**, how to share and unshare this **blog** with a mentor.

b. Information about PebblePad privacy and security.

c. Guidelines on professional practice emphasising what is appropriate to include and what should be omitted from the posts.

During the activity:

For mentors:

☐ You will receive an email when the member of staff you are mentoring first shares their **blog** with you.

☐ Log onto PebblePad.

- ☐ In **current activity** on the right of the screen, select **new received/updated asset**.
- ☐ Select the **asset** (**a blog**) that appears in the left pane.
- ☐ Select **view this asset**.
- ☐ Read the **posts** (recent **posts** appear at the top of the **blog**). Add **comments** to individual **posts** by selecting **post comment**. When you have added your new comment, select submit. Remember that this is a professional conversation and that the new member of staff is unfamiliar with the organisation and may be new to the profession.

Instructions to the learner

You can adapt these instructions to your learners and to your context

Using the URL provided in your induction pack, log onto PebblePad.

- ☐ Go to **create new**. Select **more** and then **blog**. Give the **blog** your name as a title. In the **description**, add brief details about your current role.
- ☐ For step 2 choose a **banner**.
- ☐ For step 3 select **view and post to blog**. A new window opens and in the top right hand corner, select **post new**. Introduce yourself to your mentor in the text box that appears and select **submit** to add this **thought** to your **blog**.
- ☐ In the **view** of the **blog**, you will see your **thought** added to the **blog**. Close this window. Now select **send to person**. Using **add a contact**, search for your mentor by name. They will already have a PebblePad account. **Send** the **blog** to your mentor with **comment permissions**.
- ☐ When you want to add a **post** to your **blog**, go to **view, my assets** and then select the **blog**. Choose **view** and post to **blog**.
- ☐ The first time you send your **blog** to your mentor, they will receive an email notification. Thereafter, your mentor will be able to view the **blog** as you add to it.
- ☐ Should you want to send your mentor a reminder to view your **blog**, or in the unlikely event you want to withdraw permission for your mentor to **view** your **blog** follow these instructions:
  - ▫ Go to **view**, my **assets** and select **blog**. In the right hand pane that appears, select the **share** tab. Highlight your mentor's name.

- To send a reminder click on the **bell icon** – this will send an email reminder.
- To withdraw permission to view, click on the **bin icon**. Your mentor will no longer be able to view your **blog**. You can re-share at a later date if you wish by using **send to person**.

The activity in context

This activity is a composite of common learning designs that are used widely by PebblePad practitioners.

Planning Personal and Professional Development

theme 03

There is a general expectation in higher education that learners will be encouraged to engage with the process of reflecting upon their learning and achievements and plan for their future development. In the UK this is usually described as Personal Development Planning (PDP) but in other countries and contexts, may also be described as Career and Employability Development (CED) or, in a staff development context, Professional Development (PD). For ease of reading, we have adopted the term PDP in this chapter. Whatever the description, the general approach is one that the UK Quality Assurance Agency describes as:

> *...a structured and supported process undertaken by a learner to reflect upon their own learning, performance and/or achievement and to plan for their personal, education and career development. It is an inclusive process, open to all learners, in all HE provision settings, and at all levels. (QAA, 2009)*

The idea behind the PDP approach is that learning is lifelong and life-wide, and that only when learners can identify gaps in their knowledge and skill set, or identify why they have been successful, can they plan their future direction.

ePortfolios have been viewed by many as the ideal technology to support the PDP process. PebblePad goes one step further, designing a personal learning space with prompts for reflecting upon learning built into every asset. This integrated design makes PebblePad the ideal tool for putting reflective learning theories, which underpin PDP, into practice. Through the assortment of wizards, such as action plans and meetings assets, the learner can build a picture of themselves over time in a continuous cycle of learning. The personal learning space is designed to capture the process and evidence that are at the heart of PDP across the range of learning contexts that a learner encounters.

Action planning and reflecting upon experience are important, but an essential ingredient for success is that PDP activities are developed in a structured and supportive environment. PebblePad offers tools that allow for sharing of assets and that invite feedback from trusted peers or a member of staff, such as a personal academic tutor, supporting and assisting the learners as they progress. This structure and dialogue with the learner can help those who are just embarking on their learning journey to understand the value and purpose of the personal development tasks.

It is usually left to the discretion of the institution or professional organisation whether PDP is assessed within a course of study or not. If PDP is not an assessed component of a course, creating an environment where personal development is a valued and meaningful process is a challenge for many lecturers. Explaining the value of the process to your students can help students understand the benefits of engaging with it. Dr Alyssa Phillips, who has submitted one of the activities for this chapter, describes the process to her students in this way:

> The personal development process is designed to improve your capacity to understand what you are learning, and also to reflect, review, plan and take responsibility for your own learning. PDP activities encourage you to become a more effective, independent and confident self-directed learner. It is hoped that through PDP you will develop a positive attitude to learning throughout life.

A PDP method of approaching development is becoming familiar in continuing professional development circles, with many professional bodies using this 'core learning process' (QAA, 2009) as part of their approach. The activities that follow illustrate how this core learning process can be supported using PebblePad. Activity 3.2 offers some detail on how the process can look in practice for the benefit of those who are less familiar with the practice of personal development planning.

Looking for more ideas ?

If you are interested in *Planning Personal and Professional Development*, you might find further useful activities in *Themes 4: Developing Academic Study Skills, 10: Preparing for Employment* and *6: Experiential Learning*.

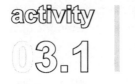

Helping learners engage with personal development planning (PDP)

This activity is designed to encourage first year undergraduate students to engage with Personal Development Planning (PDP) through using PebblePad. This is a compulsory first year academic skills course unit that helps students to understand the value of the process and what is involved. It is an assessed piece of work, signalling to the students that this is an important component of their current and future academic study.

Activity Overview

Low	Assets	
Beginner		
Low	Other Assets	
Semester		
Class		

What challenges might this address?

Engaging undergraduates in reflective learning and in PDP can be a challenge. Some students do not immediately understand the meaning and purpose of these processes in a degree course and it can take a little time for them to take responsibility for their own progress. Added to this pedagogical challenge, there are also the practical challenges in traditional approaches to PDP. Paper-based forms and questionnaires are not always filled in, may be lost or there may not be a clear strategy for keeping the records and for giving students feedback.

Using PebblePad, students start to value the activity and the timely feedback provided by the tutor on their reflections. An assessed online portfolio means that all the activities can be kept in one place. Students can see, and request, tutor feedback and the evolving nature of the process is evident as the webfolio itself develops.

Students can share their assets with anyone they want, or they can keep them private – it is their choice. This means they keep ownership of their work – an important principle for personal development planning. Using PebblePad, students are able to engage with their PDP at times to suit them, as they can access PebblePad from any computer with an Internet connection or via a mobile. Additionally, of course, students can take their webfolios and assets with them when they graduate (PebblePad lets students download files in a variety of file formats).

Learning design

Students are introduced to PDP at the start their course. In a face-to-face session they learn about the purpose of PDP and how to use PebblePad. Students are asked to fill in a PebblePad skills audit profile that asks them about themselves and their expectations of university. During this introductory session the assessment criteria for the assignment are discussed.

Later in the course students also have to complete another profile that ensures they reflect on the specifics of their degree course. During the programme, students are frequently reminded by the tutor to engage with PDP using PebblePad. They are encouraged to use other assets to record their learning, but it is up to the individual student to choose the most appropriate asset for the activity.

In the second part of the course, students present a selection of evidence/assets in a webfolio demonstrating they have engaged in PDP. They submit this for assessment and feedback. Students are required to write around four themes. These themes are described to the students in the following way:

1. **My expectations of my course and student life.**
    Here you need to reflect on your initial expectations of your course and the place you are studying, and describe how these expectations have changed over the academic year.

2. **Managing and planning my course.**
    Here you need to reflect on how well you have managed your course, particularly working between different areas of study.

3. **How I have developed my academic and transferable skills.**
    On this page include any reflections about how you have developed your skills over the academic year, through your studies, as well as through your extra-curricular activities.

4. **My plans and targets for level 2 and beyond.**
    Include here reflections about what you hope to achieve during the remaining part of your course (and beyond) and any actions you need to take to help you achieve this.

There is a page for each of these themes in the webfolio template that is shared with the students in the introductory face-to-face session.

Before the assignment due date students are invited to a face-to-face session for further reinforcement about the purposes of PDP activity, the assessment criteria and for technical help in building a webfolio. Students are required to submit their webfolio to a PebblePad gateway for assessment and feedback.

Tutor actions

What you need to do in PebblePad to set up the activity

Prior to the activity:

- ☐ Create an assessment **gateway** and set to lock on the assignment due date.
- ☐ Add students to the **user group**. The default permissions do not need to be changed.
- ☐ Create two **profiles**. The first needs to ask the students about themselves and their expectations. The second needs to be more discipline-specific. These **profiles** can be returned to at intervals throughout the course and updated.
- ☐ **Publish** the **profiles** to the student **user group** in the assessment **gateway**. When students log on they will be able to view the profiles in **create new**.
- ☐ Create a **webfolio template** with a page for each of the themes and add it to the **gateway** with **copy permissions**.

During the activity:

- ☐ In the face-to-face introductory session, show students a completed **webfolio** submission.
- ☐ At regular intervals throughout the course remind students to complete and update their **profiles**.
- ☐ After the assignment due date has passed, **grade** and give **feedback** on the **webfolios**.
- ☐ Remember to **release** the **grades** and **feedback** when all marking has been completed.

Instructions to the learner

You can adapt these instructions to your learners and to your context

- ☐ Log onto PebblePad.

- ☐ Go to the **gateway** and **copy** the **webfolio** template. This template is now in your **asset store**. This **webfolio** template is the **asset** you will use to submit your assignment at the end of this course. During this course you are going to be creating assets that you may choose to include in this **webfolio.**

- ☐ Go to **create new** and **more** and then **profile**. You will see a **profile** called 'About me and my expectations'. Fill this in. You will return to this **profile** and add to it as you progress through the course.

- ☐ Once your study is underway, go to **create new** and **profile**. This time chose the **profile** named 'About my discipline'. Again you can add to this **profile** as you progress through the course.

- ☐ As the course progresses, use a variety of **assets** to record your progress, such as the **meeting asset** or keep a **blog** of your learning journey.

- ☐ As the assignment due date draws near, **edit** the **webfolio** template and link to evidence you have created during your study such as the completed **profiles**.

- ☐ Send the **webfolio** to the assessment **gateway**.

- ☐ You will receive an email notification when your tutor has graded your **webfolio** and given you feedback.

The activity in context

This activity is based on one that is delivered to first year undergraduate students studying Combined Studies degrees at the University of Manchester. Students are introduced to PDP and PebblePad in the first weeks of their degree course in a compulsory first year academic skills course.

Staying the course: action learning and planning as strategies for student support

This activity is designed to develop essential transferable skills for vocational and academic development throughout a university programme, in this example a Business and Management degree. Using PebblePad action plans, learners practise setting goals and deadlines for their degree studies which can be evidenced and monitored in PebblePad by tutors and peers. They develop an eportfolio to reflect on the many skills that they are developing during their time at the university, which provides a vehicle for planning ahead for future studies. Individual work is assessed, but there is an expectation that there will be peer to peer communication and support through the sharing of blog posts written around specific themes. The peer to peer sharing takes place in action learning sets and consists of a blog/journal which is assessed and included in the assignment webfolio, showing evidence of reflecting on what they and their peers are learning about managerial practice.

To help readers who are less familiar with the processes of personal development planning (PDP), this activity includes some detail about how the activity could run in the learning setting.

Activity Overview

👥	Low	Assets
📖	Beginner	
🗨	Low	
🕐	Semester	
👥	Groups of 4	

What challenges might this address?

Retaining and engaging students is a core concern for most educational institutions. Students who are new to an education programme are often adapting to a new learning environment where they have to adjust to unfamiliar approaches to study, at the same time as meeting the criteria for assessment. The more the learners understand the assessment process and the value of feedback on improving performance, the more they are likely to achieve from their studies and the more they are likely to stay the course.

This poses at least two key challenges for educators. First, to find ways that promote student engagement with the assessment criteria that avoid unnecessary failures. And second, designing assessment to run throughout the course of study, allowing a 'chunking up' of assessment, whilst also motivating the student to engage at an early stage.

Personal development planning encourages students to recognise the importance of setting goals and planning ways to achieve them that will develop a lifelong habit of learning. Through the development of action plans and an eportfolio, the students can set themselves goals and targets to help manage their learning objectives. Students also, as part of the assessment, build up a bank of evidence that helps them to recognise and showcase their strengths and achievements in PebblePad. The assessment strategy enables participants to collect evidence throughout the course and then reflect back on it instead of engaging in one heavy assessment at the very end. Work that starts in action learning sets continues online through blog posts and peer comment. These posts are used in the final assignment as evidence of progression and learning.

This activity prepares students for a group assignment that happens later in the course in another module.

Learning design

The students on this PDP module are asked to complete a webfolio that contains evidence of action planning and engaging with a series of reflective blogs. The first activity described below is designed to help the students understand the importance of action planning. The second is designed to support the students in the process of regular reflective writing, which is shared with peers in an action learning set. These face-to-face action learning sets underpin the programme by offering an on-going supportive learning group, which continues online as students blog about their thoughts, inviting comment from their action learning set members.

1. Action planning

This activity uses the action plan tool in PebblePad and focuses on which areas the student would like to improve and additionally prompts them to think about how they can achieve their goals over a period of time.

In this face-to-face activity the learners are encouraged to move about physically and, in groups, to think about their current academic situation and where they want to be in twelve months time. This is then transferred into PebblePad in order for them to put the exercise into context. The group experiment with the hands-on exercises and gain a good grasp of the purpose of the activities prior to completing them electronically in PebblePad.

Resources required for the session include flip chart paper, coloured flip chart pens, post-it notes, laptops and a network connection to access PebblePad.

In the classroom, the tutor creates a timeline using three pieces of flip chart paper stuck together. The line starts at the present and runs 12 months ahead with dates in between.

The tutor takes the learners through the first three practical activities (instructions below) using flip chart paper and post-it notes. This activity normally takes about 1 hour.

The tutor then demonstrate how to use the PebblePad action plan tool (10-15 minutes).

Learners spend time putting what they have just done in the practical session into PebblePad and creating an assignment webfolio.

The following instructions are given to the students during this face-to-face session.

Instruction 1: Identifying personal areas of improvement
Spend a short time thinking about your current abilities, skills and achievements. What are they, what evidence do you have that supports this?
Write these on flip chart paper along with two or three areas you want to improve about yourself (in terms of study skills) whilst at the university.
Feedback and discuss these with the group.

Instruction 2: The improvement time-line
Using post-it notes write down the following and stick them on the timeline:
1. Your current situation (where you are now in terms of study skills).
2. Your ideal situation (where you want to be by next……….).
3. Identify key steps/resources and people you need to help you get there and post them up on the timeline.

Instruction 3: Personal SWOT (Strengths, Weaknesses, Opportunities, Threats) analysis
On flip chart paper make a grid and in each quadrant write:
Strengths: Describe your personal strengths in relation to your issue.
Weaknesses: Describe your personal limitations in relation to your issue.
Opportunities: List any resources including people that will help you achieve your plan.

Threats: Describe what barriers would hinder this plan.

Stick post-it notes in each of the four quadrants and then in groups discuss each other's SWOT areas and move post-it notes if you feel it is appropriate after the discussion.

Instruction 4: PebblePad Action Planning

Transfer and translate what you have covered on the flip charts today into the PebblePad action plan asset and add it to the webfolio you are going to create. The action plan asset will prompt you to identify the actions necessary to achieve your ideal situation. You will need to keep this updated with new action plans/achievements throughout the module for the final webfolio submission.

2. Reflective blogs

In addition to the action planning activity above, students are required to periodically write five 500 word PebblePad blog posts and share them with members of their action learning set and their tutor. The action learning sets meet face-to-face at regular intervals and use the blog posts for prompting questions and further reflection. Tutors comment regularly on blog posts.

The themes that have to be addressed in the blog and the action learning sets are:

Post 1: Personal learning style and your expectations of your course.

Post 2: Reflective practice, thinking critically and skills audit.

Post 3: Creative problem solving.

Post 4: Leadership and teamwork.

Post 5: Managing performance and change.

Both the action plans and the individual reflective blog posts with comments from peers contribute towards the final assignment and are embedded as part of the assignment webfolio. This final submission includes a reflection on the process of PDP and the journey travelled.

The tutor also creates a group blog so that general queries about the course and the tasks set can be answered.

Tutor actions

What you need to do in PebblePad to set up the activity

Prior to the activity:

- ☐ Create a **gateway**.
- ☐ Add students to the **user group**.
- ☐ Set the **gateway** to lock on the assignment due date.
- ☐ Create a group **blog** in the **gateway**.

During the activity:

- ☐ In the face-to-face sessions show students what a completed **action plan** looks like. Show students how to create a **webfolio** and how to create a link to the **action plan**.
- ☐ Add regular **feedback** to the **blog** posts.
- ☐ Encourage students to use the **group blog** to post general queries about the course and the tasks set.
- ☐ After the assignment submission due date, **grade** and give **feedback** for each webfolio.
- ☐ Remember to **release** the **grades** and **feedback** when all marking has been completed.

Instructions to the learner

You can adapt these instructions to your learners and to your context

1. Action planning

- ☐ Log onto PebblePad.
- ☐ Go to **create new** and **action plan**. Tag the **action plan** *Development*. Use the activities you have done in class to complete the **action plan**. You will have to return to this action plan to update it as the course progresses.

☐ To add a review to this **action plan**, go to **view, my assets,** select the **action plan** and then **more options**. Select **add a review** option before the assignment due date.

☐ In **create new** select **more** and **webfolio**. This **webfolio** is going to be your assignment **webfolio.** To create a **webfolio**, use the help in PebblePad to guide you. Click on the **question mark icon** to access PebblePad help.

☐ When you **add a page** to your **webfolio**, select the **tag** tab and then select *Development*. This will create a page in your **webfolio** that links to your **action plan**.

☐ If you tag any other assets Development, these will also appear in your webfolio.

2. Reflective writing

☐ Log onto PebblePad

☐ Go to **create new**, and **more** and then **blog**.

☐ Create a **blog**, and then select **view and post to blog**. In the new window that opens click on **post new**. Give the post the title of one of the blog themes given by your tutor. Write a post around this theme.

☐ **Send** this **blog** to your tutor and members of your action learning set before every learning set meeting. Give them **comment permissions**.

☐ When you receive an email that one of your set has shared with you, give them positive, constructive feedback in the **comments box**. When either your **blog** or your peer's **blog** has been updated you will see a notification in the **current activity** box when you log onto PebblePad.

☐ Visit the group **blog** by selecting **view** and **gateways**. In the **gateway** created by your tutor you can post a query about the course and the tasks set and read replies to other queries.

☐ As the due date for the assignment draws near, add your **blog** as a page in your assignment **webfolio**. In add your **pages**, click on the arrow in the **item** tab and select the **blog** icon. Choose your **blog** from the drop down list.

☐ If you have used other PebblePad **assets**, for example a **meeting asset**, you can include these in your **webfolio** to demonstrate that you have engaged with the PDP process.

☐ When you are ready to submit your assignment **webfolio**, send it to the assessment **gateway** set up by your tutor.

☐ You will receive email notification when your **webfolio** has been graded and feedback given.

The activity in context

This activity is based on work at the University of Cumbria with students on the Business and Management degree course. Course developers have worked hard to effectively integrate PebblePad into the module content in such a way that the student learners do not perceive it as a 'bolt on' to their normal academic studies. Early evidence suggests that progression and retention has improved with the use of PebblePad. Through use of PebblePad learners have been motivated to develop their learning further and look at areas of their own development that they may have not considered before.

activity 03.3 | Sustaining involvement in personal development planning (PDP) over time

This activity demonstrates how PebblePad can be used to encourage and sustain a continuing involvement in a personal development planning (PDP) process over a course of study. The students are postgraduate researchers on a professional doctorate course; the majority are members of staff in the same or an affiliated institution. They are studying part time for up to eight years.

Activity Overview

High   Assets

Beginner

Medium

Course

Groups of 4+

Students use a self assessment tool to evidence postgraduate research skills and are introduced to other PebblePad tools which enable them to share reflections with their supervisor and with their wider peer group for the duration of their study. They also participate in a group blog, which offers access to a community for shared experience and support where they can share reflections and critical incidents with their peers.

As well as keeping a record of their personal development over the duration of their study, the student benefits from immediate feedback from the supervisor, despite the distance that may exist between them, and the time between face-to-face meetings. The completed self assessment is counted as evidence of 'engagement' with the university and is an on-going record of support from supervisors. This may be important if a supervisor leaves the university, because the next supervisor can refer to the record and ensure that the student is given consistent and timely guidance and support.

What challenges might this address?

The majority of students at this level are very focussed on their research. The challenges of part time postgraduate research and working full time are such that students may find it difficult to devote time to complete personal development activities such as assessing, and reflecting on, their skill levels. It is important, however, for both the student and the assessing body to have a record of the student's development over the duration of a course – especially when the study can take years to complete.

Using PebblePad, students have one place to go to keep a record of their development and can make efficient use of their time. Using the self assessment tool, students engage in a dialogue with their supervisors to plan for further skill development. They can reflect on how their skills are developing and receive feedback and encouragement from their supervisor. The skills audit is embedded within an eportfolio with a variety of other relevant tasks that are designed to support the development of research and reflection skills. Reflective work is 'scaffolded' through a series of embedded blogs that can only be seen by student and supervisor.

A further challenge for students undertaking postgraduate research is isolation, as there are often limited face-to-face opportunities to connect with peers and with supervisors. By including a group blog to the personal eportfolio templates, students are given a dynamic link into their research cohort, who they will have met face-to-face in early sessions. Supervisors are able to talk to the cohort as a whole or have a one-to-one dialogue with students through the series of personal reflective blogs within the template. This enables a record of development all in one place, rather than trying to collate a series of email conversations.

Learning design

At the first face-to-face session attended by the whole cohort, students copy and auto publish to a gateway a webfolio template which has the research skills audit embedded as multiple pages. The webfolio also consists of reflective activities that include individual and collaborative tasks through a series of blogs.

During this session they complete the skills audit. Over the following two weeks the supervisors give the students constructive feedback directly onto the skills audit. The students are encouraged to check their webfolio regularly but a reminder email is sent to students once feedback is given.

Students are expected to act on the feedback and use the action plan tool in PebblePad to identify which areas of development to focus on and, in particular, how their research skills are being advanced. It is left up to the student whether they would like feedback on their action plans. If so, they are encouraged to link their action plans to their webfolio and this enables supervisors to view and comment.

Before the next face-to-face session three months later students are expected to update their skills audit. If they haven't done this by the session, it is done in the session. There is a structured cycle of:

□ a face-to-face classroom session;

□ skills audit updated by student;

□ supervisor giving feedback on skills audit;

□ student completing an action plan to show evidence of development (choice made by student as to whether to link to webfolio for feedback or not).

Throughout the cycle shown above, the reflective blogs are used for individual or group discussions. Reminders to complete/update the skills audit are given through the blogs too.

Each time the webfolio is updated, it is shown on the gateway and so the gateway can then be used to track student engagement by a range of relevant parties where appropriate.

Tutor actions

What you need to do in PebblePad to set up the activity

Prior to the activity:

□ Create a **gateway**.

□ Add students as users and add supervisors as tutors. The default settings on this **gateway** do not need to be changed.

□ Create a **gateway blog** and take its URL so that you can make a link to it in the **webfolio** template you are about to create.

□ Using **profile builder** create a bespoke research skills audit, based on a specific skill set for postgraduate research. **Publish** to yourself. Go to **create new** and open the **profile** you have created. Save the **profile** without editing it so that you have an empty copy of the skills audit to embed in the **webfolio** template.

□ Create a series of **blogs** around the reflective areas you wish students to engage in.

□ Create a **webfolio** and when you **add pages**, select the **item tab** and the **arrow**. Select the **profile** icon to add the skills audit as a page.

□ Using the same **add item** process add each of the **blogs** you created.

□ Create a **webfolio page** called group blog and paste the **group blog URL** as a link on it.

☐ Add the **webfolio** to the **gateway** through **manage resources**, selecting **copy** and **auto publish**. Select **notify the user group** so that the next time a student logs onto PebblePad they are asked to accept a copy of the **webfolio** template with all the embedded **blogs** and skills audit as described above.

During the activity:

☐ Give **feedback** to the students each time they complete the skills audit. Email the student to say that there is new feedback waiting to be read.

☐ **Feedback** to student will be immediately visible because the **gateway** is not locked.

Instructions to the learner

You can adapt these instructions to your learners and to your context

☐ Log onto PebblePad. As soon as you log on you will see a notice telling you that you have one asset waiting to be copied to your **asset store**. Select **view now** and then select **copy and publish**. By accepting this it becomes your own **webfolio** and gives your supervisor access to it at all times for **feedback** purposes. You will be using this **webfolio** for the whole of your course.

☐ In **view**, go to **my assets** and select the **webfolio** from your list of **assets** and on the pad that opens on the right, click **view this asset**.

☐ Click on 'skills audit' to complete it, following the instructions on screen. Remember to save your work. Your supervisor will be able to see the changes to this audit each time you update it.

☐ Once you have received **feedback**, complete a new **action plan** (in **create new**) about how you are developing your skills based on the audit and the **feedback**. To get supervisor **feedback** on this **action plan** link it to your **webfolio.**

Completing the individual reflective blogs

☐ In the **webfolio**, click the **blog** page for whichever reflective element you wish to write about. Use the **post new** to write your reflections. Prompts and ideas will be given in class.

- ☐ To comment on the **group blog** open the **group blog** page in the **webfolio** and follow the link (remember the **group blog** can be seen by all in the cohort. Your individual reflective **blogs** and skills audit can only be seen by you and your supervisor).

- ☐ Please check your **webfolio** regularly for feedback. Periodically you will receive an email reminder telling you when your supervisor has left feedback but this will not happen for activities in the **group blog**, this requires manual checking or setting up an RSS feed.

- ☐ Update the skills audit in time for the next face-to-face session.

- ☐ Regularly contribute to individual and group **blogs**.

The activity in context

This activity is based on work at the University of Wolverhampton where part time PhD students attend face-to-face sessions at the university, yet the time between sessions can be months. The length of study can be up to eight years, making it unlikely that students can be guaranteed the same supervisor throughout their course of study. Using PebblePad to record action plans and complete profiles adds continuity and a long lasting record of engagement.

activity 03.4 | Developing professional identity

The purpose of this activity is to encourage students to think more holistically about their learning, and to develop their professional identity. They create an integrated webfolio which profiles their developing academic skills during the first stage of an undergraduate degree. The portfolio informs individual academic mentoring sessions with students, which take place four times a year.

Activity Overview

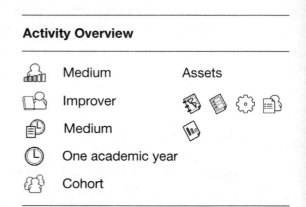

Medium   Assets

Improver

Medium

One academic year

Cohort

Over the first stage of the undergraduate degree students complete a range of activities that feed into the portfolio, presenting their development as university students and emerging professionals. While different elements or 'pages' in the portfolio are developed and assessed through different subjects, together they provide a more holistic, course-wide view of the students' first stage experience and their current level of academic skill. The overall portfolio is assessed through a 'long thin' module which spans across the first stage of the undergraduate degree (typically the first year for full time students), and draws together the industry practice, mentoring and portfolio components of the first stage curriculum.

What challenges might this address?

Most courses of study necessarily break down complex subject areas into discrete topics or modules to enable students to grasp the elements of their discipline. The difficulty facing students – and those who design the courses – is how to re-integrate learning and experiences so that students can see the 'whole picture' and think and behave as professionals. On many courses, this is something that happens in the final stages, when students are asked to synthesise their learning in retrospect.

Using PebblePad, it is possible to approach integration in a significantly different way. Since it is easy to build a webfolio piece by piece, the notion of integrating learning is introduced early in a course of study, which means that tutors can get a good idea of who the students are and what their individual needs might be. Students are able to contact individual subject tutors/mentors who can see how the student's work is developing. As well as helping students in developing their professional identity, this process can also help to identify 'at risk' students at an early stage, avoiding high attrition rates by making necessary changes or interventions before problems arise. More able students can be offered extended learning opportunities to keep them engaged.

The more that students see their informal and formal university learning experiences in a holistic way rather than in discrete 'units' which need to be passed (and realise that their tutors see them in this way as well), and the more they start to share responsibility for their learning and development, the more engaged they are likely to be and the higher their achievements.

Students have a durable, full record of their learning and development and tutors/mentors have a durable record of the mentoring process and the students' perceived value of that to their development.

Learning design

Early in the first stage of the course, students are introduced to their mentor and the processes that are used to support this aspect of their learning. They are given an explanation why this approach is effective, and the ethos underpinning it. Students copy a webfolio template and complete the introduction page (auto published to the gateway). They respond to a series of 'orientation' questions designed to prompt their thinking about why they are entering university and this specific discipline, and what they have to offer. They also complete the self assessment component of their academic skills profile (in a PebblePad profile), which outlines the expectations of them at the end of the first stage, and prompts them to think about their professional identity and areas for individual focus during their first semester. This profile, along with the assets mentioned below, are linked to the webfolio and then sent to a gateway. All the mentors and tutors on the course can see the student webfolios. This enables all involved in the course, whether their role is as a mentor or a subject discipline tutor, an opportunity to view a student's progress.

During the semester, learning experiences and assessments in each of the student's subjects serve as evidence for the academic skills profile, and are discussed at subsequent mentoring sessions. In addition, students complete a personal blog of critical incidents which help to build understanding of themselves as learners and professionals, as well as of their chosen discipline. To support the mentoring process and ensure that it is meeting student needs, students respond to a form before each mentoring session, asking what they would like from the session, and again after the session as to whether it helped them or not. During the session, both mentor and student work together on an action plan for agreed areas of focus over coming weeks, which are then reviewed at the next session.

The overall portfolio is assessed and is a collection of assets created throughout this activity.

Tutor actions

What you need to do in PebblePad to set up the activity

Prior to the activity:

☐ Create a **gateway** for the cohort and set to lock on the assignment due date.

☐ Add students to the **user group**. The default settings for the **gateway** do not need to be changed.

☐ Add tutors and mentors to the **gateway tutor group**. Use **manage tutor groups** to divide students into mentor groups. Mentors will only see the work of the students in their group, they will not be able to see the work of the whole cohort.

☐ Process owners - who may be programme leaders or unit co-ordinators, for example – might want to see the work of the entire cohort rather than just a single tutor/mentor group. To achieve this they need to be added to the **owner group** as owners can view all tutor/mentor groups.

☐ Create a **webfolio** template. Add a page called 'orientation' and, using the **webfolio editor**, include guidelines for what you would like the students to write about in their orientation section.

☐ Add the **webfolio** to the **resources** area of your **gateway** with **copy and auto publish permissions**. Select **notify the user group(s) when they login to PebblePad**.

☐ Create the academic skills profile in **profile builder**. **Publish** it to the **gateway**. It will now appear in your students' accounts when they log on and go to **create new** and then select **profile**.

☐ Create the mentor record in **form builder**. Add questions that allow the student to express what they would like to address during the mentor meeting. Add a field that allows students to reflect on the effectiveness of the last mentor meeting.

☐ Publish the **form** to the **gateway**. It will now appear in your students' accounts when they log on and go to **create new** and then select **form**.

During the activity:

As a mentor:

☐ Go to the **gateway** and view the **webfolios** that your students have created. The academic skills profile will be a page in the **webfolio.**

☐ Prior to each mentor meeting, you will receive an email notifying you that a PebblePad **form** from your student has been shared with you. This **form** will give details about what the student would like addressed during the mentor meeting. **Comment** on this to acknowledge that you have read it.

☐ During the mentor meeting, whilst sitting at a PC, ask your student to create a new **action plan** in PebblePad and complete this **asset** together. Tell your student to attach this **action plan** to their **webfolio.**

☐ View the **action plan** in the **webfolio** in the **gateway.**

☐ After the assignment due date has passed, **grade** the **webfolios** and give **feedback**. Remember to **release** the **grades** and **feedback.**

As a subject discipline tutor:

☐ You will be able to view students' **webfolios** in the **gateway** and observe their progress.

Instructions to the learner

You can adapt these instructions to your learners and to your context

☐ Log onto PebblePad. As soon as you log on you will see a notice telling you that you have one **asset** waiting to be copied to your **asset store**. Select **view now** and then select **copy and publish**. This will **copy** a **webfolio** template to your own PebblePad account.

☐ You can now rename the **webfolio** giving it your name as the title. It is automatically updated on the **gateway** so that your tutor and mentor can see your work in this **webfolio** at all times.

☐ Using the **webfolio editor**, complete the page called orientation following the guidelines. Save and close the **webfolio.**

- Now go to **create new** and select **profile**. Complete the academic skills profile. Once complete, save it.

- Now go to **create new**, **more** and select **blog**. Create a **blog** and post your reflections on the course. Add a new **post** regularly so you build a 'diary' of your learning journey.

- In **view**, open your **webfolio** and **edit it**. Add the academic skills profile using the **add your pages** and **item**. This **profile** is now part of the **webfolio** and will be updated every time you amend or add to it. Add the **blog** to the **webfolio** using the **add your pages** and **item**. This **blog** is now part of the **webfolio**. Your mentor will be able to read all **assets** linked to your **webfolio**.

- Prior to a mentor meeting, in PebblePad, go to **create new**, **more** and select **form**. Select mentor meeting form. Complete this **form** and **send it** to your mentor with **comment permission**. If your mentor comments on your **form** you will be able to see that it has been commented on in the **current activity pane** when you first log onto PebblePad.

- From the second mentor meeting onwards, fill in the field that asks 'to what extent did the last mentor meeting help with the issues you asked to be discussed?'

- During the mentor meeting your mentor will ask you to create an **action plan**. Once completed, send the **action plan** to your mentor with **comment permission**. If you want to draw on an **action plan** as evidence, you can create a **link** to it by editing a page within your **webfolio**.

- After the assignment due date you will not be able to amend or edit any of the **assets** associated with the **webfolio**. When your mentor **grades** and gives summative **feedback** on your **webfolio**, you will receive an email notification.

The activity in context

This activity is based on work in progress at Charles Sturt University, Australia, with first year undergraduates. The students' portfolio includes a personalised introduction to themselves and their background, including their prior experience in the discipline area and their key interests. They also respond to a series of questions prompting their reasons for coming to university, their early feelings and expectations, and what they think they have to offer to their cohort. The portfolio is shared via a gateway whereby each of the first stage academics are able to view the students' profile and progress at any time. In this way, staff are all privy to the same background and progress information. Just as importantly, the portfolio can then be used to inform individual academic mentoring sessions with students, which occur four times per year. The portfolio also includes elements developed through different first stage subject activities and assessments, such as a 'learning profile', the process they used to prepare their first assessment item, an initial sustainability philosophy and an outline of foundation industry skills developed during designed workplace learning experiences.

A key component of the portfolio is a self assessment and evidence-based profile of the academic skills required by the end of the first stage of their degree. During their various subjects, students are prompted to add evidence of their skill development to this profile. This is used to help students develop and implement individual action plans related to their specific learning needs during individual mentoring sessions. Students are able to customise their portfolio to suit individual needs and any additional informal learning which contributes to their professional development. They are also encouraged to comment on 'critical incidents' related to their transition to university in a personal blog. A final reflection on the year forms the last element that completes their webfolio.

Practitioner tips

Due to the large numbers of tutors and mentors potentially involved in this activity, provide all staff (including administrative staff) with an overview of how to use the gateway and how to use the webfolios to support students in their care.

theme 04 | Developing Academic Study Skills

Developing study skills that have relevance for learners is a challenge for many practitioners, and the institutional context will often have a bearing upon how this challenge is met. Some institutions have services that are specifically designed to develop study and academic skills, others embed the skills at programme level making them much more discipline-specific. Study skills can include: how to avoid plagiarism and using appropriate referencing techniques; reading and writing for academic and research purposes; and, increasingly, becoming literate with a range of multimedia devices, tools and types of files for communication and presentation.

The transition from a non-academic context to an academic one can be challenging for many learners. Moving from a school environment to one that actively encourages learners to become autonomous and independent is a process that requires detailed planning and recognition of the learner's background. Learners who are returning to study after a long break may also find that the academic landscape has changed substantially, with an emphasis on new techniques, tools and technologies that were not available when they were first studying. Strategies and tactics that have been effective in the past may not necessarily be appropriate for the course of study or discipline they have chosen today.

As you will read in the following activities, tutors and learning designers are tackling these challenges in imaginative ways, but the common thread seems to be that they are planning active learning experiences. Instead of creating reams of information and 'content' – the passive learning approach – they focus more on creating opportunities for learners to practise the required skills and to play an active part in their learning. Tasks are designed to allow learners to explore, take risks and then correct errors or misconceptions in a secure setting. The aim is to increase the level of skill at the same time as increasing learner confidence.

Control and privacy can be critical for the less confident learner. PebblePad offers learners a secure and private space where they can experiment with new skills and control who sees their work, and when. The PebblePad assets contain prompts for the learner to plan and reflect, which creates scaffolding for learning and skill development and can act as a substitute for, or an addition to, the role of a mentor. These features are particularly helpful for learners who are studying at a distance or for those who can benefit from a framework to support their learning.

Peer to peer learning can be a great source of support for new or returning learners. It is a strategy that can extend the learner's developing skill set, by engaging in a review of one another's work. It can also support the development of critical thinking skills, which is an important component of many professional development programmes and postgraduate research. The use of the anonymous review tool in a PebblePad gateway can be used effectively with groups of nervous learners who may be reluctant to share their work at first.

PebblePad allows tutors to effectively and efficiently embed digital and information literacies within the curriculum. Using PebblePad, students can engage in activities that may include the use of non-text based media (such as video or images), communicate online or present information for the web. This approach equips students with transferable skills that support lifelong learning and, when appropriate, evidence of these digital skills can be shared with future employers.

The activities in this chapter offer ways of providing students with timely, relevant and – most important – *engaging* tasks. Many tutors are now using PebblePad as a resource creation tool, which can be shared with learners through a URL without the need for learners to have their own account. By creating a bank of resources in this way, a member of staff in a study skills department, for example, can offer a resource to a student when a specific support need arises (such as guidance with referencing and avoiding plagiarism). Activity 4.1 shows how PebblePad can be used to create a resource that can be used for digital and academic skills development. Activity 4.2 takes a very learner-centred approach to tackling undergraduate resistance to writing. By contrast, Activity 4.3 illustrates how peer review and collaboration can be embedded within a programme of study to support a coordinated whole cohort approach. The final activity, Activity 4.4, uses a placement blog to capture reflections that can be used for a study assignment later.

Looking for more ideas ?

If you are interested in *Developing Academic Study Skills*, you might find further useful activities in *Themes 3: Planning Personal and Professional Development, 7: Collaborative Learning* and *5: Promoting Group Work*.

activity 04.1

Just in time resources: Using WebQuests to introduce digital and academic literacies

The ease with which you can build a website in PebblePad, without any knowledge of HTML or technical know-how, means that a site can be put together quickly as a webfolio to deliver a teaching resource, designed for students' individual needs. This is particularly helpful if you need to provide a quick response to a student who discovers a need for some form of study skill support. A bank of such learning resources can be created to be accessed by students as and when the need arises.

Activity Overview

Medium

Beginner

Medium

Variable

Individual or Class

Assets

In this activity, the resource is a webfolio created by the tutor which gives instructions for a series of learning tasks. This takes the form of a WebQuest, where learners are sent to different websites to research and learn about a topic. The WebQuest is based around an assessment task. Since this is a form of study guide, only the tutor needs a PebblePad account; students do not need an account to access and use the WebQuest. They simply use the shared URL and follow the pages and steps that are set out in the webfolio.

An individual need for a study skill might be identified either by the student, after completing a skills audit, or by their tutor because aspects of the course are a particular challenge. This WebQuest is designed to help students become familiar with unpacking assignment tasks and working with online databases including library databases, Google Scholar, and government databases. As the student completes the WebQuest they are practising their digital skills and they start to work on improving their academic literacy skills (such as referencing or how to avoid plagiarism). The webfolio can be reused with different students again and again, with additional or alternative webfolios embedded to suit different learning needs.

What challenges might this address?

One of the challenges addressed by this activity is the need to support distance students in their learning as they complete an assessment task and assisting these students to work independently as they develop their digital skills in research using online databases. As a WebQuest can be completed independently, it allows students to take control of their learning and learn at a pace that suits their needs and level.

Using the webfolio to present the WebQuest allows linking to resources, embedding of content (including videos), and interactive examples. The clean layout of the webfolio and the ability for students to access all of the information from one central location allows them to be more fully immersed in the WebQuest itself. It also encourages the students to reconsider the value of learning and teaching in online environments.

It is not only students who need to develop digital skills: this activity can provide a gentle introduction to using PebblePad tools for those teachers who are not so comfortable using technology. Manipulating the webfolio is easy in PebblePad and produces instant and pleasing results. The creator can share the resource with other teachers using PebblePad's 'collaborate' function in order to work together in the creation of the WebQuest. This can help other teachers see how easy it is to create a WebQuest (simple website) through the PebblePad webfolio tool and to build their own skills and confidence.

Learning design

The WebQuest is created by the tutor in a webfolio which is then made available to the students through a shared URL. Although PebblePad templates provide ready-made designs that will give the site a good look and feel, it is important to bear in mind the usual considerations for website design when creating the WebQuest including:

- **Layout**: What is appropriate for my student cohort? Are the menu titles clear and understandable? What accessibility and usability issues do I need to think about?

- **White space**: Does the web page look crowded or is there enough white space so that the students' eyes are not strained? Can I choose a more appropriate font to allow students' eyes to read the content more easily? Have I broken text-heavy sections with images?

- **Visual stimuli**: Have I used images and videos? Where could another image or video be added to increase engagement and break the text? Do the text and images flow well so that the student can focus on the WebQuest and not be distracted?

☐ **Colour schemes**: What colour scheme has been used? Is it appropriate for the context? Is it distracting? Is it in harmony with other colour schemes used in the online learning space or by the institution?

The precise design of the elements above will differ depending on the student group, the subject, the teacher, and the context. You can embed other webfolios that you or other colleagues have already created if this is relevant to the topic you are covering.

For the content of the WebQuest itself, here are six main components that can be used to structure the activity and organise students:

☐ Introduction: Introduce the purpose of the WebQuest and gain the students' interest. It should also give them a reason to continue through the WebQuest.

☐ Task: Set the scene for the task linked to the introduction. The goal and aim of the WebQuest should also be outlined here and may include a focus question to assist in defining the task.

☐ Resources: This section is optional. If this section is included, the type of resources will depend on the nature of the WebQuest and the students. The content of the resources section may include hyperlinks, images or articles (where permission has been granted) that the students should consult to complete the task.

☐ Process/Steps: This section provides a guide for the students to use to work through the problem. This is the section that works well with an embedded webfolio so that a submenu is created. The process/steps are broken down into manageable pieces that can be accomplished relatively easily. An example of chunking the process is as follows:
   ▫ Choose
   ▫ Search
   ▫ Summarise
   ▫ Reference.

☐ Evaluation: This is where the marking rubric or assessment guidelines for the WebQuest are placed. It is also possible to give permission for comments allowing students to provide feedback on the WebQuest and its usefulness in their learning. This can be very valuable if you plan to rework and revise the WebQuest for future student cohorts.

☐ Conclusion: The conclusion summarises the learning outcomes of the WebQuest and reminds the students of the processes they have learnt. If the WebQuest is related to an assessment task, then connecting the work completed in the WebQuest to the assessment item is essential.

Tutor actions

What you need to do in PebblePad to set up the activity

Prior to the activity:

- ☐ You will need to design your WebQuest in advance of starting to create it in a PebblePad **webfolio**. Collect and store the images, documents and articles as one zipped file so that it will be easier to **upload** these files when you start to create your WebQuest.

- ☐ Log onto PebblePad.

- ☐ **Upload** the zipped or **multiple** files you have just created. **Tag** these files with the name of the WebQuest so that they are easier to find. You can add additional tags if necessary. These files are unpackaged and now sit in your **asset store**.

- ☐ In **create new**, select **more** and then **webfolio.**

- ☐ Work through the steps in the **webfolio**, using the guidelines above to design how the content looks. You can insert the files you have created in appropriate places within the **webfolio.** Use the **info tip** tool to explain terms or phrases that may be unfamiliar to your students. This is particularly helpful for students for whom English is not their first language.

- ☐ If you are using another **webfolio** embedded within the **webfolio** you are currently creating, you can do this by adding a page and then selecting **add item** and selecting the **webfolio** you wish to embed. You can reuse **webfolios** within other **webfolios** to minimise your own workload.

- ☐ When the WebQuest is complete, **send** it to the web, and give **comment** permissions if you want students to give you feedback on the value of the WebQuest and copy the URL.

- ☐ You can now paste this URL into an email to your students or your institution's learning management system (LMS) and students can access it by just clicking on the link.

During the activity:

- ☐ If you have included your email as a contact for WebQuest enquiries, remember to check your email regularly.

- ☐ If you have given permission for **comments** you will receive notification that an asset has been updated when you next log onto PebblePad.

Instructions to the learner

You can adapt these instructions to your learners and to your context

- ☐ Click on the link given to you by your tutor.
- ☐ The tasks in this WebQuest are for you to work your way through at a time and place that suits you.
- ☐ You can change the way the WebQuest looks by clicking on **display options** in the top left hand corner of the screen. Here you can change the font and screen colours to suit your own preferences.
- ☐ If your tutor has invited you to comment on the WebQuest, please use the **comments** box to return your feedback.

The activity in context

This activity is based on work at Charles Sturt University, Australia where WebQuests are introduced to distance postgraduate students who have not studied for a period of time and a large portion of the student cohort does not have English as their native language.

Practitioner tips

If students have a PebblePad account, this activity can be designed so that students publish results to a gateway and share their work with one another, inviting comments. This can be done by giving users on a gateway permission to peer review and, if necessary, peer review anonymously.

Although it is sometimes necessary to link to uploaded files, these are always slower and more inconvenient to open than PebblePad's own assets or existing webpages. Consider whether the content of the files can be reproduced as a PebblePad asset, such as a single webfolio page.

activity 04.2 | Overcoming resistance to academic writing

Using a series of collaborative tasks and peer support, this activity aims to overcome students' fears and resistance to academic writing, and to build personal self-worth and identity. Students are shown videos that interest them (in this case, dance forms) and the academic writing skills are developed as part of a wider enquiry in their search for subject knowledge. As the students start to practise their own writing, they are

Activity Overview

🏛	Medium	Assets
📖	Beginner	⚙ 📓
📅	Medium	
🕐	Semester	
👥	Class	

encouraged by class and blog discussions to use the appropriate academic register – which might include advice about, for example, using good linking words or how to insert a reference.

The activity is learner-centred, in that all the tasks are designed to be ones that will intrigue and inspire this particular set of learners. In this example, the learners are first year dance students but similar principles could apply for students in other disciplines with some adaptation. The key point is that the learning design considers what will motivate and engage these learners and how to make the tasks interactive, collaborative and fun.

What challenges might this address?

Not all students come through a formal route to university and some may lack the essential writing skills that are required for academic study. Beginning to understand citation, referencing and the appropriate registers of academic writing can be a dry and abstract experience for students. This activity helps students to 'learn by doing'. The informal digital space of a blog allows easy revision and rewriting and it can encourage spontaneous writing, giving students confidence to express their ideas and to recognise them as valid and worthwhile. In the initial stages what they write is as important as how they write – in other words, they should be able to write free from inhibition.

This active approach is particularly appropriate for students who are learning to develop independent study skills and who may have avoided writing in the past. It demonstrates that acquiring academic study skills is not about sitting in a lecture hall writing notes off a PowerPoint presentation but can incorporate what is, for some, the more familiar and comfortable territory of Web 2.0 technologies by discussing YouTube video clips on a blog.

Developing this activity in PebblePad means that that all the information the students need – lecture notes, links, handouts – are in one place, on the group blog. Dyslexic learners can customise the colours and sizes of the text and all learners can express themselves through this feature of customising the webfolio. By adding to their paragraphs in stages, step by step, students are eased gently towards writing academically.

For tutors, the use of PebblePad means they can begin to move towards a more formative assessment of writing and develop an ongoing dialogue with learners about how they learn.

Learning design

In a face-to-face session, learners are introduced to the online task and practise writing using flip charts, coloured pens and discussion after watching a film clip. The summary of the discussions is collaboratively written, using the flip charts and coloured pens. These images are photographed and uploaded to a PebblePad group blog which is accessible to the cohort. Links to six YouTube clips are posted by the tutor as different thoughts to the group blog. The clips represent a range of dance styles and there are brief notes in the blog post to act as both introduction and guide. Students are asked to select two clips and write about them in their own blog: one piece of writing is in a colourful journalistic style, the other piece is a more formal academic style. Students are given guidelines on how to approach this task in the weekly face-to-face session.

Students share their blogs with their peers and their tutor. They are asked to comment constructively on their peers' writing.

Week by week, students add to their individual blogs, and respond to tutor feedback.

Half way through the course, six paragraphs are selected from the academic writing posts and are handed out to the students on paper without the titles of the dances or the authors. In groups, the students have to match the paragraphs to the YouTube clips and give a reasoned justification for their decision from the text and from the dances. This leads to discussion of their answers and the revelation of which clip matches which paragraph. However, the authors are not revealed at any stage. This reasoned justification then forms the basis of work on the group blog again by starting to incorporate references into their paragraphs, linking detail with contexts.

Meanwhile, each student works on their own webfolio that is confidential between themselves and the tutor via a gateway. The first page is an 'About Me' exercise, where they reflect on their past learning experiences, learning preferences and achievements by adding personal information and images. On the second page of the webfolio, the student links to their individual blog with their two styles of writing. They can continue to work on the blog posts, refining their writing and adding references until the assignment due date.

Tutor actions

What you need to do in PebblePad to set up the activity

Prior to the activity:

- ☐ Create a **gateway**. Set the **gateway** to lock on the assignment due date.
- ☐ Add students to the **user group**. The default settings for the users do not need to be changed.
- ☐ Add a **gateway blog** (found under **manage resources**). Select **show blog in my asset store**. Once created, open the blog and copy the URL. This is the group **blog**.
- ☐ In **create new**, create a **blog** template for the individual writing task. Save this and close the **blog**.
- ☐ From your own **asset store**, open the **gateway blog** and post an introduction. Add the YouTube links.
- ☐ In **create new** and **more**, create a **webfolio** for the assignment. In this **webfolio** there are three pages. The first page is called 'About Me'. Put in coloured text instructions for the students to follow. The second page is the individual **blog** for the writing task. Create this page by using **add** item and selecting the individual writing blog you have just created. The third page contains a link to the **gateway blog** (using the URL you copied earlier).
- ☐ Add this **webfolio** to the gateway resources with **copy** and **auto publish** permissions and select **notify the user group(s) when they login to PebblePad**.

During the activity:

- Upload the photographs taken of the flip chart work into your PebblePad account. Once uploaded, **send** to the **gateway blog**.

- **View** your students' **webfolios** in the **gateway** and give feedback on the pages that contain 'About Me' and the writing task in the individual **blogs**.

- As the half way point of the course draws near, copy a wide variety of the academic writing pieces from the individual **blogs** and print hard copies. Distribute the paper copies to the students for the face-to-face session.

- Check on student progress in the **gateway blog** and the **webfolios**.

- After the assignment due date has passed, **grade** and give **feedback** to each student's webfolio.

- Remember to **release** the **grades** and **feedback** when all marking has been completed.

Instructions to the learner

You can adapt these instructions to your learners and to your context

- Log onto PebblePad.

- As soon as you log on you will see a notice telling you that you have one **asset** waiting to be copied to your **asset store**. Select **view now** and then select **copy** and **publish**. This **webfolio** template is now copied to your **asset store** and you can edit it.

- In **view** and **my assets**, click on the **webfolio** template. To add to the 'About Me' page, click on **edit asset**. In the **webfolio editor** delete the instructions and add your own information. You can include images where appropriate. Your tutor will be able to see your work at all times, but other students can only see the **group blog**.

- Click on **view asset** to see what you have written about yourself as your tutor will see it. This is also where you can **view** and **post** to the **group blog** (there is a hyperlink in the page called group **blog**). The YouTube video links are here for you to play and then choose which one you are going to write about.

- You now need to start your writing pieces. In **create new** select **thought**. Give the **thought** the **title** of the type of YouTube resource you have chosen from the **group blog**.

☐ When you have written your **thought**, **send** it to your writing **blog**. If you want to revise your writing following feedback from your tutor, create a new **thought** and repeat the process of writing and sending it to your **blog**. Over time, think about how your writing is changing.

☐ After the assignment due date has passed, you will not be able to edit the individual **blogs** or the **webfolios**.

☐ You will receive an email notifying you that your tutor has given your work a **grade** and **feedback**.

The activity in context

This activity is based on work with first year dance students at the University of Wolverhampton in the UK, some of whom come to university through non-academic routes. PebblePad has allowed the tutors to begin to move from a single mode of delivery of information about academic writing towards a more formative assessment of writing and it has offered the opportunity for an on-going dialogue with learners about how they learn.

Practitioner tips

⚠ Be aware how much time it takes to leave feedback on students' work, especially when working with over 20 students.

⚠ Using PebblePad for developmental formative work is not like asking a student to work through a CD Rom and come back when they have completed the tasks but works best when structured activities accompany on-going tutor feedback.

⚠ Tutor feedback on a blog can end rather than further discussion if too 'correcting'.

⚠ Consider mocking up some academic paragraphs that are not quite as hard as journal articles to ease students in gradually.

⚠ Be aware that a younger generation of learners are not all automatically 'comfortable with computers'.

Developing a collaborative 'knowledge portfolio'

This activity is designed to develop higher order study skills by engaging students in researching and interpreting information for presentation to others. The learners are second year university students on a theory-based module.

Students develop 'knowledge portfolios' together with others in their group and then they peer review the work of other groups, providing developmental feedback in PebblePad. This process serves two purposes: it demonstrates student understanding of the task requirements and it provides each group with an opportunity to improve and enhance the reviewed portfolios. The collaborative nature of the task prepares students for the skills they will need in the real world of academic research.

Activity Overview

🏛 Low		Assets
📖 Improver		📄 🎴
📣 Low		Optional Assets
🕐 Semester		👓
👥 8+		

What challenges might this address?

When a module is content-rich, as in this example, practitioners can be tempted to 'deliver' content in a didactic style, which tends to be a passive experience for students. Using PebblePad the practitioner has options for designing an active learning approach. In this example, students are asked to engage in actual research: interpreting and re-presenting information related to the research question to support the learning of others. This approach is engaging for students and it offers opportunities to develop transferable academic and digital literacy skills.

Learning design

The student cohort is divided into groups and each group is assigned a research topic associated with the key themes of the course. The task for each group is to create a webfolio, which presents resources, supporting information and interpretation about their specific topic.

Students are shown how to create an action plan to assign the tasks within the group. They plan the structure of the final webfolio presentation and they record discussions about how they will present their work.

On a specific date, the group webfolios are sent to a gateway. All students can see the webfolios and have permission to comment on each others' contributions. The tutor provides guidelines to the students about how to critique work, how to give constructive feedback and how to make suggestions for further information or resources that may help their peers in the next stage.

Based on this feedback each group has the opportunity to amend their original webfolio. The webfolios are assessed by the tutor after the assignment submission date and the tutor gives formative feedback. The webfolios are then used to write an individual assignment and can be drawn upon as an ongoing subject resource.

Tutor actions

What you need to do in PebblePad to set up the activity

Prior to the activity:

- ☐ Create a **gateway**. Set the **gateway** to lock on the earlier **webfolio** due date.
- ☐ Add students to the **user group**. Give users permission to **publish**, **view** and **comment**.
- ☐ If there are a large number of students in the cohort, use **manage tutor groups** to divide the students into groups.

During the activity:

- ☐ Visit the **gateway** and view the **webfolios**.
- ☐ Once each **webfolio** has comments from other groups, add your own feedback.
- ☐ After the first **webfolio** submission date, unlock the **gateway** so that the groups can now amend and enhance their original submissions.
- ☐ If necessary re-lock the **gateway** to either **grade** the **webfolios**, or to ensure that they are available as a resource for every student completing their assignment.

Instructions to the learner

You can adapt these instructions to your learners and to your context

- □ Once you know which research topic group you are a member of, arrange a meeting with your group. Agree roles and responsibilities.

- □ One member of your group will log onto PebblePad and create an **action plan**. The **meeting** wizard can be used as well, if applicable, to record the face-to-face meeting.

- □ **Send** this **action plan** and **meeting asset** to all the members of your group, with **collaborate** permissions. You can create a list of the group members in **my community** and **add a group**. This will guarantee that you do not omit anyone from your group when you send **assets** in future.

- □ All members of your group need to add to the **action plan**.

- □ In **create new**, one member of your group creates a **webfolio** and **sends** it to the whole group giving **collaborate** permissions. Individual contributions will be logged in the **page history**, so your tutor will be able to see if you have engaged with the creation of the **webfolio** or not.

- □ Attach the **action plan** as evidence of working together as a group.

- □ On the advertised submission due date, **send** the **webfolio** to the **gateway**.

- □ You have permission to **view** the other groups' **webfolios**. Carefully read their work and **comment** on their work, giving constructive feedback. This may take quite a long time so remember to allow for this.

- □ During the review period you will not be able to amend your **webfolio.**

- □ Once the review period is over and every **webfolio** has received feedback from other groups, your tutor will leave feedback.

- □ At the end of the review period, you will be able to edit your **webfolio.**

- □ In **create new**, one member of the group needs to create a second **action plan** saying how you intend as a group to respond to the comments and feedback. Link this **action plan** to the **webfolio** (do not delete the earlier **action plan**).

- □ Change the **webfolio** in accordance with your second **action plan** and feedback from the review period.

- □ This **webfolio** and all the **webfolios** from all the groups are a valuable resource that you can use when writing your assignment. The tutor will lock the **webfolios** at a certain date so that they cannot be edited or added to.

The activity in context

This activity was inspired by work at the University of Wolverhampton School of Technology in the Department of Architecture and Product Design where academic staff are working with undergraduates to encourage the development of independent learning, group work, lifelong learning, and digital literacy.

Practitioner tips

The peer reviewing could be assessed, in which case change the users' permissions to peer review in the gateway.

Exemplar webfolios can be reused as a resource for future students or as an example of what can be achieved through team work.

Engaging with reflective writing

This activity is intended to help students who may struggle with the reflective writing component of a practice placement. Each student keeps a reflective blog over a five week placement applying principles of critical reflection to their decision-making for an uncomplicated caseload of patients. Students are expected to demonstrate how they have applied and related theory to their practice. The blog is shared with a visiting academic tutor and four peers from their cohort who form a peer support group. The posts in the blog are used as evidence in a summative, written assignment completed when the students return from placement.

Activity Overview

Low		Assets
Beginner		
Low		
Semester		
4+		

What challenges might this address?

Students who are learning to become autonomous clinical practitioners need to demonstrate critical reflection on their placement learning and their ability to use clinical reasoning. For a significant minority, developing the required reflective writing skills can be challenging. There is an ongoing debate about 'assessed reflection' because some students feel assessment constrains what they can write. Reflection acknowledges a need for continuing improvement and this can seem to be at odds with the need to demonstrate required competence for grading.

Embedding a formative blog into the placement enables students to record and critically reflect on their experiences, without the pressure of grading, and to improve their reflective writing in response to peer and tutor feedback. Students are more likely to engage with the blog as they see a clear purpose in developing their skills. During the placement the students improve in their ability to write honest and professional accounts of their practice and the challenges they face. Their grades for their final summative writing task also improve because they have created in PebblePad their own, authentic evidence to draw upon. Just as important, however, is the fact that the students start to value reflection as a tool to aid their learning and development.

The students' blog posts alert the tutor to any students who may be struggling with elements of their placement and the peer support element creates a community of practice where students can practise giving and receiving feedback.

Learning design

The students in this activity are already familiar with PebblePad as they have been using it to maintain their continuing professional development portfolios since the start of their course. Before going on placement they are reminded how to create a blog and how to create posts. Students have been introduced to reflective models earlier in the course, and are encouraged to apply one of these to their writing. They are told that they have to make a minimum of weekly posts to record their decision making, identify learning needs and support their professional development. The blogs are shared with an academic tutor and four peers from the cohort who are also on placement (not usually at the same place) forming a peer support group. The tutor and the peers comment on the posts in the blog.

The purposes of maintaining the blogs are shared with the students in the session before the placements begin. The students are told that writing the blog and sharing it with supportive peers will reduce feelings of isolation whilst on placement and will be a means of mutual encouragement as they apply all that they have learned on the course to real patient cases. In addition, students are told that the weekly posts will be a substantial part of their preparation for the final assignment, which is written up once the placements are over.

Tutor actions

What you need to do in PebblePad to set up the activity

Prior to the activity:

☐ There is very little preparation needed for this activity but you do need to check with your students that they are confident they can create and post to a blog and that they know how to share with you and their peers.

During the activity:

☐ Your students will share their **blog** with you and their peers and should be making a **post** at least once a week.

- ☐ To view your students' **posts**, log onto PebblePad.

- ☐ If one of your students has updated their **blog, new received/updated assets** (under current activity) will be in bold. Click on **new received/updated assets** and the newly updated received assets will appear.

- ☐ Click on the **blog** to read it. New **posts** are at the top of the page.

- ☐ To **add a comment** to a **post**, click on **add comment** at the end of the post. You may want to make your comment **private**, particularly if the student is discussing a sensitive issue or is struggling with an aspect of their placement. If you make your comment **private**, only you and the student can see the **comment**, the student's peers cannot **view** the **comment**.

Instructions to the learner

You can adapt these instructions to your learners and to your context

- ☐ Log onto PebblePad.

- ☐ In **create new**, select **more** and then **blog**. Give the **blog** the title 'Placement Learning' and put a brief description of the placement e.g. location and specific department.

- ☐ For **step 2** choose a **banner** to suit your character.

- ☐ For **step 3** select **view** and **post to blog**. A new window opens. In the top right hand corner, select **post new**. This is where you add your reflection on the placement in the text box that appears and select **submit** to add this thought to your **blog**. In your **posts**, refer to particular incidents during the placement, record your decision making and identify your learning needs. Each **post** will be saved in your **asset store** as an individual **thought**.

- ☐ Select **send to**. **Send** this **blog** to the peers who will have been chosen to support you on placement and your tutor. Give them all **comment permissions**.

- ☐ To add to the **blog** whilst on placement, log onto PebblePad and click **view**.

- ☐ Select **my assets** and then select the Placement Learning **blog**. Select **view and post to blog**.

- ☐ Every time you add a **post** to your **blog**, your peers and your tutor will be able to **view** it. If necessary, you can send an email reminder to your peers and tutor that you have posted to your blog. To do this, select **my assets** and then your **blog**. Click on the shared tab that appears on the right. Highlight the name of the person you wish to send a reminder to and click on the **bell icon** to send a reminder. An email will be sent to this person.

☐ Your peers will be sending you their **blogs**. The first time one of your peers sends you their **blog**, you will receive an email notification. You will be able to **view** each **post** they make and add a **comment**. You can see if one of your peers has updated their **blog** by looking under **current activity** when you first log onto PebblePad, and **new received/updated assets** will be in bold if there has been an update.

☐ Click on new received/updated assets and the newly updated **received assets** will appear.

☐ Click on a **blog** to read it. New **posts** are at the top of the page.

☐ To add a **comment** to a **post**, click on **add comment** at the end of the **post**. Your comments will need to be encouraging and constructive.

☐ When you return from placement and you start writing your assignment, you will be able to read your **posts** and use them as evidence and as prompts to deeper reflection. Your tutor will tell you the correct way of citing your **blog** in your assignment.

The activity in context

This activity is based on work at Manchester Metropolitan University with level five and level six students on the BSc Physiotherapy programme. In order to be eligible for membership of the Chartered Society of Physiotherapy (CSP) these students have to complete a minimum of 1,000 hours of clinical practice in six placements over the final two years of the programme. These placements are compulsory programme units and are undertaken in a variety of clinical settings under the supervision of an experienced practice placement educator. The students are expected to manage a caseload of patients that provides them with opportunities to apply and relate theory in to practice. Whilst completing the placements, the students must work in partnership with a range of healthcare professionals, promote patient-centred care, plan appropriate treatment interventions and maintain accurate records.

The Practice Placement units are all assessed by a combination of placement performance graded by the practice placement staff (75%) and a reflective writing essay graded by academic staff (25%). The reflective writing element gives the student an opportunity to reflect on a set topic in context and evaluation has shown that students found the use of a formative blog allowed them more freedom to develop their reflection without having to meet marking criteria. The academic tutors valued the opportunity to encourage the students to reflect at an appropriate depth by commenting on their reflective writing.

Practitioner tips

If you are working with large numbers of students you might prefer to manage your access to the blogs through a gateway.

Promoting Group Work

For the purpose of this next set of activities, we are defining group work as planned group activity where learners work collectively to achieve an agreed goal over a set period of time – usually weeks or months. This emphasis on the shared fixed term outcome is what distinguishes our definition of group work from collaborative learning. Of course, any collectively produced output involves a degree of collaboration (see 7 *Collaborative Learning*) but there are additional skills required for effective group work. These skills include taking the initiative, resolving conflict without having to appeal to the tutor, and mutual recognition of the diverse skills set within the group membership.

The ability to work in a team is a valued attribute for employers and for most professions, and educational programmes need to demonstrate that they are developing the group work skills of their students.

The advantage of effective groups, whether in an educational setting or in the workplace, is that individuals can work collectively on complex and large-scale activities that would be difficult or impossible alone. A successful group nurtures a sense of identity and belonging and encourages its members to share information and resources. From a pedagogical standpoint, effective group work can enable peer review and sharing of expertise – making it especially useful for adult learning. The downside to group work is that interpersonal conflict is common when there is pressure to achieve an outcome in a set period of time. Managing the tension between 'task' and 'process' is where the learning happens because successful groups attend to relationship-building and good communication as well as achieving outcomes.

Whilst a group task is easily presented at the end of a group project, monitoring and capturing individual contributions to the group task is notably difficult to do and even more difficult to assess. In particular, the contribution of those with strong interpersonal skills who are managing conflict, listening, questioning and supporting others can be overlooked in conventional outcome-focussed assessments. The risk of this approach is that learners who feel their contribution is not recognised or valued may be tempted to fall back into a more individualistic way of working, which defeats the intention of the activity.

The challenge for educators, then, has been to find ways to monitor and assess the process of the group task, as well as the outcome. Carefully designed assessment can give value to the interpersonal and communication skills that learners demonstrate as they negotiate the task, as well as to the content and resources that they contribute. In this way, the learner is introduced to the different dimensions of performance that are being assessed, which includes transferable skills such as: communication; the ability to schedule and deliver on time; the ability to adapt and be flexible; and the willingness to participate in shaping goals and plans. These are the skills that potential employers are interested in, and it is important to demonstrate them as part of the assessment.

PebblePad supports the assessment of group work process – the interactions that happen between group members, the decisions that are made (and how they are made), the discussions that are held, the disputes that are managed, the plans that are agreed. All of these aspects of the group process can be captured using PebblePad assets such as the meeting and action plan wizards, the blogs and the webfolio. Tutors monitoring or assessing a group product through PebblePad have the tools to observe the extent to which a student has played a part in the task. The tracking of versions in a webfolio, or the original author's name on an asset, blog post or comment can offer reassurance that contributions won't go unnoticed. This level of scrutiny can be useful to shift the emphasis away from the end product and back to continuous evaluation and sense-making of the evolving process. The ease with which progress can be monitored by a tutor without undue interference can be adjusted to suit the maturity of the group. For groups that are struggling it is easier to offer support and guidance at an early stage to avoid problems later.

Whether campus-based or entirely online, it would be hard to imagine a group exercise that did not take advantage of affordances offered by the online environment since the ability to work as a group online as well as face-to-face is becoming increasingly important. Faced with a group task, most learners nowadays would employ some online means of communication to keep in touch with the group, whether this is email or some form of messaging. Some learners might also employ Web 2.0 tools for collaboration and storage. Using PebblePad, learners can keep all their group activity in one secure and reliable place, which has the added advantage of providing an audit trail of the whole group conversation, as well as a window into the group process as it unfolds.

The following activities address the challenges of monitoring process and motivating all students in the group to contribute. Not all the activities use PebblePad as the means for producing the group task, some use PebblePad to document process and as part of the planning needed to reach the group goal.

Looking for more ideas ?

If you are interested in *Promoting Group Work*, you might find further useful activities in *Themes 7: Collaborative Learning, 8: Self and Peer Review* and *10: Preparing for Employment*.

activity 05.1 | Agreeing a Team Learning Contract

This activity is an excellent precursor to a more complex group assessment activity. The instructions here include a face-to-face session, but it could be adapted for distance learning. A Team Learning Contract is created in PebblePad which allows easy access, exchange and modification of the contract. The PebblePad form and submission to the gateway allows the tutor to track where teams are up to in constructing their learning contract, and identify teams that might need more help.

Activity Overview

Low	Assets
Beginner	
Low	
Session	
Groups of 4-5	

What challenges might this address?

Effective teamwork requires the team members to agree on workload, timeframes, and decision-making processes. Students are not always experienced in effective teamwork and may need initial support and instruction to manage the challenges. A learning contract is a strategy that can help students to consider in advance how they will manage the team dynamics and agree on what action should be taken if a team member does not comply with the agreed plan. A paper-based version could be used, but the disadvantage is that it will not be readily available and it is likely that it will not be referred to after it has been created. Using a form in PebblePad prompts students to consider and discuss the terms of the contract. The form can be completed, shared and modified until a specified date in the PebblePad environment.

Learning design

Students are introduced to the skills necessary for effective team working in a face-to-face session. They are then divided into small groups of 4-5. As a group, they have to create a Team Learning Contract in PebblePad, using a form template created by the tutor.

At first, the students have a print-out of the form, which they fill in together. One member of the group is responsible for logging onto PebblePad and completing the Team Learning Contract online and then sharing this with the other team members and their tutor, via a gateway. Members of the group have collaborate permissions so the Team Learning Contract can be modified and negotiated for a limited length of time, before the gateway is locked. Team members can use the comment box to query one another and clarify meaning before reaching a consensus. These Team Learning Contracts are then used as the basis for further group work.

Tutor actions

What you need to do in PebblePad to set up the activity

Prior to the activity:

- ☐ Create a **gateway**. Set the **gateway** to lock on the date that the Team Learning Contracts have to be complete.
- ☐ Add students to the **user group**. The default settings for the users do not need to be changed.
- ☐ In **form builder**, create a template for the Team Learning Contract. Ensure that you use the subheadings to prompt the students to think about a range of skills needed for effective teams.
- ☐ **Publish** the **form** through the **gateway**.

During the activity:

- ☐ Print out the Team Learning Contract template and give one copy to each team.
- ☐ Visit the **gateway** to check on the progress of the teams. You can give feedback, but this activity requires a light steer from the tutor to check if the groups are successfully completing the Team Learning Contract.
- ☐ Continue to check the **gateway** for teams who have not submitted to identify which teams might be having problems.
- ☐ After the deadline for completion of the Team Learning Contracts, remind the students that these contracts form the basis of the next group activity.

Instructions to the learner

You can adapt these instructions to your learners and to your context

- ☐ In your team, discuss the paper copy of the Team Learning Contract that your tutor has given you. In a face-to-face setting, negotiate the various aspects of the contract, and reach agreement on how the team will fill in the fields when they logon to PebblePad.

- ☐ Agree which member of the team is responsible for logging onto PebblePad and completing the contract (a PebblePad form) on the team's behalf.

If you are the person responsible for completing the Team Learning Contract in PebblePad:

- ☐ Log onto PebblePad.

- ☐ Go to **create new** and **more** and select **form**. You will see a form entitled 'Team Learning Contract'.

- ☐ Complete this **form** and **send to** your team, with **collaborate permissions**.

- ☐ Send to the **gateway**. Your tutor will now be able to see the Team Learning Contract.

All team members:

- ☐ When your colleague has shared the PebblePad Team Learning Contract with you, you will receive an email notification.

- ☐ Log onto PebblePad and click on **view** and **received**.

- ☐ Click on 'Team Learning Contract' and then select **collaborate on this asset**. It will then be stored in **my assets** and you have permission to edit. You can now modify the Team Learning Contract so that, by the deadline, you have a contract that you can all adhere to. All team members will be able to view the additions you have made to the 'Team Learning Contract'.

- ☐ Use the **comments** to discuss the issues you are being asked to agree upon as a team.

- ☐ Your tutor can see how your team is developing the contract by looking in the **gateway**.

- ☐ You will not be able to modify or edit this Team Learning Contract once the deadline for completed contracts has passed.

- ☐ You will be using this Team Learning Contract for future group work.

The activity in context

This activity is based on work at LaTrobe University with second year undergraduates.

activity
05.2

Creating a design proposal for assessment

In this activity, students are required to develop a proposal which has financial value for a client; which is assessed both by their tutor and by an external client.

Working in small groups, students collaborate on the development of the proposal. The success of the group task is evaluated against criteria related to the assignment brief, the way in which the group worked together and the individual contribution of each group member.

Activity Overview

Medium		Assets
High		
Medium		
Semester		
Groups of 4+		

The group produces a video presentation in which they articulate how they have met the various elements of the design brief. The effectiveness of the group processes is demonstrated through records the group maintains of its meetings and decisions. Students keep a journal in which critical incidents, personal contributions and reflections on the process are recorded.

What challenges might this address?

The focus of group work is often on the product and the final presentation, rather than the process, as this is easier to assess. Furthermore, without a properly scaffolded process linked to assessment, some students do not feel confident enough to assert themselves fully within a group whilst others may feel their contribution is undervalued by the assessment that focuses only on the final outcome. Using PebblePad, it becomes possible to monitor and measure individual contributions to group projects which helps students to become more engaged in the process and helps tutors to keep track of what is happening in the group.

Employers value experience of group work and collaboration and will want to see evidence of how a student has contributed to successful group projects (or learnt from less successful ones). The role of an external stakeholder in this activity provides an authentic voice to the assessment. In particular the 'client' can relate how real world teams and real world processes mirror (or otherwise) the activities experienced by the group.

Learning design

In the early stages of the course the tutor explains:

- the significance of working in teams
- the value that employers place on group working skills
- the necessity for all group members to contribute to the overall success of the team.

This learning design is written to capture evidence of these three dimensions.
An assignment brief is developed by the tutor, providing direction for the group project. Students work in small groups with the aim of developing a proposal to match the assignment brief. The group is required to:

- create an action plan outlining how they will work together to complete the task
- hold and record a minimum of three 'project' meetings
- write a précis of the proposal
- record a short 'elevator pitch' style video of their proposal.

All of these assets are to be presented in a collaborative webfolio. The group sends the webfolio to the course gateway as soon as the first action plan is completed. The webfolio will then be edited and developed over time allowing timely and iterative feedback to be provided by the tutor (and/or external client).

In order to capture their individual contributions, critical incidents and reflections on the group process, each student makes regular posts to their personal project blog. These blogs are submitted to another course gateway according to the deadline set by the tutor. The tutor visits each student's blog at timely intervals to ensure they are making regular posts. This enables the tutor to identify possible difficulties early in the course and to provide formative feedback.

The tutor and/or the external client visit each group's webfolio during the development process to evaluate progress, provide expert commentary, and, in the case of the tutor, intervene in the event of any group discord.

At the end of the process, feedback and a group grade are provided through the webfolio. Individual feedback and the individual component of the overall grade can be provided on the student's blog.

Tutor actions

What you need to do in PebblePad to set up the activity

Prior to the activity:

- ☐ Create a **gateway**. Add students to the **user group**.
- ☐ Set the **gateway** to lock on the assignment due date.
- ☐ Add the external client to the **gateway** (probably in the **tutor group** as an **external user**) with **view** and **feedback permissions**.
- ☐ **Upload** the assignment brief to the **gateway resources**. Both the students and the external client will be able to see these in the **gateway**.
- ☐ Create a sub gateway, for the personal **blogs**, by **duplicating** the **gateway** you have created. The students will also be users in this **gateway**. If you do not want the external client to view the personal **blogs**, remove the client from the sub **gateway** by going to **users and permissions** and **add/edit** for the **tutor group**.

During the activity:

- ☐ Monitor both **gateways** and give **feedback** on the **webfolios** and the personal **blogs**.
- ☐ When the assignment due date has passed, **grade** the **webfolios** and give **feedback**. **Grade** the students' individual contributions via the **blogs** on the sub gateway.
- ☐ Remember to **release** the **grades** and **feedback** when all marking has been completed.

Instructions to the learner

You can adapt these instructions to your learners and to your context

- Log onto PebblePad. Click on **view** and **gateways**. In the **gateway** designated for your assignment you will be able to access the assignment brief from the **resources** section. Read it carefully.

- One student in your group needs to create a **webfolio** for the assignment. The person responsible selects **create new**, **more** and create a **webfolio.** Once created, send to the other members of the group with **collaborate permissions.**

- Decide who will record the **action plan**. This person needs to go to **create new** and select **action plan**. Once the **action plan** is created, edit the **webfolio** and link the **action plan** as the group's first piece of 'evidence'. Then send the **webfolio** to the assignment **gateway**. Your tutor and the external client can now view the **webfolio.**

- In turns, record each meeting using the **meeting** record wizard. Add these to the **webfolio** (which automatically updates the **webfolio** on the **gateway**).

- Meanwhile create a **blog** and post your first **thought** according to the deadlines set. The **blog** should be sent to the sub **gateway**.

- Each subsequent post automatically updates the **blog** on the **gateway**. Only your tutor can see this **blog**.

- How and when you respond to feedback on your **blog** (or on the group **webfolio**) will be communicated by your tutor.

- You will receive an email notification when the final **feedback** and **grades** have been released by the tutor. These are automatically added to your assessed **assets** and can be viewed from your **asset store**.

Key points

- Only work published to the **gateway** can be seen by the tutor/external client (they cannot see any of your other work in PebblePad).

- Only you can see your work, or work you have collaborated on, on the **gateway**.

- Once the assignment is completed you can use any of the work you created or collaborated on as evidence of your learning or experience.

The activity in context

This activity is a composite of common learning designs that are used widely by PebblePad practitioners.

Practitioner tips

Use *Activity 5.1: Agreeing a Team Learning Contract* as a way of introducing your groups of students to thinking about how they will work together and reach agreement and consensus.

activity 05.3 | Assessing individual and collective contributions to a group project

The purpose of this activity is to encourage students to use the online tools in PebblePad to manage a group project outside the classroom. Each small group is given a question to research, in this example it is an 'evidence-based practice' question. The group collects and critically analyses articles that will contribute to a final written paper created in a webfolio. PebblePad action plan and meeting tools are used to support the group process. Students include a self assessment of their contribution to the written paper (the webfolio) and they record their activity in a blog, which can be used as further evidence of how and when they contributed to the group work.

Activity Overview

Medium	Assets
Beginner	
Low	
Semester	
Groups 4+	

What challenges might this address?

Group work can be challenging for students; sometimes there are difficulties with communication and differing expectations around individual contributions. Students may not be on campus meaning face-to-face communication and collaboration is difficult to arrange. Another challenge for students is evaluating peer contributions, or grading members of the group. The tools available in PebblePad can assist students with these challenges:

- individual contributions to the group project are recorded in a personal blog which is useful for the tutor and for student peer assessment;

- time management tools such as the meeting wizard help to highlight when the project is on track;

- online collaboration enables revision at draft writing stage which allows for revision and improvement of the final manuscript;

- share permissions and improved communication enhance group work.

Learning design

The students in this activity undertake an evidence-based practice project that involves them working in a group to answer an evidence-based question. Their main task is to identify, read and critically analyse articles that research the question. They summarise their collective reading in a written assignment that is submitted as a webfolio. In the introduction to the assignment students are asked to sit in their groups around a PC or laptop. The tutor explains how PebblePad will document the progress of the group, enhance communication between group members, and show the extent to which an individual has contributed to the final written paper. It is stressed that the self assessment part of the assignment will need to be demonstrated by PebblePad assets created throughout the process (and not just near the assignment deadline).

Students are then encouraged to start planning and recording their first action plans in PebblePad whilst at the PC. One member of the group logs onto PebblePad and creates the first action plan and shares it with the rest of the group giving them collaborate permissions.

In the action plan, the group identifies when and where the group will meet next. When these meetings take place, they are recorded using the meeting wizard. The reflections in the meeting prompt the students to consider the group's progress.

Students create their own personal blogs which they use to capture their individual progress, and to collect resources that will potentially be used in the final written paper. These blogs are shared among group members.

Drafts of the final written paper are created using a webfolio. All members of the group have collaborate permissions for this webfolio. The group has to decide when the webfolio is ready to be submitted, and when they agree the webfolio is complete, they send it to the gateway to be assessed. Students also compile and send a 'self assessment webfolio', which summarises their individual contribution to the group task and their further reflections. They have to draw upon a range of evidence that spans the duration of the project. Tutors mark and give feedback on both the final written paper and the student self assessments.

Tutor actions

What you need to do in PebblePad to set up the activity

Prior to the activity:

- ☐ Create a **gateway**. Add students to the **user group**. The default settings do not have to be changed.
- ☐ Set the **gateway** to lock on the assignment due date.

During the activity:

- ☐ In the face-to-face introductory session, demonstrate how relevant tools – such as **action plan** or **meeting** wizards – can support the group work. Recommend that assets are tagged to enable searching at a later date.
- ☐ When the assignment deadline has passed, **grade** and **feedback** on both the group written paper and the individual student **webfolios**.
- ☐ Remember to **release** the **grades** and **feedback** when all marking has been completed.

Instructions to the learner

You can adapt these instructions to your learners and to your context

- ☐ In the introductory face-to-face session, one member of your group logs onto PebblePad and goes to **create new** and **action plan**.
- ☐ As a group, decide on the steps you need to take in order to complete the assignment. Complete the **action plan** wizard.
- ☐ **Send** this **action plan** to all members of the group, giving them **collaborate permissions. Collaborate permissions** allow all members of the group to edit the asset.
- ☐ After every group meeting, one person is responsible for recording the meeting in the **meeting** wizard and sending this to the members of the group with **collaborate permissions**.

All members of the group:

- ☐ Log onto PebblePad. Select **create new**, **more** and then **blog**. Create a **blog** and **post** to it, with your first thoughts about the group assignment. This **blog** is your individual record of the group's progress and a place for you to share resources for the written paper with the rest of the group. This **blog** will form evidence of your engagement with the group assignment so update it regularly.

- ☐ Send this **blog** to members of your group with **comment permissions**. **Comment permissions** allow all members of the group to comment on your **blog** (but not edit it).

- ☐ When a member of your group has shared a new **asset** with you, you will receive an email notifying you that there is a new **asset** to **view** when you next log onto PebblePad. When an **asset** has been updated, there will be a reminder that there is a **new/updated asset** when you log onto PebblePad.

For the final written paper

- ☐ One member of the group needs to create a **webfolio** and **send** it to all members of the group with **collaborate permissions**. This **webfolio** is used to create the final written paper.

- ☐ As members of the group add to the **webfolio**, the history of the **webfolio** is updated, showing who has contributed and when.

- ☐ Agree who is responsible for sending the final written paper (**webfolio**) to the gateway.

For your self assessment

- ☐ Create a new **webfolio**, giving it the title of your name and 'self assessment'. Following the assessment criteria closely, identify evidence of your engagement with, and contribution to, the group's final written paper. It is anticipated that you will use your individual **blog** for some of the evidence, and the **action plans** and **meetings assets** for the rest. Link this evidence to this 'self assessment' **webfolio**, and add an assessment of your performance. Send this **webfolio** to the **gateway**.

Your tutor will **grade** and **feedback** on both the group final written paper and your self assessment. You will receive an email notifying you when grades and feedback are available.

The activity in context

This activity is based on work with students studying Radiation Therapy in Medical Radiations at RMIT University, Australia. Students conduct an 'Evidence-Based Practice' project in their second year of studies. This project requires students to work in small groups to develop and research an evidence-based practice question. Each member of the group participates in the collection and critical analysis of articles to contribute to a final written paper that answers the evidence-based practice question. The project runs over the semester, with weekly one hour tutorials to support student learning. This activity takes place in the second week of semester and is designed to assist the students with their project by introducing them to the tools in PebblePad that may be useful for group work. At this stage, groups are finalised and the development of a research question is well underway.

activity 05.4 | Working together in online sketchbooks

The purpose of this activity is to engage a group of performing arts students in a variety of tasks that they would encounter as a member of a team in the world of work. Each group has to produce a single, coherent website that will appeal to a specific audience as part of their final assessment. Students use the webfolios like online sketchbooks to explore ideas about colour, design and use of space and multimedia.

Activity Overview

👥	Low	Assets
📖	Medium	🎟️ 📄 🐭 ⚙️
📅	Low	
🕐	Course	
👥	10+	

What challenges might this address?

Working with others is a key employability skill needed in any performing arts workplace. No matter how promising students are, many find it a challenge to work in a group on a joint project. In the future, this can be potentially problematic for these students who are expected to be able to work effectively with others upon graduation.

By moving the delivery *and the discussion* of group work learning into webfolios, students are able to express and explore the fraught dynamics of working in a group to produce a single output – in this case, a webfolio that is a website for a dance company. The webfolio is an important part of their final assessment and can act as a catalyst to ensure the students demonstrate their professionalism and consider the audience in their work, which are essential considerations for their discipline.

Learning design

Each group is required to design and make a 'website' using PebblePad's webfolio tool. This website should present the group as a dance company. The company then uses the webfolio as a tool through which they articulate ideas and working processes in relation to developing their final performance project. Students need to show evidence that they have been thinking about how they address an audience for their performance, as they would in a real life situation, and consider presentation and design such as use of images, colour, layout etc, as they would in employment.

This work is associated with a taught module which explores the relationship between live and filmed performance, and students learn camerawork and editing alongside choreographic and performance skills. Assessment for this course is 80% for a group performance, which is filmed by the students, and 20% for a supporting webfolio with evidence of individual engagement. The students have to capture the group performance, upload the video to YouTube and link to this from the webfolio 'dance company'.

Students are divided into groups and given the assignment brief. As part of the preparation for the group performance, they have to collaborate on an action plan wizard and record meetings using the meeting wizard. They are required to create and submit the webfolio as a group, and submit an individual blog which records the process of planning the performance and creating the webfolio. They link the action plans or other assets used to their blogs, and are therefore able to reflect on the process in a private and secure space. Although the webfolio does not need to be submitted before the assignment deadline, the blogs are submitted at the start of the activity so that the tutors can monitor progress and identify problems with group dynamics early in the process.

Tutor actions

What you need to do in PebblePad to set up the activity

Prior to the activity:

- ☐ Create a **gateway**. Add students to the **user group**. The default permissions do not need to be changed.
- ☐ Set the **gateway** to lock on the assignment due date.

During the activity:

- ☐ At regular intervals go to the **gateway** and read the **blogs**. Remind students if they have failed to submit their **blog**. Give feedback to the students via their **blogs**.
- ☐ Once the assignment due date has passed, **grade** and give feedback to the **webfolios** and the **blogs**.

□ Remember to release the **grades** and **feedback** when all marking has been completed.

Instructions to the learner

You can adapt these instructions to your learners and to your context

Once you have been given the assignment brief, arrange to meet with members of your group. You will be using a number of assets in PebblePad. If you need help creating any of them, click on the **question mark icon** which will take you to the help section in PebblePad.

For the group performance

□ As a group, agree an action plan. One member of the group logs onto PebblePad and goes to **create new**. Complete the **action plan** and **send** it to all the members of the group with **collaborate permissions**.

□ After every meeting, one member of the group records the discussions in a **meeting** asset and **sends** this to the group, with **collaborate permissions**.

□ When a member of your group has shared a new **asset** with you, you will receive an email notifying you that there is a new **asset** to **view** when you next log onto PebblePad. When an **asset** has been updated, there will be a reminder that there is a **new/updated asset** when you log onto PebblePad.

□ The recording of the performance is uploaded to YouTube.

For the group website

□ One member of the group logs onto PebblePad and goes to **create new** and **more**. Select **webfolio.**

□ As a group, decide on how the **webfolio** should look and feel. You need to consider your audience and the style that would suit them. You can create your own banner if you want, or choose one of the standard **webfolio** banners.

□ In the **webfolio editor**, create a link to your YouTube performance.

□ Add appropriate text as detailed in the assignment brief.

□ Add a **webfolio** page for credits, giving details about which jobs the crew have been responsible for.

□ One member of the group is responsible for sending the **webfolio** to the **gateway** by the assignment due date.

For your individual blogs:

- □ In **create new** and **more**, select **blog**. Save it.

- □ Choose a banner.

- □ Select **view** and **post to blog**.

- □ A new window opens, and, in the top right hand corner, select **post new**. Write about the group project, reflecting on your contribution to date. **Post** to the **blog** once a week for the duration of the group project. To return to the **blog** select **view** and **my assets** and click on the **blog**.

- □ After your group has created an **action plan** and once it has been sent to you, link the **action plans** as evidence to your **blog**. Repeat this for any other group **assets** shared or created by you.

- □ Send your **blog** to the **gateway**. Only your tutor will be able to read your **blog**. Members of your group will not be able to see it, even though you have linked other **assets** to it.

- □ Your tutor will **grade** and **feedback** on both the group **webfolio** and your **blog**. You will receive an email notifying you when grades and feedback are available.

The activity in context

This activity is inspired by work with performing arts students at the University of Wolverhampton, UK who are completing a BA Honours degree in dance. It has featured in the JISC publication, *Effective Assessment in a Digital Age* (JISC, 2010), where Dennie Wilson, senior lecturer in Dance, explains:

Despite careful teaching, we were finding that promising students were not fully achieving their potential in group work. We needed to build their conceptual understanding and enable transfer of that understanding into their assessed work. Video was a natural medium to use: the module explores the relationship between live and filmed performance, and students learn camerawork and editing alongside choreographic and performance skills. So, in 2008, we produced a sequence of video podcasts that are fully integrated into learning and teaching on the module.

Combined with the e-portfolio system, PebblePad, the video podcasts have transformed the way students respond to group work. All work associated with the module is located on PebblePad, and can be downloaded onto iPods, and students have both individual pages and a group webfolio on PebblePad. Students access their learning resources via PebblePad, build up a dynamic account of their development as a group and as individuals in their webfolio, and use the system's blog to reflect on elements of dance choreography included in the podcasts. Tutors can track individuals' contributions to group work and intervene when necessary.

The impact of the two technologies has been considerable. Students' choreographic achievement has been enhanced by anytime, anywhere access to the podcasts, and the single, integrated environment provided by PebblePad has produced more agile and creative responses. The webfolios, rather like online sketchbooks, enable students to explore ideas about colour, design and use of space and multimedia, making the task a pleasure rather than work. Most importantly, students engage more deeply with their learning, develop greater conceptual understanding through peer and self-review and, as a consequence, achieve more.

Experiential Learning

Experiential learning allows learners to use an experience or practise a skill in a conscious manner and to then reflect upon their practice and their ability to perform this skill. An integral part of experiential learning is designing the opportunity for learners to identify gaps in their knowledge and as a result of this, plan for future personal development. It is the reflective elements of these activities that ensure learners focus on learning, and not just the acquisition of a skill.

In each of the following activities, learners master a skill under the supervision of an experienced practitioner within an educational institution. However, experiential learning can be a valuable approach in a variety of educational contexts, including placement settings or non-formal settings such as the workplace.

As part of the activities, learners are encouraged to support one another through dialogue and feedback. Sharing knowledge and reflections through PebblePad offers learners the opportunity to make sense of the experience and plan future progress, supported by constructive and timely feedback from peers and tutors. Tutor feedback in PebblePad can be given soon after the experience and then referred to at a later date as the need arises. Learners can use PebblePad to store records of their performance (for example, a video or an audio file) and use these records as evidence of ability and as a prompt to reflect further on their learning.

Each tutor involved in the activity can easily track the progress of a large cohort of students and multiple tutors or mentors can access and cross-check student submissions to enhance the group cohesion. For the educational institution, the benefits are that the taught curriculum becomes visible and students start creating personalised, quality evidence of competence in all areas of the curriculum.

The activities described here suit a range of learning styles, so they can address the needs of a large cohort of learners whilst allowing for a highly personal approach to learning. The recursive nature of experiential learning, complemented and supported by PebblePad, encourages students to focus on areas of improvement, to aim higher and subsequently achieve better results.

Each activity in this section can take place over several weeks or longer, enabling a gradual accumulation of skills and reflections. At the end of the activities, learners have a valuable, easily accessible resource in their PebblePad account that they can use or modify when they apply their learning in the workplace.

Looking for more ideas ?

If you are interested in *Experiential Learning*, take a look at the related activities in *Themes 3: Planning for Personal and Professional Development, 11: Learning for the Workplace* and *10: Preparing for Employment*.

activity
06.1

Constructing a skills diary

In this activity students develop independent learning through reflection on experience using a process of monitored practical activities requiring peer and self assessment. This activity uses a range of PebblePad tools, grouped together in a single webfolio that, as the course progresses, develops into a valuable resource for the student.

Activity Overview

Medium	Assets
Proficient	
Medium	Optional Assets
Year	
Cohort	

What challenges might this address?

In experiential learning, key challenges include how to surface students' learning as they apply theory to practice, how to encourage reflection and how to capture this process for assessment. Traditional paper-based systems are not well suited to this approach as they have a number of inherent limitations: sharing and providing feedback is slow, transportation and storage is cumbersome, and students can mislay their work. These factors and others may lead to a lack of engagement from users. A framework for constructing a skills diary is one way to address this with feedback mechanisms being a strong motivational factor for high levels of learner engagement.

Using the assets in PebblePad, students can work within a structured process that prompts a reflective narration of their learning experiences whilst constructing a resource that will potentially be useful in future study and employment.

For the tutor, there are a number of benefits. Students are more aware of skills development and submissions are easier to retrieve and comment on. In addition, the format of the webfolio provides a rich multimedia record that is both authentic and accessible for assessment.

Learning design

Prior to a practical session students are introduced to the required skills via an appropriate medium such as a video or live demonstration. This is followed by a facilitated practical skills class. In this class an experienced practitioner gives advice, addresses issues of technique and skill and ensures safe and effective practice.

Students are organised into small groups to practise the skills themselves. During this practice session the students video and/or photograph each other as they perform the skills outlined. After the class, each student selects the most appropriate PebblePad asset type to document the feedback they have received from peers. They upload the video/ photos taken in class into their PebblePad account and link the video/photo evidence to the asset. They also add their reflection on their mastering of the skill. Students create a webfolio and the theme of each page is one of the skills practised in the practical skills class. The students are required to create a link from each page in the webfolio to the asset type created for each skill, and in a separate webfolio page provide a narrative of the culmination of skills, linking their learning to broader course learning outcomes. Early in the course the webfolio is then submitted to a gateway to enable the tutor to view the work as it develops.

At this stage they are confirming self assessment of their current skill level. The tutor gives each student formative feedback through a PebblePad gateway. The student then develops an action plan based on the reflections and feedback and links this to the webfolio page for the appropriate skill. The skills diary can then be added to, or modified, as further skills are developed.

The complete skills diary can be used as evidence of skills acquisition for assessment purposes.

Tutor actions

What you need to do in PebblePad to set up the activity

Prior to the activity:

- [ ] Create a **gateway** for the cohort and, if appropriate, set a submission deadline. Add students to the **user group**.
- [ ] The default **gateway** permissions do not need to be changed for this activity.

During the activity:

☐ Give formative feedback to students as they update their skills diary, ideally this should be as frequently as practical.

Instructions to the learner

You can adapt these instructions to your learners and to your context

☐ Log onto PebblePad.

☐ Select **create new** and decide which **asset** type you are going to use to record and reflect on the practical skills activities. This may be an **ability**, an **experience** or another asset depending on the skill. Record and reflect upon the skills activity you have just completed, including the peer feedback you received in class.

☐ Select **upload file** and upload the videos/photos taken during the practical skills class. Remember you should always try to keep file sizes reasonable so anyone viewing your work can quickly download it. This is one of the reasons that PebblePad has file size limits.

☐ Now link these files to the **asset** you have just created by selecting **view** and **my assets** and then selecting the **asset** you have just created to record and reflect. Select **more options** and then **add/edit link**. You now have the option to link to the files you have just uploaded. Click the **green tick** to save and close once you have done this.

☐ In **create new** and **more**, select **webfolio**. Give the **webfolio** your name as a title. Follow the numbered steps to create your **webfolio**. Add a **webfolio page** for each of the skills you have to show evidence of mastering, plus a page for your narrative commentary. In each page, link from the **webfolio** to the skills assets you have created over the course and other commentary or evidence that shows you have mastered these skills.

☐ After you have completed the first skill in PebblePad, send your **webfolio** to the **gateway**.

☐ Your tutor will give you feedback on your **webfolio** as you add to it.

☐ Create a new **action plan** and use this to plan your development based upon feedback.

☐ Link to this **action plan** from your **webfolio.**

□ You do not need to re-send this to the **gateway** (it updates automatically to the **gateway**).

□ This skills diary now belongs to you to develop and refer to throughout the rest of the course and can be used to showcase your skills to potential employers.

The activity in context

The idea for this activity is drawn from the experiences of staff and students at LaTrobe University, Australia. Second year students, studying to become physiotherapists, were involved in a range of learning activities to promote skill development. These activities included watching videos of their peers performing clinical skills, performing the skills themselves in a facilitated practical session, unsupervised practice with peers, and then assessment of clinical skills with formative feedback. Students were also encouraged to use or create a range of resources to enhance their learning, and also as evidence of their development. Students were asked to construct a skills diary to capture the stages of skill development and establish an appropriate plan of action from identified learning needs. In addition to the reported benefits for students, it is anticipated that the fieldwork educators will benefit as students will be better prepared for, and able to reflect on, upcoming clinical learning experiences (Year 3 and Year 4).

Practitioner tips

Offer advice to students on privacy and consent issues when they are uploading photos and videos that include images of other people.

Warn students about file size limits for uploading and offer guidance on how to reduce file sizes.

activity 6.2

Practising reflection for a professional portfolio

For this activity, students collect evidence that supports claims of achievement and experience the benefits of keeping a professional development portfolio. They are guided as they engage in reflective tasks to self audit their skills development, receiving formative tutor feedback. A single webfolio brings together their whole course activity.

Activity Overview

High		Assets
Proficient		
High		
Programme		
Cohort		

What challenges might this address?

This activity is one that can help to develop a learning model that goes beyond minimum competency, fostering deep learning and the development of expertise.

In many disciplines, students need to be introduced at an early stage to the concept of the professional development portfolio to establish their future professional practice and identity. This is often combined with a need to replace traditional models of top-down delivery with learner-centred models where students identify their educational needs and are given opportunities to meet them. Learner-centred models must also align with the professional assessment requirements and, although great value is placed on prior experience in experiential learning, there are times when previous knowledge can inhibit new learning – or where poor skills technique has to be 'unlearned'. The challenge then is to identify and correct misconceptions and to guide the student in replacing opinions with evidence in supporting claims of achievement.

Using PebblePad, students have a clear understanding of what is required of them and can see how they are progressing towards completion. Students who engage in this activity benefit from continuous assessment and the ability to share their work with their peers, which combine to encourage students to aim higher. Since students can access PebblePad anywhere, anytime, they have more freedom to choose how and when they engage in their reflective work.

Learning design

Students are shown an example of a webfolio and made aware that this asset, and the blogs within it, will be used throughout the duration of the course. In a face-to-face session students are required to demonstrate a variety of techniques and skills through simulation. These simulations are video recorded. The videos are then shared with the students once the face-to-face session is finished. PebblePad is used in close conjunction with these simulation techniques.

The techniques the students are developing are complex and require multiple attempts to master. Each technique is recorded in a dedicated blog that is used to record all activity relating to the technique, including every attempt undertaken via a simulation. The blog acts as a way to both record the attempts and to self audit the level of competence in the skill. This self auditing process identifies knowledge and performance gaps, and highlights any learning needs. The simulation and reflective posts in the blogs are repeated until the student has mastered the skill with the tutor providing ongoing feedback as each attempt is recorded. There are defined points in the course for validation of competence where the tutor validates the work and may provide additional feedback. The final reflection in PebblePad focuses on personal growth and strategies for future development.

This series of tasks is repeated for each skill that the student has to master with each skill having its own blog record. Over the duration of the whole course, student activity (including the video evidence) is collected in a single webfolio where the multiple blogs make up the core structure. Higher level achievers can submit their webfolio for an additional award, providing a reflective commentary on their progress throughout the whole of the course via a reflective webfolio page.

Tutor actions

What you need to do in PebblePad to set up the activity

Prior to the activity:

- □ Create a **gateway** for submission of **blogs**.
- □ Add students to the **user group**.
- □ Use the **manage tutor groups** to put students into manageable groups. The default gateway permissions do not need to be changed for this activity.
- □ Create a **sub gateway** for submissions of **webfolios** for higher level award

- (this **gateway** will probably not be used until the end of the course). Set the **gateway** to lock at a date near the end of the course, or just after.
- ☐ Create a separate **blog** for each skill that needs to be mastered.
- ☐ Create a **webfolio** template and when you **add your pages**, select the **item** tab and the **arrow**. Select one of the **blogs** you have just created. Repeat this step to embed each **blog** as a new page.
- ☐ Upload the **webfolio** template to the **gateway** resources with **copy** permissions.

During the activity:

- ☐ Visit the **gateway** and give formative feedback to students as they update their **blogs**.
- ☐ At the point in the course where mastery of skills is confirmed:
  1. Validate all **blogs** that demonstrate the student has mastered the skill and meets requirements.
  2. Archive all the **blogs** that demonstrate competency has been attained, using the date as the name of the archive. You can remove the validated **blogs** from the **gateway** as you have a copy of them in the archive.
- ☐ At the end of the course tell the students whose work is of a high standard, that they can apply for the higher award by submitting their **webfolio** to the sub **gateway**.

Instructions to the learner

You can adapt these instructions to your learners and to your context

- ☐ Log onto PebblePad.
- ☐ Select **view** and **gateways**. Go to the **gateway** and select **copy** for the **webfolio** template. This copies the template into your PebblePad account. You can now start to edit the template. Give the template the title 'Your name' and student number. Save your changes.
- ☐ In **view** and **my assets** you will see a **blog** for each skill you have to master. Click on the relevant **blog** and post to this **blog** each time you attempt to master this skill. You can attach the simulation video file to each post using browse.

- Send this **blog** to the **gateway**.

- Each time you attempt to master this skill, post to your **blog**. The **gateway** will automatically update.

- You will receive regular feedback from your tutor.

- When your tutor thinks you have mastered a skill, the tutor will validate your **blog** at the next validation point.

- Repeat the process of adding to the relevant **blog** for each skill you have to master.

- Open the **webfolio** you were given at the start of the course. This **webfolio** now contains a page with a **blog** for each of the skills you master. If you are applying for the higher level award, add a reflective commentary and submit this **webfolio** to the appropriate **gateway**.

The activity in context

Variations on this activity are evident in many learning contexts. The inspiration for this was drawn from Flinders University School of Medicine, where health professional students on a graduate-entry programme (i.e. previous degree required) need to demonstrate their mastery of basic and advanced life support training, which is integrated throughout the four years of the programme. Many students arrive with some experience, usually gained through traditional CPR/first aid courses. The level of mastery required of health professionals is far beyond this, which presents challenges related to unlearning of poor technique.

Using PebblePad has meant that it is much easier to be accountable to academic and professional bodies such as the resuscitation council(s), course accreditation bodies and the professional registration board.

Practitioner tips

Keep on top of student submissions and visit the gateway regularly. Look on the gateway to see when students have updated their blog.

Use the gateway to monitor student progress. Early identification of underperforming students allows early intervention and reduces problems later in course.

Using simulated scenarios to develop evidence-based reasoning

The purpose of this activity is to support postgraduate students in developing a range of professional skills, encouraging evidence-based reasoning, decision-making and reflective practice.

Students engaging in this activity use simulation-based scenarios and video to demonstrate advanced management skills. PebblePad enables students to reflect on their learning close to the experience and to gather evidence of their skills mapped to a professional competency framework.

Activity Overview

Medium	Assets
Proficient	
Medium	
Course	
Cohort	

What challenges might this address?

Experiential learning is important as a way of applying theory to practice in a controlled environment but one of the challenges is how to capture simulated practice for later reflective learning. At postgraduate level, equipping students with the skills to problem solve unpredictable cases is a pedagogical challenge which can be addressed by videoing simulated skills practice and by requiring students to use evidence-based reasoning to create an effective management plan.

In traditional learning settings, records of simulated practice and reflections are often stored in different places with the result that the impact on learning is lessened. The challenges, then, tend to be both pedagogical and administrative. Learners need to acquire the critical and reflective skills to develop their understanding of the simulation-based scenarios; they also need to organise their reflective work, records and coursework.

Students using PebblePad can gather their evidence in one place or format. Using video in the classroom means that an authentic record is available for debriefing, replacing paper-based forms. By reflecting on the video in PebblePad they can bring together their actual experience of a scenario with their subsequent reflections on it.

Learning design

At the start of the course students are arranged into groups. Each group of students is given a simulation-based scenario. The group undertakes a range of tasks to solve, plan and evaluate the scenario. Then, on an individual basis, each student completes a management plan that outlines how the scenario will be handled, based on a combination of theoretical evidence from their coursework and on the particular circumstances presented in the scenario. The learning outcomes for this task are mapped alongside the professional body's competency framework. Some of these simulations are video recorded and used immediately during a simulation debrief session. This encourages immediate reflection on action, which enhances the consolidation of learning. Following the debrief, students upload small excerpts of the video scenario and complete a PebblePad form that is the evidence-based management action plan for the simulation they have just undertaken. Students also use a blog to reflect upon their performance and identify areas for their own development. Students can revisit these resources at a later date and reflect upon their performance and the management plan they have created. The forms, the videos and the blogs are presented in one webfolio using the 'tag' tool to identify the appropriate resources created by the student for each simulation. This webfolio can then be used as evidence of the course meeting the professional body's standards if the need arises.

As the activity is repeated with different scenarios (all given a different 'tag'), students are encouraged to use PebblePad to develop, collaborate, share and store learning and assessment activities. Blending the simulation videos with the PebblePad reflections now enables students to provide evidence of continuing reflective practice. The webfolio can then be used as a resource to recall, re-play and reflect at a convenient time for the individual. This resource can be a useful reference tool when the students go on placement.

Tutor actions

What you need to do in PebblePad to set up the activity

Prior to the activity:

- □ Create a **gateway**. Add students to the **user group**. Use **manage tutor groups** to divide your students into small groups.
- □ Give **publish**, **view** and **comment** permissions to the **user group**.
- □ Create a **form** that will be the management plan template. **Publish** this **form** to the **gateway**.

- □ Decide on the names of the **tags** that the students will use to organise their resources.

During the activity:

- □ Ask the students to send their **webfolios** to the **gateway**.
- □ After each simulation, give feedback to each student selecting **comment on this page**.

Instructions to the learner

You can adapt these instructions to your learners and to your context

- □ Log onto PebblePad.
- □ Select **upload file** and upload the video of the simulation you have been given by your tutor. Create a new **tag** for this, using the term recommended by your tutor.
- □ Go to **create new**, **more** and select **form**. Select the relevant form created by your tutor. Complete this **form** and **tag** it with the tag you created in the last step.
- □ Go to **create new**, **more** and **blog**. Work through the steps to create a **blog** and then select **view and post to blog**. Click on **post new** to post a **thought** reflecting on the simulation you have just completed and the management plan you have written. **Tag** the **blog** using the same tag.
- □ Go to **create new**, **more** and select **webfolio.** Work through the steps and instead of adding a new page to the **webfolio**, click on the **tag** tab. From the list of your **tags**, select the relevant **tag** for this simulation. All the resources you **tag** with the selected tag will appear on the **webfolio** page automatically.
- □ Send the **webfolio** to the **gateway**. You only need to do this once as the **gateway** will automatically update when you add to or amend your **webfolio.**
- □ The process of tagging resources and then creating a new page in your **webfolio** can be repeated for each simulation.
- □ At regular intervals, go into the **gateway** and view and comment on your peers' **webfolios**.

The activity in context

This activity can support high level learning in multiple contexts and across different disciplines. It is based on work that is being developed with level seven students on a two-year MSc (Pre-registration) Physiotherapy programme at Manchester Metropolitan University in the UK. Whilst undertaking two units, students are expected to clinically reason and problem solve simulated cardio-respiratory cases to plan and evaluate the assessment and treatment of patients with complex, less predictable pathologies of the cardio-respiratory system. During these units the students are required to demonstrate and document safe and accurate physiotherapy assessment and treatment in order to plan holistic, patient focused and evidence-based care.

The students participate in a range of low, medium and high-fidelity simulated scenarios during their two-year course. These activities are linked to clinical cases that the students have to manage with appropriate physiotherapy interventions. Some of these simulated scenarios are video recorded to facilitate post-event reflection and further group work activities. The students work together to peer review their simulated practice and develop an evidence-based management plan, linked to a reflective blog within their portfolio.

Practitioner tips

Ensure that the digital learning material is blended together to facilitate learning outcome achievement – this avoids the technology being viewed as a 'bolt-on'.

Make the video simulations available as close to the scenario activity as possible. Delays weaken the opportunity to promote and engage the students with related reflective practice.

Compress the videos so that they are under 10mb in size. Some learners may need assistance when reducing video file sizes and using video editing software.

Try to avoid long videos that lead up to the critical element. Short focused videos ensure focused reflection and planning.

theme 07 | Collaborative Learning

By 'collaborative learning' we are referring to learners who are working together on a joint endeavour to share their knowledge and experiences. Collaborative learning can take place *formally* through carefully designed activities or *informally* where professionals form networks to share knowledge and practice. A collaborative group can be a community of practice, or a group of students encouraged by their tutor to learn from one another for the duration of a course.

The terms 'collaborative learning' and 'group work' can be conflated. For assessed group work, a level of collaboration is necessary to achieve a result. However, successful collaborative learning does not have to involve formal assessment, particularly in a professional, work-based context. (For activities that address *assessed goal-oriented* group work, please go to *Theme 5: Promoting Group Work*.)

PebblePad enables collaborative learning as an active, social process. Benefits of collaborative learning include the opportunity to encounter a range of perspectives – often across organisational and geographical boundaries – and the chance to discuss topics with a diverse group of people who may bring in new and unexpected ideas to the collaborative task or challenge. Novices may learn from 'experts' and more experienced members can benefit from the questioning and challenge that new learners bring to accepted norms and ways of doing things. These benefits are a reason why so many employers now look for graduates who can demonstrate that they can work collaboratively, in a spirit of co-operation. These are trends that are emphasised in the *2011 Horizon Report*:

> *The world of work is increasingly collaborative, giving rise to reflection about the way student projects are structured. This trend...is being driven by the increasingly global and cooperative nature of business interactions facilitated by internet technologies. The days of isolated desk jobs are disappearing, giving way to models in which teams work actively together to address issues too far-reaching or complex for a single worker to resolve alone.*

> *(Johnson et al., 2011)*

Meaningful collaborative activities can contribute to the development of graduate attributes such as team work, problem solving and critical analysis. They can also support professional development and evidence-based practice through networking and knowledge-sharing.

PebblePad supports these activities in a number of ways. By enabling collaboration and communication, distant learners are less likely to feel isolated and unsupported. In PebblePad, tutors and peers can engage in review and feedback in a secure and reliable environment. Users, particularly those who have heavy demands on their time, can be confident that the time and effort they invest in participating in the collaborative activity is not going to be lost. By recording their experience in PebblePad, users can keep a record of their participation, reflecting back on their experience at a later date. This record can be either completely private, or elements can be shared when necessary.

Because collaborative learning requires a tolerance of diverse perspectives and viewpoints, it is important to create a climate that allows every participant to play an equal part. When designed with appropriate support, collaborative learning can suit a range of learner needs and appeal to a diverse student profile. In all of the following activities, the tutor's role is to establish ground rules that are negotiated and owned by all participants and to create a safe, secure environment that encourages participants to share, exchange and co-create knowledge.

Looking for more ideas ?

If you are interested in *Collaborative Learning*, you might find further useful activities in *Themes 5: Promoting Group Work*, *8: Self and Peer Review* and *4: Developing Academic Study Skills*.

activity 07.1 | An eJournal Club for professional development

This is a professional development activity that builds on work-related learning through web-based discussions of topical interest, encouraging knowledge transfer and the application of evidence-based practices. The eJournal Club (eJC) is hosted in PebblePad in a webfolio, with an article of the month on a separate page, each with an associated blog to harvest comments and foster discussion. It is a facilitated resource, with an

Activity Overview

Medium		Assets
Beginner		
Medium		
Open-ended		
Community		

eJournal facilitator playing an active role in encouraging learners to engage in peer review of the published articles and to develop their online critical appraisal skills. Learners may be drawn from across the world and across institutions and can register their involvement over a period to suit them – typically monthly or annually.

What challenges might this address?

Most educational institutions face the challenge of needing to attract new students. This activity offers one way to build a reputation with employers and professionals as a provider of high quality, flexible professional development. The eJC allows the university to showcase its postgraduate and professional development provision to a global audience, using PebblePad.

Whilst the importance of communities of practice for professional development is widely accepted, it can be difficult to find ways of keeping the momentum going across institutional and geographical boundaries. This activity offers a credible and creative approach to professional development and addresses this dilemma of how to develop and sustain a community of practice.

The eJC provides an ideal environment for the development and exchange of knowledge through online social interaction. Using the PebblePad blog for each article allows learners who may contribute part way through the month to easily pick up threads of the discussion and follow lines of argument and debate. This is made possible by the eJC facilitators who supply well-crafted questions for the blogs, helping to structure and organise discussions. Some of the benefits of using PebblePad for this activity are:

- Facilitators and learners have a secure and reliable method of engaging with the eJC.

- Learners and eJC facilitators can readily see the contributions of all eJC participants.

- Learners can access the eJC at a time, place and pace of their choosing.

- eJC facilitators (and learners – in the context of peer feedback) can provide timely feedback, reinforcing learning, responding to queries and encouraging further contribution and discussion. There is a clearly visible record of this feedback.

- Learners have a durable record of their learning and experience as evidence for continuing professional development (CPD).

Learning design

This eJC activity is conducted entirely online and begins with the creation of a webfolio with embedded associated blogs that, once created, are shared with learners by sending the webfolio to the web. A PebblePad account is not necessary for the learners participating in this activity. Once a month, there is a carefully selected article shared with the group of learners who then discuss it in the light of their own practice. There is a webfolio page for each of the following:

- **Introduction**: The aims and scope of the eJC are provided in promotional material and repeated in the introduction to remind participants of the ethos of the journal club. This introduction outlines what the tutors can expect from the learners, and what the learners can expect from the tutors.

- **eJC Guidelines**: This webfolio page describes how the eJC will operate each month. The page includes guidelines on netiquette and codes of conduct regarding issues such as patient confidentiality. Additionally, learners are told how to sign each post.

- **A page for each 'article of the month'**: Each webfolio page contains the full reference of the article, a copy of the abstract and a link to the full article (with publisher's permission). A blog is linked to each 'article of the month' page. It is in this blog that the discussions take place, although each webfolio page does have a comments option so learners can ask about processes or practical matters as well.

- [ ] **Resources**: This webfolio page contains information on how to engage critically with the article and how to evidence participation in the activity for continuing professional development purposes.

On the 'article of the month' page, learners add their contribution to the discussion using the comments box in the blog. They are encouraged to respond to other learners' comments as well. The activity is guided by a 'facilitator', not necessarily the person who created the webfolio. The facilitator changes from time to time, and sometimes there is a guest facilitator who may be a former student. The facilitator is responsible for responding to each student's contribution in the early part of the month, weaving a summary of the contributions at the end of the activity and sending email reminders alerting learners to a new article, or that the activity is drawing to its conclusion.

Tutor actions

What you need to do in PebblePad to set up the activity

Prior to the activity:

- [ ] You will need to design the eJC in advance of starting to create it in a PebblePad **webfolio.** Collect and store the documents and articles as one zipped file so that it will be easier to **upload** these files when you start to create your eJC.
- [ ] Log onto PebblePad.
- [ ] **Upload** the zipped or **multiple** files you have just created. **Tag** these files with the name of the eJC so that they are easier to find. You can add additional tags if necessary. These files are unpackaged and now sit in your **asset store**.
- [ ] Create a **blog** for each of the monthly tasks.
- [ ] In **create new** and **more**, select **webfolio.** Create a **webfolio.**
- [ ] In the **webfolio**, create a page for each section (as detailed in learning design above). For guidance on style, take a look at *Activity 4.1: Just in time resources: Using WebQuests to introduce digital and academic literacies*.
- [ ] In the 'article of the month' page, add a link to the relevant article and one of the **blogs** you have just created.
- [ ] Send the **webfolio** to the web with **comment permissions** and **copy the URL**.

During the activity:

☐ Share the URL via a welcoming email with your learners and guest facilitators.

Facilitator instructions:

☐ Follow the link to the eJC using the URL shared by the webfolio creator in the welcoming email.

☐ In the **blog**, start the discussion off and then **comment** on each contribution for the first few weeks, remembering to sign off each post with your name if you have not logged onto PebblePad. As learners become more comfortable with the online environment it may not be necessary to **comment** every time a student contributes. Send out emails to learners when a new article discussion is about to start and as a reminder to join in.

☐ At the end of each task associated with an article, provide a summary that weaves the contributions together and gives an overview of the article and the responses.

☐ Send an email to the learners when you have posted this summary in the **blog**.

Instructions to the learner

You can adapt these instructions to your learners and to your context

☐ Your tutor will send you a link to the eJournal Club (eJC) by email. Click on this link.

☐ The **webfolio** you can see will guide you through the eJC and advise you on how to respond to the monthly readings and tasks.

☐ You can contribute to the online discussions by going to the **blogs** which are on each 'article of the month' page and make a **comment** in the comment box. Remember that unless you sign your **comment**, it will appear as an anonymous contribution. Please respond to other learners' **comments** as well.

☐ You will receive email reminders when a new task is starting.

☐ On the 'Resources' page in the **webfolio** there is information about how you can demonstrate ongoing professional development, using the tasks as evidence.

The activity in context

This activity is based on one that is in use at Sheffield Hallam University, in the UK. The learners are post-registration/postgraduate practitioners working in radiotherapy and oncology from all over the UK and a number of overseas countries. Some of the learners are undertaking this activity as part of, or supplementary to, the study of distance learning postgraduate modules. The remainder are undertaking this as CPD activity. The development was prompted by feedback from learners on their postgraduate courses which indicated that journal clubs set up in-house in the health service were problematical, poorly attended and often were disbanded as a result. The challenge was to provide an online opportunity to participate in a journal club which allowed learners to access the provision at a time, place and pace of their choosing. The eJournal Club is also a way of engaging potential applicants to postgraduate courses (from UK and overseas) in a CPD activity which helps familiarise them with Sheffield Hallam University staff and PebblePad, whilst hopefully providing a quality learning experience as a stepping stone to embarking upon Master's level study. As this is a CPD activity and not an integral part of a course or award, and as such not 'teaching', they had to secure an agreement with publishers to use their articles for this purpose and agree a fee per article. They found it was best to be flexible about the opportunities for participation and now offer an annual registration fee (at reduced cost), six monthly, three monthly or monthly registration.

Practitioner tips

You can use the webfolio again with another cohort. In your asset store, copy the webfolio and remove the links to the blogs and any additional comments on other pages. Create a new set of blogs and link these to the 'articles of the month' pages.

activity
07.2

Creating digitally enhanced patchwork text

This activity is based on a 'patchwork text assessment'.

The essence of a patchwork text is that it consists of a variety of small sections, each of which is complete in itself, and that the overall unity of these component sections, although planned in advance is finalized retrospectively, when they are 'stitched together'.... Each of the short pieces of writing is shared within a small group of learners as part of the teaching-learning process. At the end [of the course] learners add a reflexive commentary to the short pieces they have already written, which they may also, if they wish, revise and edit.

(Winter, 2003)

Activity Overview

Medium	Assets
Improver	
Low	
Course	
Groups of 4+	

A digitally enhanced patchwork text assessment offers the opportunity for regular formative feedback through the online medium and learners are required to integrate multimedia into their patchwork text, encouraging them to make full use of the PebblePad environment. Each 'patch' is a piece of text that is written in response to a theme or topic and corresponds to a learning outcome of the module. The analogy with patchwork helps the learner to recognise that each patch can be an independent piece of work, but when they are seen together, the work takes on a different dimension and significance. The final activity is a reflective commentary, 'stitching' together the patches and the emerging themes.

The activity is particularly suitable for a part time course with working people as it allows learners to pace their workload, whilst also developing a community of practitioners through peer dialogue. The structure of the assessment with points for regular feedback retains the rigour required at postgraduate level, although it could be used at any level of learning. This version of the activity blends face-to-face and distance learning but it could be adapted for distance learning.

What challenges might this address?

Collaborative learning is especially important for people who are learning at a distance or who are combining work and study. Learners may be quite independent in the way that they approach their study tasks and the times at which they are able to complete their study but most learners enjoy the experience of learning within a community, knowing that they are working alongside peers who are facing the same highs and lows of the study programme. Collaborative learning is one way to develop this sense of being part of something bigger – and this activity mirrors that concept in the way it is designed – each part of the work combines to a bigger final piece. The peer review aspect of this activity is also an important way of building community and of using the strengths and insights of the learning community (the action learning set in this example). PebblePad's comment functions enable this peer review to take place securely and PebblePad also enables the learners to communicate one-to-one, or in a small group whether they have the time to meet up or not. The ability to share at a point when the author feels confident, and withdraw that permission when another patch is being developed, only to share again later, is easy in PebblePad.

This activity also addresses other issues that are familiar to most educators. Given the chance, a proportion of most student groups will leave writing the assignment until the last minute. When they also have competing work or family priorities this can prevent some learners from meeting the assignment deadline. This activity enables learners to work steadily throughout the module and it encourages them to be more organised. The notion of cumulative patches enables a longer period of time for reflection on emerging themes and allows time for formative feedback and for the learners to revise and review their submissions. This is a complex form of assessment and PebblePad eases what could potentially be an administrative nightmare. Supporting the process of developing the assignment, as well as the final output, is straightforward in PebblePad. Another advantage is that if learners take an authorised break from studying, tutors can use PebblePad to retrieve archived assignments from earlier study, which makes continued support for students a simpler task.

Learning design

In this activity the entire course revolves around the assessment, with each face-to-face session addressing one of the learning outcomes for the course. The assessment is a series of patches, each one written around a specific theme and presented as a stand-alone piece of work. A typical patch is 1,000 words. Learners are required to link their patches to evidence from their practice to support their claims. In addition, learners have to include a non-text based artefact, created by them, as evidence of their learning (such as a photograph or an audio file). The aim of this is to ensure that learners are starting to think about audience, digital presentation and visual messages. The final activity is a reflective commentary, 'stitching' together the patches and the emerging themes. The whole assignment is created in a webfolio, with a page for each patch and a page for the final activity.

Details of the assessment, the marking criteria and the themes of each patch are provided in the course handbook. Learners are introduced to the digitally enhanced patchwork text assessment at the very start of the course.

Learners form action learning sets in small groups. Following a face-to-face session, learners write a patch and learners share their draft patches with members of their learning set and invite comments at regular intervals. Following this peer review, learners are asked to share patches with their learning set tutor who gives formative feedback on each patch individually, as a cumulative process. The tutor feedback can only be viewed by the author and the other tutors.

The first session takes place in a computer lab and learners are shown how to access the template webfolio, copy it, and personalise it. They are also reminded how to link to evidence, upload a multimedia file and how to share assets with their learning set. Learners are advised about how to create a coherent webfolio and how to give and receive formative feedback. Learners give their feedback based on the marking criteria, which has the added benefit of ensuring that they read and understand the marking criteria early on in the module. Learners have the opportunity to revise their draft patches in the light of feedback before submitting them for summative assessment at the end of the course.

The webfolios are auto published to the gateway so there is no last minute panic about where to submit. It is the learners' choice whether the comments from peers remain on the final webfolio submission. The webfolios are then graded and feedback is given to each student using a feedback form with the marking criteria.

Tutor actions

What you need to do in PebblePad to set up the activity

Prior to the activity:

- ☐ Create a **gateway**. Set the **gateway** to lock on the assignment due date.
- ☐ Add learners to the **user group**. The default settings for the users do not need to be changed.
- ☐ In **create new**, **more**, select **webfolio.**
- ☐ Create a **webfolio** with a page for each of the patches and a page for the final reflective commentary. You can put the learning outcomes as text in each page. Use bold coloured text so that your learners can read and then delete this text without it impairing their own writing.
- ☐ Add the **webfolio** to the resources area of your **gateway** with **copy** and **auto publish** permissions and select **notify the user group(s) when they login to PebblePad**.
- ☐ In the **gateway**, under **resources**, add a **feedback form** based on the assignment's marking criteria.

During the activity:

- ☐ In the first face-to-face session of the course, demonstrate how to access the **webfolio** and personalise it.
- ☐ Regularly visit the **gateway** to view updated **assets** and leave **feedback** on the draft patches. **Feedback** is not seen by members of the learning set.
- ☐ When the assignment due date has passed, **grade** and leave summative feedback on the **webfolios**. Use the **feedback form** you created to give consistent feedback to each student.
- ☐ Remember to **release** the **grades** and **feedback** when all marking has been completed.

Instructions to the learner

You can adapt these instructions to your learners and to your context

- [ ] Log onto PebblePad. As soon as you log on you will see a notice telling you that you have one asset waiting to be copied to your **asset store**. Select **view now** and then select **copy** and **publish**. This **webfolio** template is now copied to your **asset store** and you can edit it. This template belongs to you and no one but your tutor can see it until you decide you are ready to share it with members of your learning set.

- [ ] In **view** and **my assets**, open the **webfolio** and edit it. In the **webfolio editor** you can delete the guidelines that your tutor has inserted and start to write your own text. You can **upload** multimedia files (provided the file size is less than 10mb) and insert them into your **webfolio** pages.

- [ ] When you have completed a draft patch, **send** it to members of your learning set giving them **comment permissions**.

- [ ] The first time a member of your learning set shares their **webfolio** with you, you will receive an email notification. Thereafter, when the **webfolio** is updated and added to, you will see a notification on your PebblePad homepage under **new/received updated assets**. Read your peers' draft patches and give them constructive comments based on the assignment's marking criteria.

- [ ] You do not need to send the **webfolio** to your tutor. Your tutor will see your work as you progress and will give you feedback. Members of your learning set will not be able to see the tutor's feedback.

- [ ] If you do not wish for the **comments** made by your learning set members to remain on your assignment, you can delete them.

- [ ] You can withdraw **view** and **comment** permissions at any time. To do this, go to **view** and **my assets**. Select your patchwork text **webfolio** and, in the pane on the right, select the **shared** tab. You will now see a list of the peers you have shared with. Click on a name and, to **unshare**, click on the **bin icon**. This removes permission to view your **webfolio.** You can re-share at a later date if you wish by resending the **webfolio** with **comment** permissions.

- [ ] On the assignment due date your **webfolio** will be locked and you will not be able to edit it or any linked **assets**.

- [ ] You will receive an email notifying you when your **webfolio** has been graded and summative feedback given by your tutor.

The activity in context

PebblePad is an ideal way of creating a patchwork text assessment. The inspiration for this activity is drawn from the University of Cumbria, UK, where a postgraduate certificate in learning and teaching in higher education uses a patchwork text assessment. Participants in the course are all part time, work-based learners who are making the transition from one profession, such as health, to teaching in a higher education context. This group of learners are typically new in post and have a number of demands made upon their time. Using PebblePad for the patchwork text offers a number of key benefits: it gives participants the opportunity to support one another in the creation of the assignment whilst at a distance from one another; it also introduces the online medium to some who, until this point, have not used elearning in their practice. One of the challenges for the course team has been to encourage participants to use non text-based artefacts in their practice, such as multimedia files. Using PebblePad for the assessment has enabled participants to upload a variety of files and consider the issues around the type of presentation tools they select with their learners.

Practitioner tips

If a grade is contested by a student, it is useful to have the tutor's formative feedback to refer to at a later date to show that the student had opportunities throughout the course to improve their work.

activity
07.3

Helping students to continue learning beyond the classroom

This activity uses collaborative blogs to help groups of students to develop their thoughts and understanding between fortnightly problem-based learning (PBL) sessions. The trained problem-based learning group facilitators also facilitate the group blogs. Individuals end up with a personal archive of their learning journey on the module and the group blogs give each student a perspective of how the other students in their group interpreted the case.

Activity Overview

Low		Assets
Beginner		
Low		
Course		
Groups of 15+		

What challenges might this address?

Encouraging students to continue their learning outside the classroom is a difficult challenge for educators. One way to achieve this is to introduce a collaborative learning task to build a commitment to continuing involvement with a topic. In this activity, each student is required to contribute to a group blog to post their further thoughts about cases that have been discussed, encouraging their further involvement with the PBL cases between group sessions. Using PebblePad supports this continuing group discussion as well as greater reflective learning. The blog tool is particularly suited to enabling peer and tutor feedback.

Learning design

Students participate in fortnightly PBL sessions in groups of 15-20 with a trained facilitator. Each session is based on integrated cases to stimulate broader thinking and discussion across subject themes.

Following each session, students are required to complete a PebblePad thought to describe their own personal learning experience in the PBL session. They are encouraged to include a summary of their learning and how the activities and discussion in the session contributed to this. Each student must then add their asset to a shared group blog that has collaborate permissions. This blog is created and managed by a nominated group representative; this person is also responsible for ensuring all have contributed. Students take turns to oversee this activity. Students have to read each other's posts before the next face-to-face session to obtain a perspective on their peers' views as well as their own.

At the beginning of each PBL session, the facilitator reviews a small sample of the blogs, focusing on any common themes arising from the entries and any questions. They seek to use this first period of the session to reinforce learning from the previous session and link it to the current session.

At the end of the course, as part of the summative assessment, students reflect on one case that has been covered and refer to their own posts compared with other students' perceptions.

Tutor actions

What you need to do in PebblePad to set up the activity

Prior to the activity:

- ☐ Create a **gateway**.
- ☐ Add students to the **user group**. Give the students permission to **publish** and **view**.
- ☐ Use **manage tutor groups** if you have a large cohort of students.

During the activity:

- ☐ Visit the **gateway** before each face-to-face session to review the **blogs** and select a small, representative number to discuss.

Instructions to the learner

You can adapt these instructions to your learners and to your context

- ☐ At the end of the first face-to-face session, meet with the rest of your group to decide when members of the group will take turns for creating and submitting the fortnightly collaborative **blog** to the **gateway**.

When it is your turn to create and send the collaborative **blog** to the **gateway**:

- ☐ Log onto PebblePad and select **create new**, **more** and then **blog**. Give the **blog** the name of your group and the session number you are reflecting upon.

- ☐ Send this **blog** to every member of your group, giving them **collaborate permissions**. You will have to do this early in the fortnight so that everyone in your group can send their **thoughts** to this **blog** when they have written them.

- ☐ Send out a reminder to members of your group if the date of the next fortnightly session is drawing near and they haven't added their post.

- ☐ Before the next face-to-face session send the **blog** to the **gateway** for your tutor to read. He may use the **blog** as an example in class.

To contribute to the blog:

- ☐ Log onto PebblePad.

- ☐ In **create new**, create a new **thought**. Add your reflection on the last PBL session.

- ☐ Send this **thought** to the **blog** shared by this session's representative.

- ☐ In **view**, and **my assets**, open the **blog** and read the **thoughts** from other members of your group.

- ☐ If you want to read **posts** from other groups, go to the **gateway** to view them.

- ☐ Once the face-to-face session has finished, do not send new **thoughts** to the **blog** for that session. You are encouraged to view it at a later date as it is necessary for completing your assignment. Your tutor will choose one case that has been covered and you are required to reflect on your post for this case and compare it to the posts made by others.

The activity in context

This activity is based on work at the University of Birmingham with Year 1 undergraduate medical students who are engaged in fortnightly group learning activities throughout their academic year. The aim of introducing PebblePad was to increase interaction on the case studies between sessions. A requirement of the course is encourage greater reflective opportunities and feedback between students and tutors/facilitators. PebblePad has been instrumental in encouraging greater reflection on the group experiences by each of the students, and capturing this for comparison and review in subsequent sessions.

Practitioner tips

The facilitators need to be confident in accessing and reading the blogs so ensure that they have training before the activity.

Check that every group blog is discussed at some point in the sessions so that students know their contribution is likely to be selected and discussed. This retains interest and motivation to contribute to the blog.

theme 08 | **Self and Peer Review**

In *Chapter 3: The Principles of PebblePad*, we discussed how the learner is at the heart of PebblePad and users are managing their own learning in a personal space where learning is 'done by me' not 'done to me'. In keeping with these principles, it makes sense to involve learners in the assessment process, where they have a voice in their own assessment and that of their fellow learners. Learners' involvement in the assessment process can include self or peer reviewing, grading peers' work and/or giving constructive feedback. Prior to the rise of the Internet, organising self and peer review could be an administrative challenge. Now, introducing self and peer review is a realistic and relatively simple approach that can be used effectively to support learning.

Self and peer review can bring many benefits, preparing learners for lifelong learning. Being able to consider one's own performance, and measure this against a standard set of criteria is a key employability attribute. Formal self assessment is an extension of the cycle of reflective learning, discussed in *Theme 6: Experiential Learning*. Being able to reflect upon one's own performance and consciously make a judgment about effectiveness or quality of the work is a valuable skill. Articulating a critique of one's own performance requires scrutiny of one's own work and approaches, reinforcing the learning that has taken place. If self review is part of an assessment, then this approach can ensure that the learner has considered how their work meets the assessment criteria.

The Quality Assurance Agency for Higher Education in the UK (QAA) sees peer assessment as an effective method of supporting student learning, where peer assessed activities enable

> *...students to understand assessment criteria and deepens their learning in several ways, including:*
>
> a. *learning from the way others have approached an assessment task (structure, content, analysis) and*
> b. *learning through assessing someone else's work, which encourages them to evaluate and benchmark their own performance and to improve it.*
>
> *Peer assessed activities can be used in a variety of learning situations, including practical work and in large or small classes.*
>
> *(QAA, 2006)*

As mentioned earlier, organising self and peer review is a much simpler administrative process than it has been in the past. PebblePad is not only designed with the learner in control, it can also scaffold and facilitate the review process. A tutor can easily create and share a self review form based on the assessment criteria. Large numbers of students can then complete a review of their assignment and attach it to their submitted work. This foregrounds the assessment criteria, drawing learners' attention to the marking scheme, which brings focus to their study and increases the likelihood of submitting final work that meets the assessment requirements.

Forming judgements about the work of peers – and giving constructive feedback – is an attribute that continues to be important throughout life and is an essential skill in all professions. Although the process of presenting one's work for review by peers can be daunting, it is easier to practise and gain confidence in a secure environment such as PebblePad.

In its most simple form, peer review is achieved through sharing and commenting on each other's work. More complex or sophisticated reviewing can take advantage of the anonymous review tools in a gateway, ensuring a degree of impartiality if necessary.

Although PebblePad simplifies as well as supports self and peer review, it is still important to recognise the complexities of the process. Guidelines for reviewing need to be clear and understood by the learner and, in many cohorts, tutors need to be available for support and to answer queries. Using a blog to air concerns about the process can be an effective and transparent method of engaging learners in the assessment criteria from the start of the course. The culture of the discipline also needs to be taken into account. The spirit of sharing and giving constructive feedback may not be effective in a discipline that is competitive, just as reflection is not an integral part of every discipline. This should not deter practitioners from using peer review activities with their learners; it just means that the complexities and attitudes to critiquing others' work will need careful and sensitive introduction.

Looking for more ideas ?

If you are interested in *Self and Peer Review*, you might find further useful activities in *Themes 5: Promoting Group Work, 7: Collaborative Learning* and *4: Developing Academic Study Skills*.

Self and peer critique of treatment plans

The purpose of this activity is to help students develop the ability to evaluate their own work and the work of their peers, using an assessment rubric. For clinicians, the ability to critique treatment plans is an important work skill but this activity is suitable for any students who need to develop the ability to self assess and to assess the work of their peers.

In this activity, students use complex medical software and scenario-based learning to plan a large number of treatment regimes for patients. Real clinical case studies are provided by the university's clinical partners. Students keep a webfolio spanning the programme, which illustrates the development of skills of increasing complexity. During their clinical placements, students are exposed to slight variations in work practice and they are encouraged to reflect on these variations and share their clinical experiences with their peers during class, inviting formative feedback. Once students have completed one or two treatment plans, they engage in self and peer assessment.

Activity Overview

Medium	Assets
Improver	
High	
Semester	
Class	

What challenges might this address?

This activity addresses two key challenges for the whole process of self and peer review:

- It helps students to engage with, and understand, the assessment criteria at an early stage in their study.
- It enables students to gain an insight into how their peers are approaching the requirements of the course – and to learn from that.

Self evaluation and self assessment are important elements of many courses that prepare students for professional work. Students who become familiar with the course assessment criteria early on in the programme are more likely to improve the quality of their submissions.

The peer review process means students are able to see how their peers have displayed their work, which assets their peers consider best illustrate learning outcomes required and alternative ways to display their work and construct their portfolio. There is also the opportunity to discuss the assessment rubric and how the criteria will be applied. If there is capability and time, examples of best practice can be displayed and discussed with the group. Further action can be taken if there are areas where the whole class received low grades and questions can be put back to the class about how to improve these areas and what additional resources/assets could be used to support learning/evidence.

PebblePad's design means that it easily supports the processes of self and peer assessment. The form builder can be used to develop bespoke assessment tools (or rubrics); gateways and 'share' permissions enable students to share and comment on each other's work.

Learning design

The following learning design is repeated every semester for the duration of the whole course. Students experience a variety of different work practices during clinical placement. In class, they write up their treatment plans and are encouraged to reflect on the variety of cases, sharing their clinical experiences with their peers and inviting formative peer feedback. Classes are run as two hour supervised computer laboratory sessions, with students required to spend time outside of class to develop their treatment plans. Students work within the discipline-specific planning software and their PebblePad webfolio at the same time, annotating a webfolio with images from the planning software and reflective text for each treatment technique planned. This learning activity occurs several weeks into the semester when students have completed one or two treatment plans.

The end of semester assessed webfolio is a collection of treatment plans. To reach completion, students:

- participate in self assessment and award themselves a grade using an assessment rubric shared through the course gateway;
- use PebblePad to share their webfolio with a nominated peer;
- participate in peer assessment of the webfolio and complete the assessment rubric for their peer and give a grade, and use PebblePad to provide a copy of this back to their peer;
- complete a reflective exercise about peer assessment and participate in class discussion;
- submit the webfolio to the gateway for the tutor to grade.

Tutor actions

What you need to do in PebblePad to set up the activity

Prior to the activity:

- ☐ Create a **gateway**. Add the students to the **user group**. The default permissions do not need to be changed for this activity.

- ☐ On the **gateway** settings, set a date when you want the **gateway** to lock.

- ☐ In **form builder**, create a self assessment form, using the assessment criteria as the basis for your fields. Remember to add a field for a grade.

- ☐ In **form builder**, **copy** the self assessment form, and rename the copy 'peer assessment'. You may need to edit the instructions to make the **form** relevant to the audience.

- ☐ In **form builder** create a third form that is a reflection on the peer assessment process. Questions can include the following:

  - ▫ What did you find the most difficult aspect of participating in the peer assessment process?

  - ▫ What do you see the advantages of peer assessment for eportfolio assessment could be?

  - ▫ What do you think the limitations are?

  - ▫ Do you think that participating in the peer assessment process has helped you understand the assessment criteria?

  - ▫ Do you think that it is difficult to give feedback to a peer? Why or why not?

  - ▫ What role does your relationship with your peer (e.g. friendship) play in this process with regard to being able to be objective?

  - ▫ Was any of the feedback provided by your peer unexpected?

  - ▫ Did you think that the assessment was indicative of the current quality of your eportfolio?

  - ▫ Do you think that students should take part in assessing their peers?

  - ▫ Did you feel comfortable assessing your peer? Add Why or why not?

  - ▫ How do you plan to implement the suggestions made in this feedback session?

- ☐ Publish all **forms** to the **gateway**.

During the activity:

- **Grade** and give **feedback** to the eportfolio submissions once the assignment due date has passed. You will need to give a rationale for the grade you have awarded, particularly if it is substantially different from the grade the student and their peer have awarded.

- Remember to **release** the **grades** and **feedback** when all marking has been completed.

Instructions to the learner

You can adapt these instructions to your learners and to your context

- Log onto PebblePad.

- In **create new**, **more**, select **webfolio.** You will be creating your eportfolio in the **webfolio** asset for the duration of the semester.

- In class after working on your treatment plans, send your **webfolio** with **comment permissions** to a nominated peer for formative feedback.

- When a peer shares her **webfolio** with you, **comment** on her work, using the assessment criteria as a guideline.

- Your tutor will tell you which nominated peer's work you will be assessing formally at the end of the semester. When you have been told who is your nominated peer, send your **webfolio** to them.

- When you **receive** your nominated peer's **webfolio**, and after having read it, go to **create new** and select **form**. Choose the peer assessment **form**. Complete this for your peer, remembering to add a grade, and **send** it to them with **copy permissions**.

- You will need to add both your assessment of your peer's work and the assessment of your work from your nominated peer to your **webfolio.** Do this by clicking on **view**, selecting the **webfolio** and then **add your pages**, **add item**. Repeat this step for each form. Do not alter the form that contains the assessment of your work.

- When the assignment due date draws near, go to **create new** and **form**. Select the self assessment **form**. Read your **webfolio** carefully and identify where and how you meet the assessment criteria. Remember to add a grade. Complete the self assessment and then, in your **webfolio**, add the self assessment **form** as a page to the **webfolio.**

☐ Repeat this last step for your reflection on the peer assessment process.

☐ To submit your **webfolio** to the **gateway** for assessment check that your **webfolio** includes:

  a. A copy of the assessment your nominated peer has sent to you.

  b. Your assessment of your nominated peer's work.

  c. Your self assessment.

  d. Your reflection on the peer assessment process.

☐ When you have all these as pages in your **webfolio, send** the **webfolio** to the **gateway**.

☐ You will receive email notification when your tutor has **graded** and given **feedback** on your work.

The activity in context

This activity is based on work in progress at RMIT University, Australia, with students who are studying Radiation Therapy in Medical Radiations. They plan radiation therapy treatment regimes for patients with cancer based on real clinical case studies. Critiquing plans and self evaluation are important for professional Radiation Therapists, and the tutors have noticed a marked improvement in the quality of submissions after the process of self and peer review. They also find the exercise useful in inspiring confidence for those less confident with computers.

activity
08.2

Anonymous peer review of research plans

This activity provides a way of improving planning for small scale projects. Students work in groups of four and select a research topic related to their subject. They produce a plan that describes how they will conduct the research. The plans are then made available anonymously to others in their 'research group' and students give constructive feedback to the other three members of their group. Based on the feedback from other members of their group, students reflect on their original action plan and identify any changes they will put into action to improve the research outcomes.

Activity Overview

Low   Assets

Beginner

Low

Semester

4+

What challenges might this address?

Encouraging students to plan their desktop research thoroughly is important to the final research outcomes. Students often start the process too late to demonstrate their full abilities and do not think through all the details of their plan. When a group is large it can be hard for a tutor to provide effective and timely feedback.

The creation of a plan in advance reduces the anxiety of beginning the research with a 'blank sheet' and the interim feedback from peers improves the learners' chances of achieving a desirable mark. The development of this activity allows the tutor to offer a more effective learning experience without a noticeable increase in workload. Workload may even be reduced as students are less likely to need to resubmit their plans.

Involving students in providing feedback to others makes them more discerning about their own work, leading to improved performance. The peer review element gives them a better understanding of the assessment criteria and how these might be met through the development, and critique, of an action plan.

This activity works best when coupled with a short face-to-face session on constructive feedback prior to the peer review activity.

Learning design

This activity takes place over the course of one semester. The course tutor develops a series of related topics for the students to research. These research topics are created as 'tutor groups' in a module gateway.

An overview of the assessment criteria and the research topics are added to the gateway resources where they can be accessed by all students.

Students self-subscribe to the gateway and choose the topic they wish to research. By week six, they produce an action plan detailing how they will conduct their research, including the resources and methods they will utilise. They send their action plan to the gateway. Peers in the research group can view the action plans in the gateway but, because the tutor has selected anonymous peer review, the author is hidden from view. Students are given one week to provide helpful and constructive feedback to the other three members of the group. By the end of week eight, each student must add a reflection to their original action plan identifying what they have learnt from the peer feedback and identifying the changes they will action to improve the research outcomes.

Once the review period is over, the view permissions for students are withdrawn on the gateway. The final research reports are uploaded to the gateway for assessment. If the quality and context are appropriate, the tutor can choose to use a selection of the peer feedback as summative comments through use of the comment bank.

Tutor actions

What you need to do in PebblePad to set up the activity

Prior to the activity:

☐ Create a **gateway**. Add students to the **gateway user group**. Give the students permission to **anonymously peer review** and select **hide author details**. Select **self subscription** for the **user group**.

- □ Select **manage tutor groups**. Create a **new group**, giving it the title of one research topic and a limit to how many students should be in the group. Repeat for each research topic.

During the activity:

- □ At week 6 check that all students have submitted their **action plans** and monitor the feedback being added through the review process. Excellent examples of feedback can be copied and pasted into the **comment bank** under **gateway resources**. This can then be re-purposed/re-used for the final assessment.
- □ Once the review period is over, go to the **gateway** and withdraw the student **user group view** and **review permissions** leaving them with only **publish** permission. Inform the students that the permissions have been changed by going to **manage gateway** and **send a message** to all **users**. Users will receive an email from you. Tell the students that they can now submit their final research reports.
- □ **Grade** and **feedback** on the assignments once the assessment due date has passed.
- □ Remember to **release** the **grades** and **feedback** when all marking has been completed.

Instructions to the learner

You can adapt these instructions to your learners and to your context

- □ Log onto PebblePad.
- □ From **view**, go to the **gateway** and **self subscribe** to the research group that interests you most. Beware that popular research topic groups will fill up fast.
- □ In **create new**, create an **action plan** giving details on how you are going to complete your research assignment.
- □ Send this **action plan** to the **gateway**.
- □ From **view**, go to the **gateway** and view your peers' **action plans**. You will be able to leave anonymous feedback. Remember to be constructive and encouraging in your feedback.
- □ Once you have received feedback from all your peers, go to **view** and select your

> **action plan**. Update the **action plan**, based on feedback you have received.

- ☐ You are now in a position to write your research report. Once you have done this, **send it** to the **gateway**. Your tutor has changed user permissions so you will only see your assets.

- ☐ When your tutor has given your work a **grade** and **feedback**, you will receive an email notifying you.

The activity in context

This activity is a composite of common learning designs that are used widely by PebblePad practitioners.

Practitioner tips

The 'anonymity' features on the gateway allow for many variations of this or related activities. However, the 'promise' of anonymity to your students carries an additional burden of responsibility so make sure you understand the various settings – all of which are explained in the gateway tipsheet 'assessment on gateways'.

One variation of this activity is not to use the action plan as a precursor to another asset but to continue to develop the action plan (or other document) iteratively as a result of the peer review feedback.

As users can belong to more than one tutor group it is possible to have the students peer review the work of members of an entirely different group (and research topic).

activity
08.3

Developing professional discourse through blogging

In this activity, students use blogs to practise expressing and sharing ideas with a peer audience. Developing the ability to enter into professional conversations with peers is an important skill for most students who are preparing for professional work. Hosting the blogs on a group gateway enables learners to view and respond in mutually supportive exchanges. This activity can be used with large cohorts of over 100 students.

Activity Overview

Low	Assets	
Beginner		
Low		
Semester		
Cohort		

What challenges might this address?

When undergraduate students arrive at university it may be the first time they have been required to express themselves as 'emerging professionals'. Suddenly they are being asked to think of themselves beyond being a 'learner' and adopt a new professional role such as a teacher, clinician, engineer or scientist. Using PebblePad personal blogs, students can start to articulate their evolving understanding of their discipline and professional philosophy in a supportive and confidence-building group of peers. This adds a powerful social dimension when it is linked to a gateway.

Making the blogs accessible for peer comment means that learners are practising the skills of debate as well as gaining confidence and reassurance in the company of peers who are working to the same objectives. A further benefit of using the blog is that learners can include photos, graphics, audio and video which create a rich multimedia learning log.

Learning design

This activity is used as an ice-breaker during an introductory course module. Students work together in the computer laboratory and create a blog, adding photos of themselves and personalising the appearance of the blog.

The entire cohort can be over 100 students, comprising five tutor groups. To ensure blogging in a public space does not appear too daunting, gateways are created for each group with 'view' and 'comment' permissions. At the outset, the blogs are published to the gateway and each student selects two learning buddies to follow for the following ten weeks. At least one new post, of at least 250 words, is expected each week. Students are told that blog entries should relate to their learning and their future practice. Posts can contain links, multimedia files and attached assets. Students read their learning buddies' blog posts in the gateway and add comments that are professional in nature.

Although the activity is compulsory, it is not assessed because the idea is to create a shared learning space to experiment. At the end of the module the tutor gives a 'pass' grade to students who have completed the activity by writing the blogs and by being a supportive peer to their learning buddies. The tutors provide further feedback if appropriate and encourage the students to keep their blogs intact so that they can refer back to them in their Year 2 module.

Tutor actions

What you need to do in PebblePad to set up the activity   ⚙ 🚪

Prior to the activity:

- ☐ Create a **gateway**. Add students to the **user group**. Give the student **user group view** and **comment permissions**.
- ☐ Use **manage tutor groups** to divide the students into manageable groups.

During the activity:

- ☐ In the first face-to-face workshop show the students a **blog** created by a former first year student. Emphasise the benefits of writing for an audience of peers as well as for a tutor.
- ☐ Visit the **gateway** periodically to monitor activity in the **blogs** and comments being given by the learning buddies.
- ☐ At the end of the semester **grade** the **blogs** (making a note of the extent to which the learning buddies have been commenting) with a pass mark and give feedback encouraging the students to value the **blog** and use for future reference.
- ☐ **Archive** the **blogs**.

Instructions to the learner

You can adapt these instructions to your learners and to your context

- ☐ Think about the design of your **blog** and the images you want to use to illustrate it.

- ☐ Log onto PebblePad.

- ☐ Go to **upload** and upload digital photographs to illustrate your **blog**. These photographs are now in your **asset store** and can be used repeatedly in future **assets**.

- ☐ In **create new**, **more**, select **blog**. Create a **blog** and choose a **template** that suits you, or create your own **banner**. If you want to create your own **banner**, select **create new template** and then choose one of the photographs you uploaded into your **asset store**.

- ☐ **Post** to your **blog**. Each entry needs to be 250 words. Your writing needs to focus on your learning and future practice. Remember your audience as you are writing.

- ☐ **Send** your **blog** to the **gateway**.

- ☐ In **view**, select **gateway**. You can **view** and **comment** on the **blog** your learning buddies have created. Give positive and encouraging feedback to your buddies, focussing on their achievements.

- ☐ At the end of the semester your tutor will give you a pass mark if you have contributed to your **blog** every week and commented on your learning buddies' **blogs**.

- ☐ You will be able to refer back to your **blog** as your studies progress.

The activity in context

This activity is being used at the University of Worcester with learners on the BA Qualified Teacher Status (QTS) course. Many of the students are straight out of school and are wrestling with new perspectives and frames of reference. These present a challenge on emotional, social and cognitive levels and the blogging activity provides a valuable tool for clarifying and articulating early ideas. Peer access and review is a positive motivator for many, rather than writing purely for their tutor. Although it is difficult to quantify, it appears that the contribution across the group is of higher quality, in terms of reflective thinking, than the previous paper-based individual journals. This may be because students invest greater thought into their blog entries as a sense of audience is created through the gateway.

theme

09

Preparing for Accreditation

Being accredited by a professional body is a prerequisite for practice in many professions and industries. Sector-wide recognition of a particular standard of achievement ensures safe practice and minimum levels of competency and quality across the profession. Even when accreditation isn't a condition for practice, it makes sense for today's employees to gain formal, professional certification if they want to stay current and up to date with developments in their sector. Today's employees may change jobs many times, but they are less likely to change professions. Gaining accreditation demonstrates that a learner is committed to their own development and lifelong learning. Whether essential or not, the process of gaining professional accreditation and maintaining it can be enhanced through use of PebblePad, providing a secure and durable record that can be shared with validators and scrutinised whenever required.

If a course of study is accredited by a professional body, the transition from newly qualified graduate to professional is overseen by the institution, and the responsibility for registering is taken by the course administrators. Alternatively, programmes of study can prepare students to apply for professional status upon graduation, and the responsibility for applying for professional status lies with the learner. Whichever process is in place, PebblePad can support the application process offering benefits to the learner and the institution supporting them.

To retain professional accreditation, members of a body usually have to demonstrate that they have maintained, or improved upon, the competences they reached when newly qualified. One way of demonstrating this is by collecting evidence of continuing professional development (CPD) at regular intervals. Using PebblePad to record and reflect upon a variety of professional development activities provides the accrediting professional body with an overview of how the member has ensured that their practice is up to date and that they are fit to continue practising. In addition, using PebblePad to support CPD can be an effective way of presenting specialist knowledge and skills.

Some professional certification can be awarded through portfolios that demonstrate competence in the required criteria of the profession. Two of the authors of this book, for example, chose to use PebblePad to present their eportfolio application for certified membership of the Association for Learning Technology (CMALT). There is also a small but growing interest in using PebblePad as an emerging method of claiming prior learning amongst some educational institutions who are developing formal processes to support the recognition of prior learning (RPL) or accreditation of prior experiential learning (APEL).

As well as bringing benefits for individual users, the use of PebblePad can streamline the processes of accreditation for the institution and the professional body. PebblePad gateways can collect and validate a newly qualified professional's work or a declaration of on-going professional development. Members' work can be monitored efficiently and at specified times for quality assurance processes, and there is also the facility to show specific submissions to external examiners or bodies for a time limited period.

As you read the activities that follow, notice how working towards accreditation is designed as a reflective process, which usually continues beyond the lifetime of the activity. Once a learner has developed assets and an eportfolio in PebblePad, they are able to continue to build on their webfolio to meet continuing requirements for job applications or professional development. In the last activity featured here, we have given some detail to the design to show how becoming familiar with the professional framework prepares graduating students for their future as registered teachers.

Looking for more ideas ?

If you are interested in *Preparing for Accreditation*, you might find further useful activities in *Themes 3: Planning Personal and Professional Development*, *10: Preparing for Employment* and *11: Learning for the Workplace*.

Preparing a portfolio for professional development

This activity describes how to use tags in the preparation of a professional portfolio.

At the beginning of a course of study, learners are introduced to the concept of developing a portfolio, which is clearly structured according to professional or industry frameworks and standards of attainment. Regular meetings with tutors support the learners in developing a PebblePad webfolio, using tags. A key programme learning outcome is that students develop the ability to identify their own learning needs and take responsibility for evaluating their personal learning and professional development.

Activity Overview

Low	Assets
Improver	
Low	
Programme	
Cohort	

This activity works well when it is combined with personal development planning activities (see *Theme 3: Planning Personal and Professional Development*).

What challenges might this address?

Embedding employability into the curriculum is a key challenge for all educational providers. There is a need to demonstrate that their curriculum is responding to changes in the workplace and it is providing opportunities to develop relevant skills and knowledge. The professional portfolio is one strategy for addressing the need to show evidence of attainment of key skills. Using frameworks that are identified by employers and/or professional bodies means a portfolio can be used in a variety of contexts for job applications, accreditation and assessment.

Paper portfolios do not meet the needs of students today, who keep most of their documents and resources in electronic format. PebblePad allows students to gather evidence in a variety of media that can be kept together in one place and easily re-used for different purposes.

Learning design

Within two weeks of the course start date, students have a face-to-face session in a computer lab, where they are introduced to the concept of a professional portfolio and how PebblePad is used to support this. It is important to clearly distinguish between PebblePad as the space in which the students work and the professional portfolio as the particular asset they are creating. Students new to PebblePad may need reassurance that they don't share their whole PebblePad account with anyone else but that they can select and present aspects of their work as appropriate. The students are introduced to the term 'tag' and are required in the session to create tags that represent a skills framework constructed from the standards of the professional body. Using the professional framework helps students become acquainted with terminology that is familiar to potential employers.

The students are required to maintain their professional portfolio using PebblePad throughout their three year undergraduate programme. They use it to record their learning experiences and engage in reflection activities, to prepare for job applications and, ultimately, to prepare for their professional career. To ensure that they engage with this process, personal development is embedded throughout the programme.

Students are supported by a personal tutor and regular meetings are timetabled throughout the academic year. At each of these meetings the tutors remind the students about the professional portfolio and encourage the students to share assets with them.

To support student learning and reflection, the programme team encourage the students to use the tagging functions to evidence the skills framework that forms the structure of their professional portfolio. This ensures that the assets will be stored in a structured format that will make it easier for the students to manage their professional portfolio and present evidence for CVs and job applications.

Tutor actions

What you need to do in PebblePad to set up the activity

Prior to the activity:

☐ Agree across your course team the **tags** your students are going to use for the whole course.

During the activity:

☐ In the face-to-face introductory session show the students how to **tag assets** and how to combine **tagged assets** in a **webfolio.** In this session it needs to be made very clear to students the importance of maintaining their professional development portfolio, otherwise they may fail to engage.

☐ When a student sends you a **webfolio** prior to a personal tutor meeting, **comment** on their work and progress.

Instructions to the learner

You can adapt these instructions to your learners and to your context

☐ Log onto PebblePad.

☐ Go to **tools** and then **my tags**. Create a new **tag** for each skill identified by your tutor.

☐ Now go to **create new**. Start a **thought**. **Tag** it with one or more of the skills you have created as a **tag**. After finishing the thought, this will now be available to search in your **assets** under the **tag** you have used.

☐ To search for **assets** under a specific **tag**, go to view and then **my assets** and **open tag cloud**. A list of your tags appears. Select the **tag** you want to search in, and a list of associated **assets** will appear.

☐ Now go to **create new** and **more**. Select **webfolio**. Create a **webfolio** following the steps. If you need help, click on the **question mark icon** to read the PebblePad help pages. When you have to **add pages** to your **webfolio**, select the **tag** tab. You can collate **assets tagged** with one skill on a page. Choose the **tag** you want to appear on the page. This will be useful when you have to identify evidence of skills for a potential employer.

☐ Prior to meeting with your personal tutor share your **webfolio** with her. Use the **send to** tool to share with her, giving her **comment** permissions. When your tutor has commented on your **webfolio**, you will see that an **asset** has been updated on your PebblePad home page under **current activity**.

☐ When you come to apply for a job, use the **tags** to search for evidence of the essential and/or desirable skills you have accumulated during the course. If applicable, create a presentation **webfolio** which draws upon your assets to provide evidence of your skills and knowledge and **send to** the potential employer. You can do this by clicking on **add a contact** and then **external user**.

The activity in context

This activity is based on work at Manchester Metropolitan University where the BSc Physiotherapy programme is using PebblePad as part of the Joint Information Systems Committee (JISC) funded 'Supporting Responsive Curricula' (SRC) project. The purpose of the physiotherapy strand of the project is to use PebblePad and a key skills framework to enhance students' employability. Tutors encourage students to keep their undergraduate portfolio (which they call a personal development portfolio) structured with a key skills framework constructed from the standards of the Health Professions Council (HPC), the NHS knowledge and skills framework (KSF) and the Chartered Society of Physiotherapy (CSP). This structure is important as it is meaningful to potential employers. One of the most significant drivers for this project was the rising number of applications for Band 5 physiotherapy posts where sometimes vacancies are advertised for very short periods of time (in some cases jobs close in a matter of hours). The students therefore need to be able to submit CVs and electronic application forms as quickly as possible. Searching by tags enables the students to find and repurpose material for specific job descriptions in a short time.

Practitioner tips

Students forget how to access PebblePad if they do not regularly use it so drop-in sessions throughout the year in a computer lab are useful.

Staff development is important – students are much more engaged if staff are also using PebblePad as their own professional portfolio.

activity 09.2 | Supporting feedback and dialogue for portfolio-building

This activity supports the application process of qualified members of staff for professional accreditation. In this example, the professional body specifies the outcomes that need to be met but leaves it to the education provider to decide how the outcomes will be achieved and evidenced. PebblePad is used in conjunction with a Learning Management System (LMS) to support a distance learning and development programme that provides a route to accreditation. Learners develop a portfolio mapped to learning outcomes and enter into a dialogue with their facilitator as they amend and improve their submission at a pace and at times that suit the learner.

Activity Overview

Medium		Assets
Beginner		
Medium		
Variable		
1 or many		

What challenges might this address?

Many professional bodies are moving away from costly inconvenient paper-based portfolios in favour of eportfolios. The webfolio in PebblePad offers an elegant and flexible alternative for presenting evidence of achieving learning outcomes.

A more difficult challenge for educational providers is how to support the process of accreditation for professionals who are already busy and are learning at a distance from the institution. The structure of PebblePad supports the reflective process and aligns with the professional guidance on recording professional development activities. PebblePad also offers features that allow feedback and a dialogue between the tutor and learner which is the core of this activity.

The learning design for this activity addresses the difficulties of workload management by allowing learners to take ownership of the process, working at their own pace. Those who work remotely from the educational institution can use PebblePad to receive timely feedback on areas for development.

Learning design

The learners in this activity are given a year's subscription to the scheme that includes access to the LMS and a PebblePad account. Their first encounter with the scheme is an introduction to the LMS and PebblePad, which gives access to resources related to a set of learning outcomes. Learners can access the learning materials on the LMS in their own time.

Guidance on how to gather and upload evidence into a webfolio is given in the LMS, alongside a link to PebblePad. Learners are directed to a webfolio template in a gateway. There is a page within the webfolio for each learning outcome and a claim for accreditation can be considered complete when the evidence has been shared with an institutional facilitator, and feedback from the facilitator has been acted upon. This can be a straightforward process, or it may develop into a longer dialogue between facilitator and learner. The learner may, for example, request clarification, or may enter into a discussion about how the feedback has helped them to adjust or change their practice. The webfolio pages can be amended as many times as necessary and at a pace that suits the learner (within the limits of the year subscription).

When the facilitator can verify that the webfolio is of a standard acceptable to the professional body, the webfolio is given a 'pass' in the grade box. The learner then shares the webfolio with two external referees. Each referee adds a comment to the webfolio confirming that the learning outcomes have been met. The facilitator then validates the webfolio confirming that it has met all requirements.

Once the member of staff has gained professional accreditation, the webfolio is archived and can be accessed for quality assurance processes.

Tutor actions

What you need to do in PebblePad to set up the activity

Prior to the activity:

- ☐ Create a **gateway** for the accreditation process Add learners to the **user group**. The default settings for the **gateway** do not need to be changed.

- ☐ Create a **webfolio** template, with a page for each of the learning outcomes. Add this **webfolio** to the **gateway resources** with **copy** and **auto publish** permissions. Select **notify the user group(s) when they login to PebblePad**.

◻ Ask the author of a successful application for permission to share this. Add this **webfolio** to the **gateway resources** with **view** permissions only.

During the activity:

◻ Check which webfolios are in the gateway as a means of finding out who has successfully copied the **webfolio** template.

◻ Visit the **gateway** regularly to provide **feedback** (**feedback** will be instantly released on an **unlocked gateway**).

◻ Give the **webfolio** a pass grade when it is ready to be shared with the external referees. Notify the student by clicking on **manage gateway** and **send a message**. Select **user group** – you can send an email to the student from here.

◻ **Validate** a **webfolio** when it demonstrates that the author has met all of the learning outcomes and the external referees have confirmed this in comments. Use **send a message** to notify the student.

◻ **Archive** the **gateway** to keep a record for quality assurance purposes.

◻ Send relevant documentation to the professional body confirming entry onto the register.

Instructions to the learner

You can adapt these instructions to your learners and to your context

◻ Follow the link in the LMS to log onto PebblePad.

◻ As soon as you log on you will see a notice telling you that you have one **asset** waiting to be copied to your **asset store**. Select **view now** and then select **copy and publish**. This **webfolio** template is now copied to your **asset store** and you can edit it.

◻ In **view**, go to **gateway** and then in the **gateway** created by your tutor, view the exemplar **webfolio** in **gateway resources** and use this as inspiration when you are creating your application for professional accreditation.

◻ In your **asset store**, edit the **webfolio**, providing evidence of how you meet each of the learning outcomes. In your **webfolio** you can link to evidence you have created in PebblePad: for example, a **thought**. Or you can **upload** evidence: for example, a photograph. Your **webfolio** is automatically updated in the **gateway** every time you add or amend a page in the **webfolio**. Your facilitator can see your updates as you progress.

☐ When your tutor has added feedback to your **webfolio**, the **current activity pane** will have a message in bold telling you an **asset has been updated**.

☐ Reply to your facilitator's **feedback** and describe how you intend to act upon their feedback. You may also ask for clarification if you are unsure of the meaning of the feedback.

☐ Once your facilitator believes you have met all the learning outcomes, you will receive email notification that you have passed. This is your prompt to send the **webfolio** to two external referees who have to add their **comments** confirming that the **webfolio** meets the professional body standards.

☐ Notify your facilitator by email when you have received both confirmation comments from your referees.

☐ You will receive an email notifying you that your **webfolio** has been validated. Your facilitator will contact the professional body on your behalf confirming that you have obtained professional accreditation.

The activity in context

This activity is based on work at Sheffield Hallam University where postgraduate Radiography staff are supported in their progression onto the Practice Educator register held by the College of Radiographers. The Practice Educator status is recognition of the role that qualified staff play in supporting students and staff in a practice setting. Although the College of Radiographers has provided the criteria for accreditation, the College has left the process of implementation to individual universities. Six learning outcomes must be met, and evidence offered to support any claims by the applicant. The content is assessed by the university facilitator. Staff are then recommended for accreditation and, once minimum standards are met, they are entered onto the register.

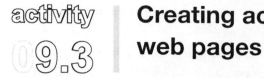

Creating accessible and usable web pages

The activity uses the PebblePad webfolio and its display options to help learners to complete a professional qualification that requires them to demonstrate their knowledge and understanding of web usability and accessibility. The activity builds a community of peer support, using a combination of face-to-face sessions, an online forum in the Learning Management System (LMS) and PebblePad. Learners are supported in writing personal narratives around learning outcomes and the webfolio assignment is designed to provide direct evidence of applying the concepts to practice. It may subsequently be used in a declaration of on-going professional development activities if required by the learner's professional body.

Activity Overview

Medium	Assets
Beginner	
Medium	
Programme	
Class	

What challenges might this address?

Demonstrating understanding of web accessibility and usability is best demonstrated in practice. Traditional ways might be, for example, to critique websites, to put together guidelines for specific impairments and to experience simulations of impaired vision, dyslexia and so on. Finding ways to show that theory is being applied to practice is more challenging.

PebblePad can meet this challenge, using features that make it an accessible and useable system suitable for a diverse range of learners who are creating and sharing assets. Outputs created by users such as a webfolio have features such as alternative text for images and customisable text size, font style and background colours. All of the HTML outputs are standards-compliant and offer complete style sheet functionality.

These PebblePad features offer opportunities to devise activities and assignments using the inbuilt accessibility tools. Learners are asked to create their own web pages that meet international standards of accessibility and usability. Together with reflective exercises that show how the learning will be applied to wider professional practice, this offers an exciting and creative way for learners to demonstrate their skills and practical understanding.

Learning design

Learners are members of staff from a variety of different employers who have volunteered to attend an accredited professional development course. The course is about how to create accessible learning opportunities for a range of diverse learners. The assignment is a narrative created in a PebblePad webfolio that fulfils the awarding body's requirements of meeting specific standards, whilst allowing the learner to recount their own unique journey. In addition, the webfolio has to model best practice in the online environment, using PebblePad's accessibility functions to create an assignment that meets sector standards.

The course outcomes are achieved through a blend of face-to-face sessions, an online forum in the Learning Management System (LMS) and PebblePad. The use of a forum and regular face-to-face sessions are important for cohort morale and for injecting a sense of pace and challenge. These methods also serve to enable peers to form a learning community, who subsequently may share their webfolios with one another. Learners use PebblePad to write their individual narratives and to submit their final assignment. This combination of learning methods reduces feelings of isolation and helps to motivate learners when they are compiling their individual webfolios.

The first activity on the course explains this unusual approach to attaining certification and helps the learners understand that the course requires a high degree of self-management and discipline. Specific PebblePad accessibility features are demonstrated, with explanations as to why they are good practice. For example, PebblePad prompts users to include full alternative text descriptions for uploaded documents including images.

In subsequent sessions, learners are repeatedly encouraged to consider the concept of writing a narrative around learning outcomes rather than simply submitting assignments or mapping evidence. In turn, this approach encourages course participants to consider different user perspectives and to reflect on the importance of designing learning or web pages with the specific needs of their users in mind.

The completed assignment is a webfolio that meets the standards required by the awarding body, in a manner that allows the learner's unique journey of learning to be told. If required, the portfolio can be used as evidence in a declaration of on-going professional development.

Tutor actions

What you need to do in PebblePad to set up the activity

Prior to the activity:

- ☐ Create a new **gateway**. Add students to the **user group**. The default **gateway** settings do not need to be changed.

- ☐ Create a **webfolio** template with pages for each of the standards. Add to the **gateway resources** with **copy** and **auto publish** permissions. **Select notify the user group(s) when they login to PebblePad.** This means that the students' **webfolios** are by default sent back to the **gateway** once a student has copied the **webfolio** from the **gateway**.

- ☐ Ask a former student for permission to use their **webfolio** as an exemplar. Add this to the **gateway resources**.

During the activity:

- ☐ Encourage the learners to share their **webfolios** with one another and **comment** on work in progress.

- ☐ View the student **webfolios** on a regular basis and give formative **feedback**.

- ☐ After the submission due date, mark the **webfolios** and give summative feedback. Remember to **release** the grade and feedback when all marking has been completed.

Instructions to the learner

You can adapt these instructions to your learners and to your context

- ☐ Log onto PebblePad.

- ☐ As soon as you log on, you will see a notice telling you that you have one **asset** waiting to be copied to your **asset store**. Select **view now** and then select **copy and publish**. This is now in your **asset store**. You will be adding to this **webfolio** at regular intervals throughout the course. Your tutor can see your **webfolio** at all times through the **gateway** and will give you **feedback** as you progress.

- Before starting to create your own **webfolio**, view the exemplar **webfolio** in the **gateway resources**. Go to **view**, **gateways** to see this exemplar. Your tutor will direct you to it. Use this exemplar to inspire you when you are creating your **webfolio**. Pay attention to the way in which the author has created an accessible, useable online environment that takes into account the reader and their potential needs. Notice how the author has used images, titles and the **info tip** tool.

- Go to **view** and **my assets**. Select your own **webfolio** and edit. Use the PebblePad help to guide you. To access PebblePad help, click on the **question mark icon** on the right of the screen. When you have completed your first page in your **webfolio**, **view** it and then use the **display options** to experience how other users may view your **webfolio**.

- As you build your **webfolio**, you are encouraged to share your work in progress with your peers. Use **send to person** to share with peers and give them **comment** permissions on your **webfolio**.

- If a peer shares their **webfolio** with you, **comment** on their progress in a positive and constructive manner.

- Once the assignment submission date has passed you will not be able to add to your **webfolio** or amend any of the **assets** associated with it.

- You will receive an email notifying you when your **webfolio** has been marked and summative feedback given.

The activity in context

This activity has been developed from work with further education teaching staff at Thanet College in the UK who are selected to complete the TechDis ITQ at Level 3, an internationally recognised qualification. PebblePad is used to capture the mapping element of the ITQ, the contact record requirements and the mapping of evidence to competences required by the awarding body (City and Guilds). The intention is that this can be then be put forward as evidence of continuing professional development to the professional body, the Institute for Learning (IfL).

activity 09.4 | A 'capstone task' bringing together theory and practice

Most of the activities in this book are intentionally generic in their descriptions, to make it easier for you, the reader, to apply the ideas to your own setting. In this activity we have retained the focus on accreditation for teaching, since this is an area which will interest many of our readers. It can, of course, translate to other contexts.

The activity shows how PebblePad can be used to support learners as they

Activity Overview

Medium	Assets
Proficient	
Medium	*plus assets created during the course prior to the capstone task*
Programme	
Cohort	

reflect and integrate all their learning throughout a programme, mapped to standards set by the accrediting body. Here PebblePad is used to prepare for, and complete, a 'capstone' task – a final year activity that pulls together learning from across a course of study and work placement. Graduating teachers are asked to create a webfolio that demonstrates their management and understanding of teaching and learning in different contexts as seventy per cent of their final grade. The portfolio is structured in such a way that the trainee teachers can go on to use it, after graduation, to present to the awarding body for professional registration.

What challenges might this address?

Bringing together, and making sense of, what has been learned is an important stage for all students at the end of a course, especially for those who are preparing for professional practice and registration. Learning on a course may be viewed (by students and by tutors) in 'silos' which do not cross over, with the result that students do not always relate what they learn to their practical experience.

Integrating formal university learning with practical placement (in this instance, a school placement) is a familiar challenge, particularly for students who may struggle to draw connections between their practical experiences and the theory that has been introduced in the formal learning setting. By introducing PebblePad at the beginning of the year, students and staff can see the opportunities for using PebblePad as a study aid, as a feedback tool and as a place to showcase and celebrate achievement attained across the course and placement. Using PebblePad for feedback means that assessment becomes formative in nature and students have a record of their learning over time. By providing detailed guidance on the use of the system, students have the technical know-how to use it creatively and are encouraged to experiment and create their unique story within the framework required by the accrediting body.

Learning design

The students on this course are required to create a webfolio that reveals their knowledge, understanding, reflections and philosophical stance. They do this by demonstrating the experience they have gained over the duration of their teaching course, including whilst on placement. The module is the final 'capstone' that is purposefully designed to draw together and explicitly recognise the learning that has taken place over a period of years.

Students on this course are introduced to PebblePad when they first enrol. They are made aware at the beginning that they will be gathering evidence of learning and recording development for the whole of their study. The PebblePad introduction is created in the institution's learning management system (LMS). It is highly structured and gives step by step details on constructing and editing a webfolio and how to send it to a gateway for assessment. The guide includes videos and screenshots. Students who need additional help receive face-to-face support in a workshop setting. Throughout the course, students are encouraged to use the variety of PebblePad assets to record and reflect upon their learning, so that when they start this capstone module they have a substantial range of evidence to draw upon. By the time they embark upon their webfolio, students are familiar with PebblePad.

The completed webfolio has to include pages that correspond to their professional body's framework of standards. The students are encouraged to see their webfolio as a resource that will enable them to cultivate clear plans for developing evidence as well as a means to present their evidence in a flexible and interactive format. For the trainee teachers in this example, the webfolio includes the following pages (though these could be substituted for different frameworks in other disciplines):

1. **Pedagogy**: Knowledge and understanding of general teaching practices, strategies and resources, approaches to teaching based on educational psychology and philosophy.

2. **Content knowledge**: Knowledge of the content and structure of their teaching subjects as defined by curriculum documents and a broad and deep knowledge of the discipline. Understanding of the influence of society and politics on what counts as worthwhile knowledge and skill.

3. **Pedagogical content knowledge**: Teaching practices, strategies and resources specific to the subject based on a deep understanding of the discipline, its structure and the ways it can be learned.

4. **Learners**: Knowledge and understanding of the students today, together with the influences on their thinking, interests, habits, values and attitudes.

5. **Planning and assessing learning**: Knowledge and skill in planning lessons, units of work, courses of study and curriculum knowledge of assessment strategies, their strengths and weaknesses, and appropriate use.

6. **Maintaining safe and challenging learning environments**: Knowledge of strategies and skills for maintaining safe and challenging learning environments as well as any evidence that this has been done.

7. **Being a professional teacher**: Broad and detailed knowledge of the role of education and teachers in society. Informed opinions about educational issues. Evidence of a commitment to professional behaviour, ethics and on-going professional development.

8. **Reflective practice**: Knowledge of principles and evidence of reflective practice.

Exemplar webfolios by former students are made available to students so that they have a concept of what the final, assessed webfolio contains and how it may look. Students are encouraged to be creative and to tell their own story. They can represent themselves and their learning in multiple ways and use a range of genres to highlight their experiences.

Assets that will be used in the final webfolio are developed over the duration of the course, which reduces anxiety amongst students about providing appropriate evidence for their learning. In addition, the formative nature of their assessment tasks allows student to see their learning develop and mature over time.

All course tutors give formative feedback to the students through the PebblePad gateway. By using PebblePad, the tutors have a window into the on-going development of the various components of the task and, if necessary, they can intervene before problems arise to offer encouragement and support. This learning design also highlights common issues which can be raised and discussed amongst the cohort.

Students submit their completed webfolio to a gateway for marking at the end of the course. The webfolio remains with the student as a resource to use or draw upon when applying for employment, showing potential employers their professional learning gained whilst studying. Because the webfolios are structured according to the standards of the professional body, students are practised in describing how their learning and practical experience relates to each of the key dimensions of the professional framework. This can be helpful for students for interviews where questions along these dimensions will be raised. The webfolio can be the basis for a presentation during an interview process, or as a link when completing an application.

Tutor actions

What you need to do in PebblePad to set up the activity

Prior to the activity:

It is important to note that these instructions are for setting up the creation of the webfolio for the final capstone task. Direction on how to engage students from their induction period through to graduation can be found in *Activity 9.1: Preparing a portfolio for professional development*.

- ☐ Create a **gateway**. Set the **gateway** to lock on the assignment due date.
- ☐ Add students to the **user group**. Add tutors to the **tutor group**. You do not have to change the default settings. If you have a large number of students on your course, use **manage tutor groups** to divide your cohort into manageable groups.
- ☐ Create a **webfolio** template with pages for each of the standards. Add to the **gateway resources** with **copy** and **auto publish** permissions. Select the **notify the user group(s) when they login to PebblePad** option to notify users that the **webfolio** is available when a user next logs on.
- ☐ Ask a former student for permission to use their **webfolio** as an exemplar. Add this to the **gateway resources**.
- ☐ Create the supporting PebblePad guides and upload to the LMS. Ensure that you include a link to the PebblePad log on page if your institution doesn't have single sign on.

During the activity:

☐ View the student **webfolios** on a regular basis and give formative feedback. If you select **feedback**, only you, other tutors and the student can see the feedback. Other people that the student may share the **webfolio** with (e.g. peers or potential employers) cannot see feedback. Collate any common issues you identify and use this as a basis for discussion in face-to-face sessions.

☐ After the assignment due date, mark the **webfolios** and give summative **feedback**.

☐ Remember to **release** the **grades** and **feedback** once the marking is complete.

Instructions to the learner

You can adapt these instructions to your learners and to your context

☐ You will already be familiar with PebblePad. If you do need a reminder of how to create assets, log onto the LMS and read the introduction to PebblePad. The resources in this section of the LMS will remain here for the duration of the course so you can access them at any time. Follow the link in the LMS to PebblePad and log on.

☐ As soon as you log on you will see a notice telling you that you have one **asset** waiting to be copied to your **asset store**. Select **view now** and then select **copy and publish**. This **webfolio** template is now copied to your **asset store** and you can edit it.

☐ You will be adding to this **webfolio** at regular intervals throughout the course. Your tutor can see your **webfolio** at all times through the **gateway** and will give you **feedback** as you progress.

☐ View the exemplar **webfolio** in the **gateway resources**. Use this exemplar to inspire you when you are creating your **webfolio**.

☐ As you build your **webfolio**, you may want to share it with more people than just your tutor. Use **send to person** to share with peers on the course or potential employers. They can **comment** on your **webfolio** if you give them permission. If you do share with your peers, they will not be able to see the tutor feedback you receive; only your tutors and you can see this feedback.

□ Once the assignment submission date has passed you will not be able to add to your **webfolio** or amend any of the **assets** associated with it.

□ You will receive an email notifying you when your **webfolio** has been graded and summative feedback given.

□ Potential employers will be interested to view your **webfolio**. You can use **send to person** and add the employer as a **contact**. Select **external user** and their email address. You can give the employer **comment** permissions if appropriate. Should you wish to withdraw permission to view your **webfolio**, you can do this by selecting **unshare**. You can do this by selecting the **shared** tab, highlighting the employer's name and selecting the **bin icon**.

The activity in context

This activity is developed from a larger and more detailed programme with students at La Trobe University, Australia. The learners are Diploma of Education students enrolled in the core subject 'Changing Contexts in Education'. This cohort consists of a range of ages and backgrounds including international students, mature aged students and those coming directly from an undergraduate degree, all with varying skills and abilities in using technology. There are approximately 250 students enrolled in the Diploma of Education.

Educational designers worked closely with the academic staff to develop learning modules for the Learning Management System (LMS) to introduce students to PebblePad. In addition to online materials, students are also offered small workshops for extra support. Students work individually to complete *Assessment task 1: Managing teaching and learning in different contexts webfolio*. This task is worth seventy per cent of the final mark for this subject and the key areas of research and evidence are centred on the Victorian Institute of Teaching's standards for graduating teachers. Many students use their final webfolio, or reconfigure it, to send to potential employers. They report that the process of organising their knowledge into the six standards prepares them well for interviews. PebblePad provides a space in which graduates can continue to gather their evidence in preparation for final registration.

theme
10

Preparing for Employment

Employers and students expect post-16 education to provide a good preparation for future employment, in addition to personal development and academic achievement. Most courses are under scrutiny to embed specific or generic employability skills, or attributes as they are sometimes called, into the curriculum or learning design. Equipping adult learners for employment may be a specific learning outcome for a course, or preparation for future employment may be embedded in other ways, such as work placements or providing short courses for professional development.

Employers look for prospective employees who can demonstrate evidence of a range of skills that will equip them to be competent in the workplace or their profession. In some disciplines, the links between professional bodies and educational institutions are very close and educational providers are already developing learning in dialogue with professional and commercial frameworks. The tension between the demands of workforce development and traditional educational practices challenges both sides to find new ways of designing relevant and responsive learning experiences that can be rigorously evidenced and assessed. One of the benefits of using PebblePad learning designs is that qualitative learning outcomes can be made visible and learning can be delivered flexibly. Both learning processes and outcomes can be supported through the PebblePad tools – thus meeting the pedagogical concerns of educational institutions and training providers, whilst also demonstrating to employers that specific skills or competences are being met.

The educator or learning designer faces a number of challenges. First is the need to show that the skills or competences are embedded into the learning design; then activities need to be designed to help students to understand the requirements of skill acquisition and to scaffold learning to attain those skills. Alongside developing skills for employment, many courses incorporate some element of higher order learning skills, or 'learning to learn'. Such skills equip students to take responsibility for their future lifelong learning, which is a pre-requisite of the 21st century worker.

Those who design or deliver learning with adults need also to support the associated process of helping students to recognise prior learning and to understand how these previous experiences can be harnessed to show evidence of employability. Students at all levels of study need supported learning activities that are designed to enable them to select appropriate evidence, reflect upon it and present it in a way that meets the expectations of potential employers.

Through the use of the PebblePad scaffolded assets, practitioners can design learning activities that bring the relevant employability skills to the fore, and allow students themselves to identify and demonstrate the extent to which they have mastered these skills. By introducing the tagging function early in a module, students can get into the habit of identifying key skills and labelling the relevant evidence. This sense-making exercise serves a dual purpose of organising a student's work and drawing attention to the fact that the student has gained competence in an area of study.

A PebblePad account can be used across all courses associated with a student, so the learner can use it to record evidence of voluntary work, non-assessed work and work experience, which then enhances the student's profile. The learner can draw upon their whole repertoire of courses and experiences to subsequently select, collate and share with a potential employer in a single presentation. This allows the learner more choice in how they present their broad experience to meet industry and professional standards and gives the employer a more holistic insight into the student's attributes.

Looking for more ideas ?

If you are interested in *Preparing for Employment,* take a look at the related activities in *Themes 6: Experiential Learning*, *9: Preparing for Accreditation* and *11: Learning for the Workplace*.

activity 10.1 | Recording and reflecting on a work placement

The purpose of this activity is to encourage critical reflection on what happens before, during and after a work placement, to identify the skills students are acquiring, how their experiences relate to the topics studied on the course, and how they might be transferable to later employment.

In this activity students keep a placement blog where they record their experiences and benefit from regular tutor feedback.

Activity Overview

🏫	Low	Assets
📖	Beginner	⚙️
📑	Low	
🕐	Semester	
👥	unlimited	

What challenges might this address?

Placements provide a valuable opportunity to close the gap between theory and practice and to find out how a course or programme is preparing students for real situations. This is often a time of rapid learning, which needs to be captured as close to the events as possible to enable the student to make sense of their experiences day by day.

Traditional methods of keeping track of student placements tend to be an inefficient use of the tutor's time. Students often misplace paper diaries and it is extra work and cost to photocopy for assessment and record-keeping.

Using the blog asset in PebblePad allows students to enter their blog posts anywhere that has an Internet connection or mobile device. There is no danger of the diary being lost and both the student and tutor can see entries wherever they are. Tutors can comment, if this is built into the activity, and students can attach further evidence (photos, images, links to other assets) as they go. When the placement comes to an end, the blog remains as a record that students can use and modify when they do further advanced assignments or when they apply for jobs.

Blogs are one of the well-used PebblePad tools, perhaps because their use is established and understood outside the personal learning space. Using a blog in PebblePad has a number of benefits. The learners can share their entries when they are ready and then enter into a dialogue with their tutor. At the end of the placement the blogs in the gateway are a formal collection of the placement experiences that can be archived if necessary.

Learning design

Before going on placement, students are shown in a face-to-face session how to create and post to their own PebblePad blog. The value of posting regularly to the blog is emphasised, with guidance on selecting appropriate evidence of learning. In the session before the placement, students are asked to create a blog and to post their first thoughts about the upcoming experience. They are then instructed to send the blog to the gateway. This ensures that the student retains a communication channel with their tutor and any difficulties in sending the blog to the gateway are addressed in the session. During the placement students post regularly and tutors respond with feedback.

Tutor actions

What you need to do in PebblePad to set up the activity

Prior to the activity:

- ☐ Create a **gateway**.
- ☐ Add students to the **user group**. The default **gateway** permissions do not need to be changed for this activity.
- ☐ Use **manage tutor groups** if a large number of students are going on placement.
- ☐ Ask a former student for permission to use their placement **blog** as an exemplar. Upload this exemplar to the **gateway** as a resource and keep the default setting as **view only**.

During the activity:

- ☐ In the face-to-face session before the placement, show students how to **create** and **post** to a **blog**. Ask the students to post their first thoughts about the upcoming experience and send their **blog** to the **gateway**.
- ☐ Give regular feedback to the student via the **gateway**.

Instructions to the learner

You can adapt these instructions to your learners and to your context

- Log onto PebblePad. Select **create new**, **more** and then **blog**. Create a **blog**.

- When you have created your **blog**, add a post by selecting **view and post to blog**.

- To update the **blog**, select **view** and **my assets**, click on your **blog** and then **view and post to blog**.

- Send the **blog** to the **gateway**. Only your tutor can see the **blog**. Each time you post to your **blog**, the **gateway** will automatically update.

- Add to your **blog** regularly throughout your placement. You can upload photograph, audio and video files if you wish, by selecting browse when you post a new blog entry.

The activity in context

Blogs are used in many contexts where some form of reflective journaling is required. This activity is based on work at Brunel University in the UK, where second year undergraduate students spend a year out in industry. They use the blog to record and reflect on their work placement on a regular basis. They share the blog with their placement tutor, who comments on their reflections. It also provides a starting point for discussion when the tutor meets the student on placement. Students refer back to their blog in their final year, when they write a report that is assessed as part of a professional practice module.

Practitioner tips

Provide a brief tipsheet on how to use PebblePad so that students can refresh their memory about how to use the software when they are actually on placement.

Invite a student from the previous year to come into the face-to-face session and share their experience.

activity
10.2

Supporting unemployed people returning to work

This activity enables unemployed people to demonstrate how their skills match up to a specification set by a potential employer. Rather than simply linking evidence to a pre-determined set of competences, this activity is based on a reflective portfolio approach which helps learners to present their evidence as a narrative showing how the skills were developed. This is a learner-centred approach where the webfolio is

Activity Overview

👤	Medium	Assets
📖	Beginner	🖊
📑	Low	
🕐	Open-ended	
👥	Class	

introduced as a collection of 'empty shells'. As they progress, learners are able to see that each entry they make helps to fill the empty spaces. The course finishes when the webfolio has been filled with appropriate evidence in each of the shells. The outcome is a story of their learning in the context of the employment environment as well as their own interests and aspirations.

What challenges might this address?

This activity is addressing both employer and potential employee challenges.

The employer needs evidence that learning outcomes relevant to their needs can be met within a certain timeframe.

The potential employees may be returning to study and, for many, this will be a new style of learning. Most of the learners enter the course expecting to be passive in the sense of the pace, direction and delivery of learning. They may also expect that achieving the qualification is enough in itself: that the qualification will do all the talking in terms of their abilities.

Using PebblePad, learners can show evidence that the employer requirements are being met. Over and above this, students are introduced to new study skills that include a degree of reflective thinking and writing rather than being purely descriptive about all they do.

They are also encouraged to draw on their wider experience to demonstrate how their lives outside formal study may be relevant to the requirements of an employer.

Learning design

The learners are currently unemployed and have been chosen by interview to complete a training course preparing them for full employment. A number will be employed at the end of the course while the remainder will have a portfolio of skills to support employment opportunities elsewhere. The learner progresses through the learning outcomes that have been negotiated with the employer, using a variety of PebblePad tools to construct a story of their learning in the context of the employment environment and their own interests and aspirations.

Each learner copies a webfolio template consisting of pages for each learning outcome required. Despite some time constraints set by the employer, learners can work at their own pace filling the webfolio when they are ready. The course is considered completed when the learner has filled the webfolio.

Learners are encouraged to progress through each learning outcome in turn. Supporting resources are available in the institution's Learning Management System (LMS). Evidence of achievement is identified during a class activity as well as private study time and these are uploaded to PebblePad. During tutor-led sessions, learners are introduced to new study skills that include a degree of reflective thinking and writing rather than being purely descriptive about all they do. The scaffolding tools in PebblePad give weight to these activities. Evidence can include, for example, scanned copies of certificates of achievement such as for first aid or for volunteering.

On each webfolio page the learner explains what they learned and how it makes sense to them in the context of their experience. An authentic and personal narrative develops as each learner showcases their wider abilities, adding further pages to capture experience that may provide new evidence of additional accomplishments.

The end product is a unique, reflective portfolio that shows how individual learners can present their learning in the context of the 'rounded person'.

Each webfolio is published to a gateway that can be viewed by tutors who will provide formative feedback as the webfolio is constructed.

Upon completing the course, the tutors confirm that the learners have met the learning outcomes. Students are encouraged to share their webfolio with potential employers.

Tutor actions

What you need to do in PebblePad to set up the activity

Prior to the activity:

- ☐ Create a **gateway** for the cohort and, if appropriate, set to lock on a specific date.

- ☐ Add students to the **user group**. The default settings for the **gateway** do not need to be changed.

- ☐ Create a **webfolio** template. Add pages for each learning outcome. Give examples on the template of the types of evidence the learners can use.

- ☐ Add the **webfolio** to the **resources** area of your **gateway**. Select **copy and auto publish** permissions and **notify the user group(s) when they login to PebblePad**.

During the activity:

- ☐ Use the **comment bank** in the **gateway** to create a range of regularly used feedback phrases to save you time. Select **feedback** and this will remain confidential between the tutors and the learner. Feedback needs to be encouraging and motivational, helping the learner to identify relevant evidence from a range of experiences. Continue to give feedback to your students as they contribute to their **webfolio**.

- ☐ **Validate** the **webfolios** as they are completed.

Instructions to the learner

You can adapt these instructions to your learners and to your context

- ☐ Log onto PebblePad. As soon as you log on you will see a notice telling you that you have one **asset** waiting to be copied to your **asset store**. Select **view now** and then select **copy** and **publish**. This **webfolio** template is now copied to your **asset store** and you can edit it.

- ☐ You can now rename the **webfolio** giving it your name as the title. It is automatically updated on the **gateway** so that your tutor can see your work in this **webfolio** at all times.

□ As you work on each learning outcome, **upload** evidence to your PebblePad account. When you are editing your **webfolio**, you can create a link to evidence uploaded. Remember that you may need to scan paper certificates and then upload them as evidence.

□ You can add new pages to the **webfolio** if you wish.

□ Your tutor will give you feedback on the **webfolio** each time you complete one of the learning outcomes.

□ When you have completed your **webfolio** your tutor will validate it.

□ You can send your **webfolio** to a potential employer by selecting **send to** and then **add a contact** and **external user**. You will need to know the potential employer's email address.

The activity in context

The idea for this activity is based on work in progress at Thanet College, UK. The College was presented with a request to provide a set of learning outcomes unique to the needs of the employer, all to be delivered inside a timeframe set by the employer. By using PebblePad they plan to provide each learner with an opportunity to present a personal contextualised portfolio and thereby demonstrate 'the wider self' beyond the achievements of the qualifications alone.

Practitioner tips

Create a gateway blog for the whole cohort and show the learners where to find it. This way you can encourage communication between learners whilst they are working on their individual webfolios.

activity 10.3 | An award scheme demonstrating employability skills

This activity, which we are describing as a 'University Passport', is an award scheme that could be used at any academic level. It is an optional activity that leads to a non-accredited employability certificate, giving learners a user-friendly way to submit evidence, whilst encouraging them to use other aspects of PebblePad to further their personal and career development. It also helps the learners to practise articulating their new skills within job applications. The Passport scheme uses a form in PebblePad to enable students to submit evidence of their experience, which is then verified and assessed.

Activity Overview

Low	Assets
Beginner	
Medium	
Open-ended	
Unlimited	

What challenges might this address?

Undergraduate students know that they will need to prove their skills for later employability, but it can be a challenge to encourage them to continue gathering the evidence of developing skills throughout their period of study. Employers are interested in the range of experiences that students bring to a new post, and with increasing competition in the job market, it is important that students are able to show the depth and scope of their skills and experiences as well as their university qualification.

The Passport student award scheme would be difficult to administer as a paper-based scheme, but using previous students' PebblePad submissions, new students can see how impressive the final presentation can be in PebblePad. This can motivate students and help them to see that preparing for employment is not something that starts when studying ends, but that it can be part of the undergraduate experience. The introduction to digital tools simultaneously introduces learners to habits of learning that they can continue to use to develop and document their employability skills, which in this learning design are referred to as 'graduate attributes'.

Learning design

All undergraduates are invited to a one hour face-to-face session during which the Passport Scheme is explained and they are introduced to PebblePad. This is usually enough time for the students to become acquainted with the software. Students are made aware of how to share their work with external verifiers and how to send their work to a gateway. A 'take away' guide is provided so that students can refer back to it at various stages of completing the Passport.

Students complete a relevant activity that links to a specific graduate attribute, fill out a PebblePad form recording this activity and then share it with someone who can verify that they carried out the experience. Because PebblePad allows internal and external mentors to access the form, this is a simple process. The mentor or verifier adds a comment to the form confirming that the activity described is correct. The student then sends the form to the Passport gateway. The Passports are awarded points and feedback given. Students repeat this experience for each graduate attribute to accrue points towards the Passport. Once a student has the correct amount of points, an employability certificate is awarded. Completed Passports can be archived and used as evidence of institutional action and commitment to graduate employability. The archive can also be used to audit which skills students are gaining and which skills need more attention in developing on an institutional level.

Tutor actions

What you need to do in PebblePad to set up the activity

Prior to the activity:

- ☐ Create a Passport Activity **form** in **form builder** for each graduate attribute so that students can accurately record their evidence for the scheme.
- ☐ Create a Passport **Gateway**. Select **self-subscription** to allow users to self-enrol onto the gateway. This means you can identify which students have chosen to join the Passport scheme. It is easy to keep an eye on students who have submitted evidence and get in touch with those who have yet to submit evidence.
- ☐ Publish the **forms** to the Passport **Gateway**.
- ☐ Create a guide for the students to take away with them.

During the activity:

- [ ] In the face-to-face session, demonstrate the process of opening a **form** and **sending to** an external verifier with **comment** permissions.

- [ ] Award points to the student submissions by using the grade box when they are published to the **gateway**, and give **feedback** (not **comment** ensuring that no one else but Passport moderators and the student can see the feedback).

- [ ] Notify the student when their submission has been awarded points by going to **manage gateway** and **send a message**. You can send an email to students from here.

- [ ] Once a student has earned sufficient points to be awarded the certificate, **archive** the **forms**.

Instructions to the learner

You can adapt these instructions to your learners and to your context

- [ ] Log onto PebblePad.

- [ ] Go to the Passport **Gateway**. **Self-subscribe** to this **gateway**. You do not need to repeat this step.

- [ ] Go to **create new** and **form**. There will be a **form** for each graduate attribute. Use each **form** to demonstrate you have met each attribute.

- [ ] Once you have completed your first activity, select and complete the **form** that most appropriately describes this activity.

- [ ] Share this **form** with your mentor or verifier by selecting **send to person** and then **add a contact** and **external user**.

- [ ] Check with the mentor or verifier that they know to put a **comment** on the **asset** you have shared with them.

- [ ] Once you have a **comment** from the mentor or verifier, send the **form** to the Passport **Gateway**. You can **unshare** the **form** with the mentor or verifier if you wish. You can do this by selecting the **shared** tab, highlighting the mentor or verifier's name and selecting the **bin icon**.

- [ ] You will receive email notification when the **form** has been given points and feedback given.

- [ ] Repeat the process of completing the **form** for each graduate attribute.

- ☐ Look regularly at your **assets** in your **asset store** to find out how many points you have been awarded for that activity.

- ☐ Once you have been awarded sufficient points by the moderator team, you will be issued with a certificate.

- ☐ You can use the **forms** again as evidence of your skills when you are applying for a job.

The activity in context

The idea for the Passport scheme is based on work at the University of Winchester in the UK. The Winchester Passport was launched at the start of the academic year 2010/11. PebblePad has made it easy to administer the scheme and keep accurate records of the number of forms each student undertaking the scheme has submitted. Students report that they enjoy using PebblePad and learn how to use it quickly. The hope is that, as more students use PebblePad, word will spread throughout the university and greater numbers will interact with the software.

theme
11

Learning for the Workplace

In a rapidly changing workplace, there is a growing need for a flexible, creative workforce who can evaluate and problem solve, contributing to – and playing a part in – their employers' success. With careful planning and partnership between employers and training providers, work-based learning can help employees develop the vocational and academic skills and competence they need to do their jobs well. It should also help develop habits of lifelong learning, where employees recognise the need to update their skills and knowledge on a regular basis and take responsibility for improving their skills, abilities and productivity.

Lifelong Learning UK (LLUK) describes the function of work-based learning as being:

> ...to provide work focused learning opportunities relevant to the workplace environment, related to the skill sets, values and purpose of the employers' business. It embraces all work focused training and development functions, and related activities. (http://www.lluk.org)

Work-based learning is found in every sector and at every level of learning. Providers can include commercial training organisations; voluntary and community bodies; and educational institutions. Invariably, the learner is part time and studying at a distance to the institution.

Designing work-based learning involves a fine balance between ensuring that the learning activities meet the demands of the employer, that they are suitable for the level of learner and that they address quality assurance and validation processes within an institution.

Work-based learning addresses the need for continued staff development; it is learning for the workplace. For work-based learning to be valuable and useful, however, the learners' needs have to be at the forefront of any learning design. For higher education providers, these needs are more specific and less easily addressed than those of campus-based students. Work-based learners are frequently under competing pressures with work, study and family commitments, and need a learning design that allows flexibility and a pace that can allow for unexpected interruptions to study.

In the following learning activities, there is a considerable amount of preparatory work for the tutor to do, either in a complementary environment such as the institutional Learning

Management System (LMS) or created within PebblePad as a resource repository. Work-based learners are often studying at a time when campus-based services are unavailable so access to help and support can be an important element of designing the learning to help keep learners on track. This may include, for example, communication with peers, or well-written study guides.

When studying within a work context it is common for a learner to feel isolated when starting to study; this is true for both students new to work-based learning and those returning to study after a long break. Using PebblePad to track student progress can alert a tutor at an early stage if a learner is struggling to engage with a course. In the activities below, learners are able to study at a pace that suits them, using practical, work related experiences to create authentic records of learning. In addition, collaborative activities within PebblePad, such as a group blog or regular and timely formative feedback from a tutor, can reduce these feelings of isolation, help students to connect with their peers and increase their motivation to continue studying.

Looking for more ideas ?

If you are interested in *Learning for the Workplace*, take a look at the related activities in *Themes 6: Experiential Learning*, *9: Preparing for Accreditation* and *10: Preparing for Employment*.

activity
11.1

Enabling the transition to advanced practice

This activity is used to develop expert practice at a high level of skills attainment. Learners are already qualified and practising professionals, who want or need to develop further skills through a blend of work-based learning and distance learning supported by a Learning Management System (LMS). PebblePad is used as a vehicle for providing sample templates, understanding and evidencing formative assessment tasks and for submission. Learners are mentored and supervised in their workplace by experts in their field.

Activity Overview

High		Assets
Improver		
Medium		Other wizards
Programme		
Cohort		

What challenges might this address?

Advanced practitioners need to update their skills on a regular basis and, as job roles change and evolve, some practitioners need to engage in advanced training for new roles. There are a number of stakeholders involved in this process:

- The learners – postgraduate professionals already practising in their field, seeking to extend and develop their roles in transition to advanced practice.

- Educators – supporting and facilitating the transition in the context of credit rated modules and postgraduate awards.

- Employers – sponsoring and supporting students, entering into a tri-partite agreement with learners and educators to guarantee mentorship, support and access to resources.

- Professional bodies – who are part of the validation process and provide accreditation for advanced practitioners.

PebblePad is used to help support the learner's development as an expert practitioner. This means developing practice knowledge that reflects their scope of practice, alongside developing autonomy. Because many practitioners are working in departments in isolation, the sharing of work through PebblePad generates a community of practitioners that encourages the exchange of practices and expertise. Learners have a readily accessible record of their learning and development that can be shared with managers when applying for advanced practice posts. The programme is developed to match the learning outcomes of the professional body for accreditation so learners are confident that their efforts will be professionally recognised.

PebblePad allows learners to re-enter the study environment and bring with them the evidence of competence they have gained so far. This can help learners manage the steep learning curve of advanced study and take ownership of the learning process.

Learning design

This module is undertaken over a number of months and offers learners a 'blended' way of studying. The learners study online and in the workplace, never visiting the institution. There are distinct synergies between these two elements of the 'blend' in that both share the characteristic of encouraging students to increasingly take responsibility for their own learning (learner autonomy) through working in partnership with others (academic and clinical learning facilitators and academic and clinical peers). The online components of the blend are a combination of the institutional LMS and PebblePad. The LMS is used as the repository for a wide range of learning materials, a means of literature sourcing and initially is the forum in which learners establish their online identities at the outset of the module. PebblePad is used as the space for:

- □ sharing of practice;
- □ undertaking formative assessment activities;
- □ providing peer feedback;
- □ evidencing learning;
- □ identifying areas of development;
- □ summative submission and summative feedback.

The module leader creates and shares with learners an 'Expert Practice' webfolio (with linked assets providing resources) to support and guide students in the undertaking and submission of assessment. Because there are no opportunities for a face-to-face induction, this Expert Practice webfolio also contains a combination of PebblePad movies, tipsheets and help tools to support learners' initial orientation around PebblePad. Learners can access this webfolio at any time in the gateway resources area. The module leader negotiates with previously successful learners to share their assessment submissions to provide ideas and inspiration and to show a range of ways in which these could be presented. Learners only have permission to view these resources.

The module is divided into sections of study with a gateway created for each section. Within each section learners undertake a formative activity in PebblePad (which the authors call a 'p-tivity') and then send it to a gateway when completed. Learners have to complete all the p-tivities. A p-tivity may be a reflection upon a critical incident or a review of a peer reviewed journal article and analysis of its relevance to practice. In the p-tivity gateways, learners can view and comment upon each other's work. Learners are encouraged to use a range of PebblePad wizards appropriate to the p-tivity to help develop their evidence to satisfy the assessment criteria for the module.

An e-moderator is allocated to a small group of learners (no more than 12 per group) to facilitate discussions and feedback on assets submitted to the p-tivity gateways. Learners are supported in developing peer feedback skills and required to comment upon the posts of at least two other learners on the module. Universal, whole cohort feedback is provided for each p-tivity via a generic feedback webfolio uploaded by the e-moderator to the relevant p-tivity gateway.

Summative assessment requires the submission of a portfolio of evidence to an assessment gateway. Evidence of undertaking each formative p-tivity is required and learners do this by creating a webfolio and linking to the evidence of completing each p-tivity.

After the assessment due date, audio feedback from the e-moderator is uploaded to each submission when graded.

Tutor actions

What you need to do in PebblePad to set up the activity

Prior to the activity:

For the gateways:

- ☐ Create a module **gateway** and add students to the **user group**. You do not need to change the default permissions for this **gateway**.

- ☐ Create an assessment **gateway** by selecting **duplicate gateway** whilst you are in the module **gateway**. Do not change the default settings. Rename the **gateway**. This ensures that the students are also users in this assessment **gateway**.

- Add a date to lock the assessment **gateway**. Add tutors to the **tutor group**.

- Go back to the module **gateway** and create the first p-tivity **gateway** by selecting **duplicate gateway**. Do not change the default settings.

- Add the e-moderators to the **tutor group**.

- Select **manage tutor groups** and create a group for each tutor (either manually or automatically).

- Change the permissions for the users in this p-tivity **gateway** to **publish, view** and **comment** so that the learners can give formative feedback to one another.

- Duplicate this p-tivity **gateway** for the remaining p-tivities. The groups and associated permissions remain the same in each **gateway**, but you do need to change the **gateway** title to reflect the p-tivity. You should now see a module **gateway** that has within it an assessment **gateway** and a **gateway** for each p-tivity.

To create resources:

- Create the Expert Practice **webfolio** within your own PebblePad account and add it to the module **gateway resources**. Don't allow users to copy the **webfolio** as it is a 'resource' that when copied will take up storage space if every user copies it into their **asset store**.

- Obtain permission from one or two previously successful students to use their summative assessment **webfolios** as exemplars. Add this to the module **gateway resources** with **view** permissions only.

- Use the **comment bank** in each gateway to create a list of frequently used feedback phrases.

During the activity:

- As an e-moderator, comment on each learner's completed p-tivity. Use the **comment bank** to save you time. Remember, if you want to ensure that other learners do not see the comments, you need to select **feedback**. Only other tutors and the learner who created the asset will see your feedback.

- Read the comments that learners leave for one another.

- On the assessment **gateway**, **grade** and give **feedback** (audio files if you wish to use this method of feedback) when the assessment due date has passed.

- Remember to **release** the **grades** and **feedback** when all the marking is complete.

- For the external examiner to view the assessment **gateway**, **add** the examiner as an **external user** to the tutor group.

Instructions to the learner

You can adapt these instructions to your learners and to your context

- ☐ Log onto PebblePad.

- ☐ Select **view** and **gateways**.

- ☐ Go to the module **gateway** and **view** the Expert Practice **webfolio.** This contains support and guidance for completing your summative assessment. It will remain here for you to refer to throughout the module.

- ☐ You are required to complete each p-tivity and need to select the most appropriate PebblePad **asset** to do so. This may be an **ability**, an **experience** or another **asset**. Select **create new** to choose the most appropriate **asset**. The help section in PebblePad provides details about **assets** and their purpose. Click on the **question mark icon** to go to the help section.

- ☐ As you complete each p-tivity, **send** it to the appropriate p-tivity **gateway**. The e-moderator assigned to each group will give you formative feedback.

- ☐ You are required to read at least two of your peers' p-tivities and give them feedback. Do this by going to the p-tivity **gateway**, selecting a p-tivity to view and when you have finished reading, clicking on the **comment** icon. Remember to give constructive feedback and be encouraging at all times. Do not make your comments **private** because the e-moderator will need to monitor the quality of feedback being given.

- ☐ You need to complete every p-tivity and give feedback to your peers for every p-tivity.

- ☐ For the summative assessment you need to create a **webfolio.** Use the p-tivities as evidence of your development and link to them in the **webfolio.** You can view an example of a successfully completed **webfolio** by a former student by going to the module gateway resources.

- ☐ When you have completed the summative assessment **webfolio, send** it to the assessment **gateway**.

- ☐ You will receive an email confirmation that you have submitted.

- ☐ When your e-moderator has graded and given feedback on your assessment you will receive email notification.

The activity in context

This activity is based on work at Sheffield Hallam University, UK, where the learners are qualified therapy radiographers (radiation therapists) who are extending and developing their roles in radiotherapy and oncology as part of the process of reconfiguring service provision in cancer services. This educational opportunity and support facilitates the development of a range of advanced practitioners undertaking roles previously fulfilled by doctors. The learners are operating and working in the context of a multi-professional healthcare team, initially with mentorship and supervision from doctors until clinical competences are achieved in their defined scope of practice.

Submitting the final webfolio to the professional body for accreditation is challenging as they have their own online submission format and negotiations are on-going to explore an alternative submission system using PebblePad.

activity 11.2 | Enabling work-based learners to study for a formal qualification

The purpose is to provide learning opportunities for work-based learners that can be accessed from the workplace and that could build towards a further or higher qualification.

Although this activity requires a fairly sophisticated understanding of PebblePad by the tutor it is designed to be easy to use, even for students who have basic IT skills. Learning content and activities are delivered within webfolios, which are then personalised by the learners, in combination with three types of blogs that allow for content delivery, collaboration, personal reflection and communication with the tutor.

Activity Overview

High	Assets
Beginner	
High	
Programme	
Groups of 12-25	

What challenges might this address?

Learners in small to medium enterprises (i.e. fewer than 150 employees) are often unable to attend courses at university. Potential learners in this group do not, typically, access higher education although they can be working in senior roles within the organisation. Traditional courses are not attractive to this group because they require a long term time commitment, are not available at a time to suit learners, are not flexible enough to meet the diverse work and other commitments of this group and do not clearly address either the employer or employees' learning needs.

The challenge for workplace learning is to design learning experiences that are:

- flexible
- accessible to learners in work
- not reliant on face-to-face contact
- related to their work
- a pathway towards a qualification.

As well as meeting these learner needs, the design must also take into account the needs of the employers.

PebblePad offers a number of solutions to these challenges. In this activity, the performance need identified by the employer is met at an affordable cost per learner per unit. At the same time, the learner becomes more aware of relevant aspects of the employer's business. Learners are able to get quick and timely feedback when they complete activities and they have flexibility on where and when they do their work. The on-going tutor support means the learner is monitored throughout the study period which helps to motivate learners and to give them the best chance of completing their study.

Learning design

This group of learners are all studying at a distance and their first contact with the tutor team and their peers is via the online course developed in PebblePad. The activity is designed for a low technology threshold for the learner; they only need basic 'Internet surfing' skills. The formal channel of communication for the whole course is PebblePad. The students are emailed instructions on how to log onto PebblePad and how to copy a webfolio. Included in the webfolio are pages with content and details of activities to be completed. There are also embedded blogs to support learner responses, group activities and communication with the tutor. The activities in the first unit of the programme are centred on three types of blog.

The activity blog is to support learner reflection on the activities relating to the unit content; the group blog is for collaborative activities related to the content and as a forum for cohort discussion; and the personal blog is used for recording critical incidents and communication with the tutor.

The pace of studying is an important factor in distance, work-based learning, and so each unit is highly structured into ten weeks of content and related activities. Every week the learners have a notional five hours to work through the content and to complete activities. At least every two weeks there are tutor facilitated activities that contribute to the group blog. Learners are encouraged to complete activities regularly each week but can do more, or less, depending on their other commitments. Learners are not fixed to any day or time in the ten week period when they must be online.

There are, on average, 3-4 activities set for each week and the tutor responds to a minimum of one of the activities each week for each learner, or group activity.

In the final week (week 10) learners complete, in the blog, a short patchwork text-based narrative of approximately 500 words that asks them to apply their learning from the unit in their workplace.

Learners who complete sufficient units to be awarded credits are asked to complete a patchwork text assessment that draws together their learning across the units in a similar way to the summaries completed at the end of each unit.

Tutor actions

What you need to do in PebblePad to set up the activity

Prior to the activity:

- ☐ Create a **gateway**. Set the gateway to lock on the assignment due date.
- ☐ Add students to the **user group**. The default settings for the users do not need to be changed.
- ☐ Add a **gateway blog** (found under **manage resources**). Once created, open the **blog**, post a welcome message and copy the URL.
- ☐ In **create new**, create two **blogs** called:
  - ▫ Activity **blog**. Post a description that the purpose of this **blog** is to support learner reflection on the activities relating to the unit content.
  - ▫ Personal **blog**. Post a description that the purpose of this **blog** is for recording critical incidents and communication with the tutor.
- ☐ Create a **webfolio** for the course. Add pages for content and add pages giving instructions for the activities.
- ☐ Embed the **blogs** in the **webfolio** as pages by clicking on **add your pages** and clicking on the **item** tab. Select the activity **blog** and the personal **blog** by clicking on the **arrow** on the tab.
- ☐ On a separate **webfolio page**, embed a link to the group **blog** using the URL you copied earlier.
- ☐ Add the **webfolio** to the resources area of your **gateway** with **copy** and **auto publish** permissions. You can also select the **notify the user group(s) when they login to PebblePad** option to notify users that the **webfolio** is available at login.
- ☐ Create a welcome **webfolio** with instructions on how to log onto PebblePad and the course **webfolio. Send** it to the web. Copy the URL.

- □ Email all your students giving them the URL that sends them to the welcome **webfolio** containing instructions for logging on.

During the activity:

- □ Check the **gateway** and, because the **webfolios** are set to auto publish, you will see which students have successfully followed your email instructions.
- □ Use the **comment bank** to create a range of regularly used feedback phrases that can save you time.
- □ Give feedback to your students as they contribute to the **blogs**.

Instructions to the learner

You can adapt these instructions to your learners and to your context

- □ Log onto PebblePad.
- □ As soon as you log on, you will see a notice telling you that you have one **asset** waiting to be copied to your **asset store**. Select **view now** and then select **copy and publish**. This will copy the **webfolio** containing all the course material and activities to your own PebblePad account.
- □ Your tutor can see your work in this **webfolio** at all times.
- □ Select **view** and **my assets**. Click on the **webfolio** and select **view**. A new window opens. Read the Week 1 instructions, content and activity pages. These will direct you to the tasks you have to complete for week 1.
- □ You will have to post to your **blogs** regularly throughout the course. Your **blogs** can be accessed by clicking on the relevant page in the **webfolio** and then selecting **post to blog** or, for the group **blog**, following the link.

The activity in context

This activity is based on work in progress on the ePSSME project at the University of Wolverhampton.

The course is suitable for learners working in small to medium sized enterprises and is designed to target learning opportunities that meet identified business needs, identified through market research. The ePPSME team were keen that learners weren't put off by the technology used, so they made learners' interaction with PebblePad as intuitive as possible and combined the learning content and learner activities into a webfolio that appears, and acts, like a webpage to use skills that basic users of IT will be familiar with.

To read more, visit their website at http://www.wlv.ac.uk/Default.aspx?page=20007

Practitioner tips

Provide mutual support for other course tutors in developing their first units through a community of practice.

Ensure the learner and tutor are aware of each other's expectations (at the start of each unit include an activity in the group blog for each to introduce themselves and their expectations).

Interaction in group work varies and is dependent on the composition of the cohort and the supportive intervention of the tutor. No two cohorts are the same.

Aim for 12 – 25 learners on each cohort, with an optimum of 16. Expect around 4 hours of tutor time per week to support and feedback to each cohort.

Advanced knowledge of PebblePad (by the tutor) and online facilitation is required.

Ensure learners and sponsors can access the learning environment before they sign up for a unit; one way to do this is through the creation of a 'compatibility checklist' that included links to download relevant software e.g. Flashplayer, Quicktime, Adobe Reader.

activity
11.3

Creating an audit report of a service/organisation

The purpose is to support the learning of a cohort of first year university students, most of whom are mature adults in full or part time work who are studying at a distance. The activity asks students to evaluate their work environment using a structured audit tool, created in PebblePad. This allows students to demonstrate their understanding of their coursework by applying it directly to their workplace and, using the webfolio, to present their findings.

Activity Overview

Medium	Assets
Beginner	
Medium	
Semester	
Cohort (can be 600+)	

What challenges might this address?

Particular challenges are presented when you are designing learning for busy, mature working people, many of whom are also parents. These groups might typically describe themselves as novice computer users, although they may be keen learners, passionate about their service or subject area, and very supportive of each other. Many will be returning to learning after a gap of some years and may need time and help to develop skills in the areas of information technology, critical reflection, independent learning and professional observations.

One learning strategy for work-based learners is to evaluate their work environment. This offers a good opportunity to apply learning to the workplace. Traditionally, completing an evaluation report might be carried out independently over a period of weeks and then submitted for summative assessment. The drawback to such an approach is that there is only minimal opportunity to check progress and to offer formative feedback to the student. For this particular group of adult learners, who need more guidance and support for their learning, the lack of formative feedback can pose a risk.

By using PebblePad, tutors are able to create a template for students to work through, track student progress and provide both formative and summative feedback. The template itself offers prompts that help to further the student's thinking. From the student perspective, this means their first university assessment task is well-supported and they are working to clear objectives.

Large cohorts of learners pose additional challenges for teaching teams when it comes to administrative tasks. An assessment item such as this activity would traditionally be submitted in hardcopy and delivered to the individual tutors (both on and off campus). This is a time-consuming process which places undue pressure on the tutors. By using PebblePad, students are able to submit the completed form to their tutor's gateway and to receive regular and timely feedback, streamlining this administrative process and allowing tutors to make better use of the marking period.

Learning design

The students use the institutional learning management system (LMS) to access their modules and the resources needed for their study. The students are introduced to the discipline concepts and are asked to consider these concepts within their own services.

The use of the LMS complements the use of PebblePad. Students are asked to complete an audit report (a PebblePad form) that has been designed to support the learning process. The questions in the audit report encourage students to apply their new knowledge within their own working environments. The students are asked to collect evidence, or create new assets to document their findings. These are then attached as evidence in their final, assessed audit report.

The complete audit report is a synthesis of knowledge and reflection based upon experience, creating an authentic learning experience.

Tutor actions

What you need to do in PebblePad to set up the activity

Prior to the activity:

- □ Create a form in **form builder** designed to encourage students to apply their new knowledge. Allow evidence to be added to each question.
- □ Create a **gateway** set to lock on the date when the final audit report is due.

- Add students to the **user group**. If you are working with large numbers of students and several tutors you could use the **manage tutor groups** option.

- Within f**orm builder** make **form** available to gateway group. Select **auto publish responses**. This automatically submits the forms back to the **gateway** as soon as the student saves their form response.

- In the **gateway** add your frequently used feedback phrases to the **comment bank**, which allows you to quickly and easily add common feedback statements which can then be personalised.

- If your students have not used PebblePad before, insert a hyperlink in the learning management system resources area to the PebblePad log on page.

During the activity:

- Give feedback to your students on a regular basis, using the **comment bank** to save time.

- Once the assignment due date has passed, give summative feedback to each student and grade each form.

- Release the **grades** and **feedback** when the marking process is complete.

Instructions to the learner

You can adapt these instructions to your learners and to your context

- Log onto PebblePad and go to **create new**.

- Select **thought** and complete it following the instructions given in the LMS module.

- Go to **create new** and this time, choose **more** and then **form**. Open the **form** that corresponds with the instructions you have been given in the LMS. Attach the **thought** you created earlier, as evidence. When you save the **form** it will automatically be submitted to the **gateway** so your tutor can provide feedback.

- At the start of your course you won't be able to complete all the **form** in one go. You will need to regularly create **thoughts** and add them as evidence to the **form** in your asset store as the module progresses. Every time you update your **form**, it is updated in the **gateway**.

- Your tutor will give you regular formative feedback.

□ Once the assignment due date has passed you will not be able to change/amend your **form** or any assets attached to it, but you will be able to view your **form** at any time.

□ You will receive an email notifying you of when the **form** has been marked and feedback given.

The activity in context

This activity is based on work with a student cohort of over 600, studying by distance at Charles Sturt University, Australia. This includes both domestic (Australian) and overseas students.

The teaching team includes one Subject Coordinator and eight tutors. Students are divided evenly across the teaching team. These academics are supported by an Education Designer and the School's Administrations Officer.

The students are mature-aged childcare workers updating their professional qualifications. They are asked to reflect on the childcare service where they work and think about how they are (or are not) providing for the wellness and wellbeing of children. Students must also consider what improvements could be made. The end product is called the *Wellness and Wellbeing Audit Report: How is your service catering for the wellness and wellbeing of children in the six dimensions of health?*

Practitioner tips

Tutors may like to share an asset of their own at the start of the semester as an 'ice-breaker' activity.

theme 12 | Action Planning and Project Management

Whatever the discipline, most courses in tertiary education aim to equip their students with the skills to become independent, autonomous learners. An important starting point for developing independent learning is being able to identify a goal, and then to create an action plan that specifies the steps and necessary resources to reach this goal.

The touch points that we discussed in the *Chapter 3: The Principles of PebblePad* tend to present the more challenging episodes in a learner's life and are rendered more manageable by breaking down the activities into smaller focused tasks. Completing a series of smaller, time limited steps, and using relevant information and reliable sources to make decisions, can seem less daunting than setting out to achieve one big goal with no planning. Smaller milestones also make it easier to monitor progress for both the learner and the tutor. This 'chunking down' process is a useful skill in a team context as it is a key component of project management, a skill area that is increasingly important in the employment market.

Application to university, completion of group projects and career development are all activities that benefit from careful preparation. Whether part of personal development planning (PDP) or just as an effective strategy designed to enhance and monitor learning, a carefully prepared action plan has a big impact upon the successful completion of a goal within a required timeframe.

The ability to envisage reaching a goal does not come naturally to everyone and it is important that this process is not left to chance. Most learners benefit from some direction and a clear structure when they are setting goals and completing their plans. Prompts that bridge the gap between the current context, where the learner is now, and the ideal situation, help to build motivation and develop focus.

When a goal is imposed upon a learner (for instance, completing an assignment), filling out an action plan has the potential to be a very dry activity. However, there are a number of tools in PebblePad that encourage learners to plan imaginatively how to reach targets in their learning journey. Obviously there is the 'action plan' wizard that prompts learners to think creatively about people and resources they are able to draw upon to reach their ideal situation. However, many of the assets have an action planning focus. For instance, the 'thought' wizard prompts the learner to reflect on what they have done and what changes they would make in the future. The 'meeting' wizard asks the learner to document meeting outcomes and dates for when these outcomes should be met. If a goal is predetermined by the tutor or the course requirements, then a shared asset is an effective and early means of checking that the learner understands the nature of the goal, and the process of reaching this goal. The 'action plan' prompts learners to pinpoint resources, and the tutor has the experience and expertise to know how reliable these resources are. This gives the student and the tutor opportunities for conversation and checking that the tutor's expectations are aligned with what the students think they should be doing.

When action plans are co-constructed within a peer group or with external stakeholders, expectations are negotiated and confirmed during the process of drawing up goals and identifying the steps to meet these goals. This process of negotiation and consensus-building is another subset of project management skills and, in this situation, the action plan is a record of the discussions, as much as a blueprint for action.

The habit of goal-setting and action planning becomes an important skill for lifelong learning and is a practice that helps to organise our busy lives. Because it deals with future possibilities rather than past events, it also lends itself to some of the most creative uses of PebblePad.

Not all action planning activities necessarily lead to developing a webfolio, but when they do, the action planning assets in PebblePad help to make the process of portfolio-building an active forward-looking process, rather than a retrospective process of selection and collection. In the preparation of this book, we used a webfolio to collate the chapters as we developed, edited and commented on different drafts. In this way, it became a tool for project management that allowed the editorial team to focus on the latest versions of files. At the same time, we could (literally) watch the book taking shape and see at a glance how well we were meeting our milestones for completion.

Looking for more ideas ?

If you are interested in *Action Planning and Project Management*, you might find further useful activities in *Themes 3: Planning Personal and Professional Development, 5: Promoting Group Work* and *8: Self and Peer Review*.

Planning for a field trip: pebbles on the path to the Long Walk

This activity is suitable for students who are undertaking an extensive preparation and planning project. The process includes an action plan and structured tasks within separate webfolios. It provides a structured format for students to provide evidence of their preparation, planning and research for a field trip, in this case an 18 day walk. Participants work individually and in groups to prepare for the trip.

Activity Overview

Low		Assets
Proficient		
Low		
Semester		
10+		

Students represent their learning in a variety of different formats using PebblePad to showcase evidence. This enables the educator to engage students with a variety of learning styles and to provide ongoing formative feedback throughout the entire process through signposted activities.

Working in PebblePad, the students plan their trip, carry out research and record what happens. The end result is a comprehensive research webfolio which shows evidence of planning and preparation. The webfolio will be useful to present to prospective employers and has potential for reuse in a variety of settings, for example as a resource for their university peers or as teaching materials for their future careers.

What challenges might this address?

Planning for a field trip is conventionally a set of tasks and text-based exercises which are not always directly integrated into real-life preparation for the trip. Once completed, the tasks are often left stagnant and unused.

There are a number of benefits to designing the planning and presentation of the work in PebblePad.

Benefits to the learner

- The use of PebblePad encourages the creativity of students who may not respond to the more traditional paper-based academic writing. Examples of innovative approaches could include digital stories showing students measuring, preparing and vacuum packaging the food that they will take on the walk. Others might take videos of their fitness regime as evidence of their preparation.

- The completed webfolio is an interactive and creative resource that can be viewed by others.

- The experience of building this resource in PebblePad will be useful for future teaching practice.

- Formative assessment helps students improve and learn from their work in progress.

- Rather than finding evidence of learning at the end of the experience, students build up their webfolio as they go, so there is less stress and the webfolio grows as they learn.

- The learner can demonstrate their awareness of safety in their planning and preparation.

Benefits to the lecturer

- The activity provides a way of interacting with students engaged in the task of preparation and planning. The lecturer has a window into the on-going preparation of the various components of the task and can intervene, encourage and support when necessary.

- It offers a feedback mechanism directly to individual learners and highlights common issues which can be shared.

- The activity increases the potential for a variety of learning styles to be incorporated into a single learning design.

- The efficiency of marking and assessing suitable evidence of learning is improved.

Benefits to the institution

- Provides a strong foundation for personal learning evidence that is unique to individuals.

Learning design

The focus of this activity is to prepare students for this challenge whilst simultaneously requiring them to conduct research into one specific aspect of the region they are about to visit. Supporting resources are hosted in the learning management system.

The students complete the Long Walk in a group of ten. At the start of the semester the membership of the group is organised and the requirements of the course are outlined in a face-to-face session. Students have to negotiate their role in the group and also what equipment they will be responsible for. This is recorded in the action plan. By the time the walk commences, students must have created:

1. An action plan called 'The Long Walk Action Plan'.

    The Long Walk Action Plan is designed to detail the necessary planning, timelines and required information necessary for a student to prepare for The Long Walk. It is a brainstorming exercise that ensures the individual is ready for this challenge. Students need to give considerable thought to this process as it will lay the foundations for completing all other aspects of preparation required for the Long Walk. The Long Walk Action Plan is evidence that a high level of consideration has been given to being prepared. In the face-to-face session students start the action plan and send it to a gateway. This ensures that tutors can monitor the students' progress from day one. It is of paramount importance that students can prove they have prepared for this challenge, for their own safety and the safety of the rest of their group. By using the gateway to view the action plans, tutors can oversee preparations and intervene if necessary.

2. A webfolio that outlines the preparation for the walk.

    The Long Walk Preparation and Planning Webfolio requires students to complete a detailed planning and preparation assignment to provide evidence that they are suitably prepared for the requirements of undertaking an 18 day walk. Students provide evidence on a range of topics that need to be considered in the preparation stages that connect to their own preparation and also their group. The webfolio gradually builds as the students work towards being adequately prepared for the Long Walk. Pages in the webfolio are given the following headings:

- ☐ Introduction
- ☐ Goals and objectives for the trip
- ☐ Group goals
- ☐ Readings
- ☐ Equipment
- ☐ Food and menu
- ☐ Physical preparation
- ☐ Plan for my leading day
- ☐ Suggested route and options
- ☐ Personal information

3. A research webfolio provides details of the research the student has conducted into one aspect of the region visited.

   The Long Walk Research Webfolio is based upon an aspect of the environment students will be encountering. Students create an interactive research webfolio with the intention of engaging others with their chosen topic. The audience for this may be their group, peers at university, future employers, members of their family. Longer term, it can be used in future teaching practice.

   There is an additional face-to-face PebblePad workshop timetabled to help students create both webfolios. Both webfolios are sent to a PebblePad gateway with view permissions so that other members of the group can read about the preparation and the research in advance of the Long Walk.

Tutor actions

What you need to do in PebblePad to set up the activity

> Prior to the activity:
>
> - ☐ Create a **gateway** for the submission of the **action plans**. Add students to the **user group**. Use **manage tutor groups** to divide the students into groups of 10. Give the students **view permissions** so that they can see the **action plans** created by each other.
> - ☐ Create a second **gateway** for the sharing of the preparation **webfolio** and the research **webfolio.** Do this by going to **manage gateway** and selecting **duplicate gateway**. Select **link groups** and give the **gateway** a new title.
> - ☐ Check the **permissions** in this second gateway so that **users** have view **permissions**.
>
> During the activity:
>
> - ☐ Visit the **action plan gateway** regularly and give **feedback** to each student. If you are repeating comments use the **comment bank** to reduce the amount of time giving feedback.
> - ☐ Before the Long Walk, read each **webfolio** and give **feedback**.

Instructions to the learner

You can adapt these instructions to your learners and to your context

You are going to create and submit three assets in preparation for your Long Walk.

> - ☐ Log onto PebblePad.
> - ☐ In **create new**, select **action plan**. You will not complete this **action plan** in one go, but it must be complete before you undertake the Long Walk.
> - ☐ In the face-to-face session, start the **action plan** and then send it to the **gateway** created by your tutor. Your tutor will now be able to monitor your progress as you add to your **action plan**. You will also be able to see the **action plans** created by others in your group.

- To add to your **action plan** in the future, log onto PebblePad and select **view** and **my assets**. Click on your **action plan** and select **edit this asset**.

- To see your peers' **action plans**, select **view** and **gateways**. Choose the **action plan gateway** to view other people's **action plans**.

- The second and third asset you have to create are both **webfolios**.

- To create a **webfolio** go to **create new** and **more**. Select **webfolio.** To complete the **webfolio**, use the **help** section in PebblePad to guide you. The **help** section is located by clicking on the **question mark icon** in the bottom right hand corner of the screen.

- Your tutor will tell you which pages to include in the **webfolios**. You are encouraged to use a variety of multimedia files to illustrate your **webfolios**. Multimedia files must be less than 10mb.

- On the date specified by your tutor, send both **webfolios** to the **gateway** created by your tutor. You will be able to **view** other **webfolios** created by members of your group. Read these as preparation for your Long Walk.

- After the Long Walk, your **webfolio** can be sent to a number of people if you have their email addresses, including prospective employers, family members or students you may teach in the future.

The activity in context

This activity has been developed and tested with first year students undertaking a Bachelor of Outdoor Education at La Trobe University's Bendigo Campus, which provides diverse opportunities for students to develop skills to work in the outdoors. One of the final activities that students undertake at the end of their first year Outdoor Education Degree is an 18 day walk in the Australian High country – *The Long Walk*. Understandably this is rather a daunting prospect for students, and for the teachers who have to prepare them for it. The walk is designed as a transition from being a participant to a position of leadership in outdoor education activities. Approximately 65 students undertake preparation and planning for the Long Walk.

Practitioner tips

Emphasise the need for students to view the task as a formative system which requires activities to be submitted to the gateway early to enable feedback to be given.

activity 12.2 | Planning and negotiating a community project

This activity encourages students to plan their project in relation to the academic and transferable skills they hope to develop over the course of a community project placement. The action plans are submitted for assessment, ensuring that the tutor has the opportunity to provide students with initial feedback on their project plans and objectives. On completion of the placement, students reflect on their experience using a PebblePad form.

Activity Overview

Medium	Assets
Beginner	
Low	
Semester	
Class	

What challenges might this address?

Whilst community placements can provide an important experience for students, many leave the planning of their group project until the last minute. The addition of a PebblePad action plan assessment task offers the opportunity to ensure students start their planning early on and to award an individual (rather than a group) grade to this project planning assessment task. The action plan tool provides an excellent template to encourage both project management and planning and also reflection on the benefits of the learning activity. PebblePad allows students to share their action plans with other key stakeholders as well as the ability to update the plans during the course of the project.

Learning design

Undergraduate students take part in group-based project placements within community organisations close to the university. The placements are designed to encourage students to develop their transferable and academic skills whilst encouraging them to become more self-directed learners. Students are expected to negotiate the project aims and objectives with the community organisation. A paper 'Project Contract' supports the students in this process and outlines the aims of the project, the contact details of all involved and any agreements about resources and allocated expenses. The contract must be signed by all members of the group and the community contact.

In the planning stages of the project placement, each student submits an individual PebblePad action plan to a gateway for the tutor to give feedback. This action plan centres on the individual's contribution to the community project and contains the students' personal goals, plans and further reflections on the group project. The action plan is graded separately from the group project.

After receiving a grade and feedback, students are encouraged to share their PebblePad action plans with other group members and with their contact at the community organisation. They are encouraged to update their action plans during the project placement.

At the end of the project placement, students reflect back on their action plans, using a form created in PebblePad.

Tutor actions

What you need to do in PebblePad to set up the activity

Prior to the activity:

- ☐ Create a **gateway**. Add students to the **user group**. The default settings do not need to be changed for this activity.
- ☐ Set the **gateway** to lock on a date close to the start of the project placement.
- ☐ In **form builder**, create a **form** that requires students to reflect upon their **action plans** after they have been on the project placement.
- ☐ **Publish** this **form** to the **gateway** you have just created.

During the activity:

- ☐ Ask your students to send their **action plans** to the **gateway** before they start their group project. Give them **feedback** and add a **grade**. If you give them **feedback**, this cannot be viewed by either other students or an external stakeholder (e.g. contacts at the community organisation).
- ☐ Release the **grades** and **feedback** when the marking is complete.

- Almost immediately, unlock the **gateway** so that students can share the action plan with their community project group before they go on placement.

- When your students have completed their placement, they will use the **form** you created to reflect on their **action plan**. They will attach the completed **form** to their **action plan**. When they have done so, their **action plan** in the gateway will have a **bell icon** indicating that the **asset** has been updated. Give feedback on these **forms**.

Instructions to the learner

You can adapt these instructions to your learners and to your context

- Log onto PebblePad. In **create new**, click on **action plan**. Give the **action plan** your name as the title and in the description outline your community project.

- Work through every step of the **action plan**. Remember that this is your perspective on the community project.

- **Send** the **action plan** to the **gateway** created by your tutor.

- When your tutor has given your **action plan** a **grade** and **feedback**, you will receive an email notification.

- To view your **grade** and the **feedback** given by your tutor, log onto PebblePad and click on **view**. Select **my assets** and **view this asset**.

- You can now **send** this **action plan** to your peers in your community project group. Select **send to person** and **add a contact**. Your peers will be PebblePad account holders. You can also share with your contact at the community organisation if you have their email address by selecting **add a contact** and **external user**. Give your peers and the contact **comment permissions**.

- When one of your peers shares their **action plan** with you, you will receive an email notification. To view your peers' **action plans,** log onto PebblePad and from **current activity** select **new received/updated assets**. Click on the **action plan** and view it. Use the **comment icon** to make a constructive comment.

- You can update your **action plan** at any time during your placement. To do this, log onto PebblePad and select **view** and **my assets**. Click on your **action plan** and select **edit this asset**.

- At the end of the placement reflect on your **action plan**. Log onto PebblePad and select create new. Click on **more** and then **form**. Select the **form** your tutor has created for this purpose and click on the **green tick**. The **form** opens in a new window. Complete the **form** and save **changes**. Close the window.

- You are required to attach this **form** to the **action plan** you created before the placement. Select **view** and **my assets**. Click on your **action plan** and select **more options**. Select **add/edit link** and then chose the **form** you have just completed. This **form** is now attached to the **action plan** and your tutor will be able to see the **asset** has been updated the next time they go to the **gateway**.

- When your tutor gives you **feedback** on the **form**, you will be able to view this on your **asset**.

The activity in context

This activity is used in a course unit entitled 'Enhancing Academic Skills', delivered to all first year Combined Studies students at the University of Manchester, UK. As part of this course unit, students engage in group-based projects with community organisations in the Greater Manchester area. This activity was introduced into the course unit as an addition to the project contract assessment task after two years of running the community project placement. While the paper contract provides an important focus for the group aims and objectives, as well as for formalising the agreement between the students and the organisations, it was felt more direction was needed in the area of project planning for students.

References

Barnett, R. (2007). *A will to learn. Being a student in an age of uncertainty.* Berkshire: Open University Press.

Beetham, H. and Sharpe, R. (Eds.) (2007). *Rethinking pedagogy for a digital age. Designing and delivering e-learning.* London: Routledge.

Biggs, J. (1999). *Teaching for quality learning at University.* Buckingham: SRHE and OUP.

Chickering, A. W. and Gamson, Z. F. (1987). Seven principles for good practice in undergraduate education. *American Association of Higher Education Bulletin,* 3-7.

de Freitas, S., and Yapp, C. (2005). *Personalizing learning in the 21st century.* Stafford: Network Educational Press.

Garrison, D. and Vaughan, N. (2008). *Blended learning in higher education: Framework, principles, and guidelines.* San Francisco, CA: John Wiley & Sons.

Ghaye, T. (2010). *Teaching and learning through reflective practice: A practical guide for positive action.* Second Edition, London: Routledge.

JISC (2010). *Effective Assessment in a Digital Age: A guide to technology-enhanced assessment and feedback.* (Available to download at http://www.jisc.ac.uk/media/documents/programmes/elearning/digiassass_eada.pdf accessed May 2011.)

Johnson, L., Smith, R., Willis, H., Levine, A., and Haywood, K., (2011). *The 2011 Horizon Report.* Austin, Texas: The New Media Consortium. (http://net.educause.edu/ir/library/pdf/HR2011.pdf)

Moon, J. A. (2004). *A handbook of reflective and experiential learning: theory and practice.* Oxon: RoutledgeFalmer.

Print, M. (1993). *Curriculum development and design.* Second Edition, St Leonards: Allen and Unwin.

QAA (2006). *Code of practice for the assurance of academic quality and standards in higher education. Section 6: Assessment of students.* Second Edition, Mansfield: The Quality Assurance Agency for Higher Education. (Available to download at: http://www.qaa.ac.uk/ACADEMICINFRASTRUCTURE/CODEOFPRACTICE/SECTION6/COP_AOS.PDF accessed May 2011.)

QAA (2009). *Personal development planning: guidance for institutional policy and practice in Higher Education. (*Available to download at: http://www.qaa.ac.uk/academicinfrastructure/progressfiles/guidelines/pdp/default.asp accessed May 2011.)

Sutherland, S. and Powell, A. (2007). CETIS SIG 9 July 2007 (http://www.jisc.ac.uk/publications/briefingpapers/2007/eportfoliooverviewv2.aspx accessed May 2011.)

Titchen, A. (2003). Critical companionship. *Nursing Standard*, 9, 33-40.

Winter, R. (2003). Contextualizing the patchwork text: Addressing problems of coursework assessment in Higher Education. *Innovations in Teaching and Education International*, 40,(2), 112-122.

Winter, R., Buck, A., and Sobiechowska, P. (1999). *Professional experience and the investigative imagination, the art of reflective writing.* London: Routledge.

Activity Index

You can use this activity index as a quick reference to determine which assets are used within certain activities; or to separate those activities that can be accomplished within a single session from those lasting a semester or more. The index allows you to identify which activities are easily and quickly prepared and see how expert your learners need to be to fully engage in any given activity. As we have stated elsewhere, activities should not be selected because they are easy or speedy or because they use a particular kind of asset – so the index is simply another way of navigating the book or narrowing down your options. The activity and PebblePad icons are explained on pages 64 and 65, with further explanation in *Chapter 2: Designed for Learning*.

Theme 1: First Steps with PebblePad

1.1 Getting to know each other in PebblePad

Low		Low		Class	
Beginner		Session			

1.2 Introducing blogging for reflective practice

Low		Low		4+	
Beginner		Semester			

1.3 Seven steps to success with PebblePad

Low		Low		unlimited	
Beginner		2 hour workshop			

Theme 2: Orientation and Induction

2.1 Using case studies to reflect on the transition to university life

Low		Low		Cohort	
Beginner		Semester			

2.2 Managing information overload during orientation

Low	Low	Cohort
Beginner	2-3 weeks	

2.3 Mentoring through online dialogue

Low	Low	4+
Beginner	3 months	

Theme 3: Planning Personal and Professional Development

3.1 Helping learners engage with Personal Development Planning (PDP)

Low	Low	Class
Beginner	3 Semester	

3.2 Staying the course: action learning and planning as strategies for student support

Low	Low	Groups of 4
Beginner	3 Semester	

3.3 Sustaining involvement in Personal Development Planning over time

High	Medium	Groups of 4+
Beginner	Course	

3.4 Developing professional identity

Medium	Medium	Cohort
Improver	One academic year	

Theme 4: Developing Academic Study Skills

4.1 Just in time resources: Using WebQuests to introduce digital and academic literacies

Medium	Medium	Individual or Class
Beginner	Variable	

4.2 Overcoming resistance to academic writing

📊	Medium	📋	Medium	👥	Class
📖	Beginner	🕐	Semester	⚙️ 🎴	

4.3 Developing a collaborative 'knowledge' portfolio

📊	Low	📋	Low	👥	8+
📖	Improver	🕐	Semester	📄 🎴 👥	

4.4 Engaging with reflective writing

📊	Low	📋	Low	👥	4+
📖	Beginner	🕐	Semester	⚙️	

Theme 5: Promoting Group Work

5.1 Agreeing a team learning contract

📊	Low	📋	Low	👥	Groups of 4-5
📖	Beginner	🕐	Session	📄	

5.2 Creating a design proposal for assessment

📊	Medium	📋	Medium	👥	Groups of 4+
📖	High	🕐	Semester	📄 ⚙️ 👥 🎴	

5.3 Assessing individual and collective contributions to a group project

📊	Medium	📋	Low	👥	Groups of 4+
📖	Beginner	🕐	Semester	⚙️ 👥 🎴 📄	

5.4 Working together in online sketchbooks

📊	Medium	📋	Low	👥	Groups of 4+
📖	Beginner	🕐	Semester	⚙️ 👥 🎴 📄	

Theme 6: Experiential Learning

6.1 Constructing a skills diary

Medium		Medium		Cohort	
Proficient		Year			

6.2 Practising reflection for a professional portfolio

High		High		Cohort	
Proficient		Programme			

6.3 Using simulated scenarios to develop evidence-based reasoning

Medium		Medium		Cohort	
Proficient		Course			

Theme 7: Collaborative Learning

7.1 An eJournal Club for professional development

Medium		Medium		Community	
Beginner		Open-ended			

7.2 Creating digitally enhanced patchwork text

Medium		Low		Groups of 4+	
Improver		Course			

7.3 Helping students to continue learning beyond the classroom

Low		Low		Groups of 15+	
Beginner		Course			

Theme 8: Self and Peer Review

8.1 Self and peer critique of treatment plans

Medium	High	Class
Improver	Semester	

8.2 Anonymous peer review of research plans

Low	Low	4+
Beginner	Semester	

8.3 Developing professional discourse through blogging

Low	Low	Cohort
Beginner	Semester	

Theme 9: Preparing for Accreditation

9.1 Preparing a portfolio for professional development

Low	Low	Cohort
Improver	Programme	

9.2 Supporting feedback and dialogue for portfolio-building

Medium	Medium	1 or many
Beginner	Variable	

9.3 Creating accessible and usable web pages

Medium	Medium	Class
Beginner	Programme	

9.4 A 'capstone task' bringing together theory and practice

Medium	Medium	Cohort
Proficient	Programme	

Theme 10: Preparing for Employment

10.1 Recording and reflecting on a work placement

📊	Low	📋	Low	👥	unlimited
📖	Beginner	🕐	Semester	⚙️	

10.2 Supporting unemployed people returning to work

📊	Medium	📋	Low	👥	Class
📖	Beginner	🕐	Open-ended	📰	

10.3 An award scheme demonstrating employability skills

📊	Low	📋	Medium	👥	Unlimited
📖	Beginner	🕐	Open-ended	📰	

Theme 11: Learning for the Workplace

11.1 Enabling the transition to advanced practice

📊	High	📋	Medium	👥	Cohort
📖	Improver	🕐	Programme	📰	

11.2 Enabling work-based learners to study for a formal qualification

📊	High	📋	High	👥	Groups of 12-25
📖	Beginner	🕐	Programme	⚙️ 📰	

11.3 Creating an audit report of a service/organisation

📊	Medium	📋	Medium	👥	Cohort
📖	Beginner	🕐	Semester	📰 💭	

Theme 12: Action Planning and Project Managing

12.1 Planning for a field trip: pebbles on the path to the Long Walk

Low		Low		10+	
Proficient		Semester			

12.2 Planning and negotiating a community project

Medium		Low		Class	
Beginner		Semester			

Index